BLACK FRONTIERSMEN

A South American Case

BLACK FRONTIERSMEN

A South American Case

NORMAN E. WHITTEN, JR.

A Halsted Press Book

Schenkman Publishing Company

JOHN WILEY AND SONS
New York — London — Sydney — Toronto

Copyright © 1974
SCHENKMAN PUBLISHING COMPANY
Cambridge, Massachusetts

Library of Congress Catalog Card Number:
Whitten, Norman E.
    Black frontiersmen; a South American case.
    "A Schenkman publication."
    Bibliography: p.
    1. Negroes in Ecuador. 2. Negroes in Colombia.
I. Title.
F3799.N4W49   1974   918.61'06'96   74-6209
ISBN 0-470-94126-X
ISBN 0-470-94127-9 (pbk.)

Printed in the United States of America

DEDICATION

Dedico este libro a la gente morena
del litoral Ecuatoriano y Colombiano

CONTENTS

PART II: AFRO-HISPANIC CULTURE

ILLUSTRATIONS

PREFACE

Most of this book presents selected material about an Afro-Hispanic culture in one of South America's last frontiers. It is a sequel to my 1965 study of a predominantly black northwest Ecuadorian community on the brink of sustained development and national incorporation. Over a decade ago, when I first visited northwest Ecuador, I found participants in this culture to be intensely interested in economic development and "nationalization." And I found non-participants in the culture equally interested in "nationalization" but also in "colonization" of the zone.

During 1964-65 I had the opportunity to work in, and visit, many Afro-Hispanic communities in the Cauca Valley, Colombia, north to Cartagena, and the Gulf of Urubá, on south through the Chocó, and especially on down the Pacific Littoral from Buenaventura to the Ecuadorian border. These experiences deeply impressed me with the potential for social and political disenfranchisement of black people in settings where competition over expanding economic opportunities existed. It became quite clear that the more prosperous a given area, the greater the black concentration in poverty zones. This relationship was so obvious that national planners and developers could dismiss black poverty zones as "resisting" development. The argument was simple: opportunities exist; black people are concentrated in areas which are relatively unproductive; therefore, black people do not know how to take advantage of expanding opportunities. Then, in 1968, I returned to northwest Ecuador to find that considerable disenfranchisement of black people was taking place, and that people so enthusiastic about development a decade ago were seriously reassessing their own life-chances.

This book is a sequel to the first in two ways. First, it elaborates the creative, continuing dynamic adaptation of one Afro-Hispanic culture to a frontier ecology. Second, it documents a process of black disenfranchisement which places the white problem in economic development as a foremost one for those classified by developers as "black" in a particular Latin American setting. Here I should state my own bias: I favor economic development, but I deplore the racism which seems to accompany it.

The book stresses aspects of one Afro-Hispanic culture which seem of greatest interest to the students whom I have taught in college courses on Afro-American Societies and Cultures. It is addressed primarily to college students, although I find it necessary to use some technical constructs which may appeal more to my colleagues with particular interest in social structure. Nonetheless, I feel that the technical discussions of such areas as ritual, family, kinship, and ethnicity are essential to avoid ambiguities and connotations attached to more colloquial styles.

I use "Afro-Hispanic" as an American English literary convenience. It denotes cultural and ethnic background and allows me to cut back and forth across the national borders of Colombia and Ecuador. The convenient designation should not, under any circumstances, be taken to imply that this is the dominant Afro-Hispanic culture in the New World, or that it manifests the "most" African and Hispanic culture traits. It is not even "characteristic" of other Afro-Hispanic systems. I do not use the concept "subculture" because, from this Afro-Hispanic standpoint, the ways of doing things described in this book are not subordinate to any other cultural system, with the important exceptions carefully documented in the final chapter .

If this book is translated into Spanish, and I hope that it will be, some literary convenience other than "Afro-Hispanic Culture" will have to be employed, for the Hispanic, or Iberian, concepts of "Afro" are justifiably taken as pejorative by the people about whom I am writing. *"Gente morena,"* "dark people," may be the best Spanish term at this time, but that would only satisfy readers familiar with the context of black life in northern South America and the Caribbean. This is not an easy problem to cope with, for it is not one of simple "translation" so much as with connotations attached to terminologies which relate culture and race in different nations, by peoples participating from many segmental positions of cultural and social pluralism. Actually, no amount of terminological hassling will solve the semantic problem which relates culture and race as discriminating mechanisms on a world-wide scale.

Any work of this nature has its drawbacks and limitations. These are the ones I recognize. First, I naturally see things through the eyes of a male anthropologist interacting primarily with male companions.

A woman's perspective is needed to provide essential complementary detail, and to complete the sketch of culture in this zone. In particular, I have inadequate data on the symbolism of birth, which is a woman-dominated event. Chapter VI would be much richer if I had appropriate access to information controlled by women.

Second, the historical and ecological work lying ahead in unraveling Afro-Hispanic cultures of Ecuador and Colombia is formidable. Many Colombians, some of whom are cited in this work, are making great progress in these directions. I have relied primarily on secondary sources, and have tried to cite sources readily available in United States libraries. When this work is revised for publication in Spanish I shall work equally hard to cite work readily available in Ecuadorian and Colombian libraries.

Third, much can be learned from a structural analysis of myth, folklore, music, and idiomatic speech. For my own part, publication of such an analysis is seen as the next step in understanding the structure of this Afro-Hispanic culture. Various suggestions of data contributing to such an analysis are given in the books by Aquiles Escalante, the doctoral theses of Thomas J. Price and David Pavy, in articles by Rogerio Velásquez and Nina S. Friedemann, and in the novels of Adalberto Ortíz, and Nelson Estupiñán Bass. I have relied on their work, and on Moritz Thomsen's book, to check data which I collected, and have been influenced by their various insights into Afro-Hispanic life.

My primary debt is to the people of western Ecuador and Colombia whose daily lives are the stuff from which everything in this work eventually derives. No amount of appreciation can return to them their contribution. Special gratitude goes to Luis Ante, Rosendo Quintero, Edelberto Rivera Reascos, Manuel Montaño, Bolívar Arisala Reascos, Petra Caicedo, Gonzalo Calzada, Teófilo Potes, and Wilfredo Requené. They did as much as any human could to make me understand the way of life which I am now trying to translate into an anthropological mode of communication.

Dr. Aurelio Fuentes Contreras and Padre Lino Campesán also facilitated my research in Ecuador in numerous ways. The unrelenting drive by both of these men to build a community of San Lorenzo with improved conditions for all people merits deepest respect and admiration. In no way are they responsible for the processes of black disenfranchisement which I set forth in this book. Rather, the processes are international in scope. The irony is that anyone now "developing" the Pacific Littoral will have to face the tendencies toward racial

discrimination which I discuss. In fact, Dr. Fuentes and Father Campesán are quite aware of the processes, and are working diligently to
combat them.

Funds for field research were provided as follows: 1961, 1963—
Public Health Service Fellowship MH 14,333, NIMH supplements
M-54447 SSS and MH 06978-01 SSS R04; 1964-1965—NIH Grant
1-S01-FR5444; 1968—Latin American Studies Grant, Washington University, St. Louis. I began working on this manuscript on NIMH
Grant No. P01 MH 15567-01, and completed it under National Science
Foundation Grant No. GS-2999. I greatly appreciate the flexibility
and academic freedom attached to the NIH, NIMH, and NSF granting procedures. Such freedom contributed much to whatever merits
this book may have. Virtually nothing could have been accomplished
in a more rigid or restrictive framework.

My host sponsors in Ecuador and Colombia are as follows: 1961,
1963, 1968—Casa de la Cultura Ecuatoriana and the Junta Autónoma
de Ferrocarril Quito-San Lorenzo; 1964-65—the Universidad del Valle,
Cali, Colombia. Many of the data on "blanco" values and racial
stereotypes in the lowlands were gathered during 1970 and 1971 while
working with the Lowland Quechua Indians in eastern Ecuador. This
project has been, and continues to be, sponsored by the Ecuadorian
Instituto Nacional de Antropología e Historia (INAH), formed in
1969. Again, the freedom of inquiry given me under this sponsorship
contributed enormously to whatever merits this book may have. The
very special degree of tolerance toward my viewpoints, even where
they differ from those of some of my academic and administrative
hosts, augers well for free international discussion of crucial issues.

In various ways the following people influenced my thinking in the
areas of cultural adaptation, social organization, and race relations. All
of them encouraged me to return to Ecuador in 1968, and helped me
organize concepts, and present data, in the framework which emerges
in this book: John W. Bennett, Joseph B. Kahl, Lee Rainwater,
Charles A. Valentine, and Alvin W. Wolfe. Others who have considerably influenced the direction this book takes, either by professional
interaction or by their publications, or both, are Conrad Arensberg,
Charles J. Erasmus, Cynthia Gillette, Nancie Solien González, John
Gulick, Ulf Hannerz, Mary W. Helms, John J. Honigmann, and
Julian H. Steward.

Neil Kleinman, Norris Lang, DeWight Middleton, Michael J. Olien,
Scott L. Robinson, Enid Schildkrout, John O. Stewart, and Margarita
Wurfl made constructive comments on one or more chapters of earlier
drafts of the manuscript. Obviously, only I am at fault for any short-

coming in analysis, interpretation, or presentation of data and theory in this work.

Mrs. Darlene Graves typed all drafts of this manuscript, and contributed to its preparation in other ways, as well. The drawings were done by Laird Starrick, the maps were made by James Pritchard, and the photographs prepared from colored slides by William T. Ward. All three have taken considerable pains to help the reader visualize aspects of life, and concepts pertaining to Afro-Hispanic culture. Again, however, any faulting of visual effectiveness must be directed solely to the author.

My wife, Sibby, has contributed comments and constructive suggestions on every draft. She has also aided me at every point in the field work and travel necessitated by collection of the information, and by her discussions with me about the meaning of experiences shared with full time participants in Afro-Hispanic culture.

N. E. WHITTEN
Urbana, Illinois
July 5, 1972

PART I:

Afro-Hispanic Adaptation

CHAPTER ONE

Introduction

A narrow coastal strip lies west of the Andean spine of northern South America. From southern Panama down through northern Ecuador this plain is extremely rainy and humid. I refer to the southern half of the plain as the "wet littoral," and the northern half as the "Chocó." Today the population of this whole Pacific Lowland area consists of primarily black, Spanish speaking people. I call the culture of the black people "Afro-Hispanic culture."

Afro-Hispanic culture in the rainy western lowlands of Ecuador and Colombia is only one representative of the many Afro-Hispanic cultures of South America, Central America, Mexico and the Caribbean. Indeed, there are other lowland and highland Afro-Hispanic cultures in Ecuador and Colombia. This book is about certain black people adapting to changing environmental conditions. It is about people creating a dynamic heritage which includes many means by which to wrest a continuing existence from their environment. It is also about competition in a changing social arena where racism accompanies economic development.

A CULTURAL PERSPECTIVE[1]

"Culture" refers to uniquely human patterns of social intercourse. Cultural patterns are overt and covert, obvious and hidden, manifest and latent, mundane and sacred. Within the dynamics of culture there are means for patterning interaction, and we call such patterning "social organization." Other forces, seen as *acting on* a particular culture bearing population, are regarded as the environment. Social organization forever adjusts to environmental constraints, and cultural patterns thereby adapt. This perspective—called cultural adaptation

—attempts to view continuity and change within a unified frame of reference. At the core of this perspective is the idea of endless *human coping* with the environment. People do not cope by individual actions alone, but through the basic mechanism of *reciprocity*. Reciprocity occurs at many levels—person to person, person to system, system to system, system to environment. Things, ideas, emotional mood, and commitments are reciprocated through social networks, within social contexts. The generalized plans of action which allow us to understand the patterning of reciprocities through time, as well as in a moment of time, we call *adaptive strategies*.

In this book special attention is given to certain creative, adaptive facets of one particular Afro-Hispanic culture. Before going on with definitional issues, let us glance at the area of our concern, and continue to define our terms, clarify our concepts, and indicate the directions which a cultural adaptational perspective on Afro-Hispanic culture will take.

In 1939 an adventurous geographer journeyed down the Pacific Coast of South America from Panama to southern Ecuador. In spite of the "hurried, uncomfortable, and hazardous" nature of the voyage, many of the observations made (Murphy 1939a) are still most pertinent. He began by noting (1939a:1):

> . . . the continental seacoast most rarely viewed and least known in every geographic aspect lies not at the antipodes but, rather, close at hand, and just beyond the threshold of one of the world's concentrated trade routes . . . This obscurity . . . has existed since the days of earliest discovery. Exploration in its broadest sense has been carried on from diverse motives at intervals that lend themselves well to a historical grouping: but the whole area—its physical attributes and its life—is still known only spottily.

In spite of large scale attempts in the mid-19th and mid-20th centuries to chart the rivers of the northern Chocó, and of southern Darién, the Pacific Lowlands of Ecuador and Colombia still lie just beyond national thresholds. In this sense geographic marginality seems an apt characterization of the area.

Agents of centralized national systems have unpredictable, sporadic, but profound effects on the Pacific Lowlands according to commercial demand for particular tropical resources. This sporadicity of demand from external markets leads to economic marginality. Economic marginality simply refers to the fact that, within the Pacific Lowlands, *surplus is sporadic* (cf. Oberg 1955, Whitten and Szwed 1970:41-49).

The concepts of geographic and economic marginality do not imply cultural, psychological, or social inadequacy. Rather, they imply a

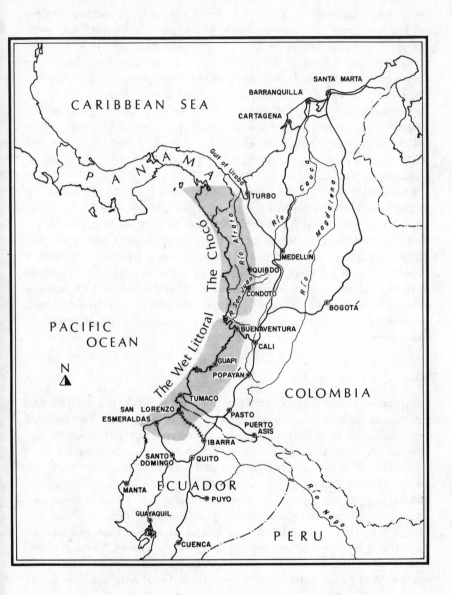

Map I: The Pacific Lowlands

relatively autonomous position *vis-à-vis* centralizing forces of state sponsored development. That such development has a powerful effect on the marginal territories, however, is quite significant. Although marginal to unfolding patterns of industrialization, and international commerce, zones such as the wet littoral are nevertheless effected by such processes. We must not confuse the marginality of a zone with the richness of the culture of people in the area. We are not talking about marginal people, or marginal culture, or "the marginal man." But we must remember that the marginality of a particular area establishes parameters for cultural adaptation. We are especially concerned with the creative aspects of Afro-Hispanic culture in the face of economic marginality.

Laced with African, European, and Indian cultural elements, the wet littoral is clearly within the influence of today's western Hispanic and Anglo industrialized world. Exploitation of the environment, then, must be set in terms of western technological and economic dominance. Such dominance is taken to be part of the environment of Afro-Hispanic culture. We must think of Afro-Hispanic culture as part of contemporary western commercial and industrial expansion. It must be understood, as far as possible, in terms of an adaptive, areal-specific internal system, whatever the historically particular roots of the system may be.

BLACK ADAPTATION

Adaptation is our key concept in portraying black life in the wet littoral, as well as in all other areas of the New World. The concept is a biological one, drawn from evolutionary theory. It refers to the *survival of a population in its environment.* The boundaries of a "population" must be defined, and many criteria could be used. In this work we take as our population the people living in the mangrove swamp-rain forest zone of western Colombia and Ecuador who participate in Afro-Hispanic culture, and who are defined as *negro,* "black," by participants in various sectors of Ecuadorian and Colombian life. These people self identify as *costeño,* "coastal," and *moreno,* "dark." The population under consideration has been expanding in the Pacific Lowlands for some four hundred and fifty years as far as we know. We do not know how large the population is, but we can place a very crude conservative guess at about a half million people in 1968.

Black people, of course, do not make up a unitary bounded social or biological organism. Nevertheless, in many and perhaps all parts

of the New World, some people defined as "black" live in regional
and national systems where a concept of "blackness" is used by cultural participants. The concept "black" implies *some* concept of non-
black. And throughout the New World *ideas of race* become entangled
with *opportunities for advancement*. We must consider the *concept* of
"black" held by non-blacks, the *degree* of non-black over black in
day-to-day social interaction, and the *actual opportunities* for cash
gain extant at a particular time, in a given area. To a great extent
these factors hinge on the *social demography* (Bruner n.d.)—"the
nature of the particular [ethnic] mix in a given context." This, in
turn, hinges on the demand by world markets for natural resources
in the wet littoral.

Having defined a population as "black" we must talk about black
adaptation. Writing about Guyana, on the east coast of South America,
the social anthropologist Raymond T. Smith (1963:46) makes a crucial point most clearly: ". . . eventually we shall have to make decisions
about such questions as what is the meaning of blackness in societies
integrated around the dominance of whiteness?" My intent in subsequent chapters is to reach a deeper understanding of blackness, as
blackness exists—adaptively—in a sector of northern South America.
I also try to delimit some major forces in the relevant environment of
black people with which they must cope, if survival is to continue.
In undertaking this task, I subscribe to the position recently summarized by Charles A. Valentine (1968:5):

> . . . through culture men collectively adapt themselves to environmental
> conditions and historical circumstances. Cultures have thus come to be un-
> derstood as adaptive responses to such conditions and circumstances. In-
> deed, environing habits and external historical influences are among the
> major kinds of factors that men cope with by means of their cultures.

Returning to the observations of Robert C. Murphy (1939b:461, 470-
471) for a moment, let us see how he summarized the adaptive aspects
of the history of people in the wet littoral:

> The greater part of the Pacific seaboard from Panama to western Ecuador
> was never effectively occupied by the Spaniards. To this day . . . the rain-
> forest area between shore line and Andes remains a region of sparse human
> population, as well as one in which the original armed contest between
> white and red men has been succeeded by a struggle, biological rather than
> war-like, in which red and black peoples are the chief competitors. (Murphy
> 1939b:461) . . . The conclusion in the sphere of human geography would
> seem to be that the negro is the fittest heir of the Chocó [read, here, "Pacific
> Lowlands" for Chocó]. He enjoys the typical "preadaptations" . . . which

imply that an organism wins out if it possesses traits that particularly suit it to a given environment or that enable it to find a new environment where such traits confer relative advantages. Transplanted from Africa, the negro has become, as regards survival, a "native" superior to his predecessor . . . Like many elements of the humid-tropical Caribbean biota, he has succeeded willy-nilly in breaking through to the Pacific seaboard at the weakest point in the continental barrier, which is the Isthmus, and has spread thence into all rain-forest terrain that attains no great altitude. (Murphy 1939b:470-471)

How Mr. Murphy's words were to forecast the first experiences and interpretations of later outsiders! Today timber buyers, gold prospectors, Peace Corps Volunteers, development experts, government officials, missionaries, novelists, poets, and engineers see the large numbers of black people exploiting the rainy environment as dominant peoples, making a "willy-nilly" conquest of this fringe region at the periphery of large international trade-routes. But, so often, black dominance in such an environment is seen by outsiders only in terms of the forest and swamp; the darker population is viewed as a successful "Caribbean biota" exploiting natural wealth for a subsistence life, at the expense of nobler Indians.

To suggest mere subsistence as a primary referent for ideas about exploitation of relevant environments and the adaptation of a population is to reason fallaciously. We must consider black adaptation not only to natural features in the environment, but also to social and political features. Opportunity potential in a given environment in a man-dominated biosphere rests on *policies* whereby exchangable tokens (money, for example), are differentially distributed. It also rests on the manner by which capital resources can expand within a particular population, and the relationship of capital resource expansion and distribution to natural resource utilization and social demography. Such distributional patterns make up what is called the *political economy*.

Black people in the wet littoral are confronted with a political economy in which economic "booms" sporadically occur and where "busts" often follow. During such booms cash is available for labor. When there is no boom, survival means utilizing and marketing natural resources. During boom periods black people enter the world of proletarian workers, but non-blackness as a desirable characteristic for upward mobility also intensifies. During bust periods subsistence life restores the positive value of blackness, but at the expense of opportunities for upward mobility. I shall be concerned in this book with the manner by which the mass of black people maintain a balance between a *proletarian strategy* and a *peasant strategy* in the boom-bust political economy. The contrast is between *investment of time and energy bringing in money* (proletarian strategy), and *pursuits bringing a direct harvest, supplemented by some cash gain* (peasant strategy). The margin allowing us to separate the two general strategies is a narrow one, but it is critical in terms of continuing adaptation of different ethnic aggregates to the natural and socio-political environments. The difference is in the degree of opportunism when a boom occurs. At any time, for example, we may find two families attending to the same means of natural resource utilization. For example, men may be hunting wild peccary, while their wives harvest manioc tubers. The peasant perspective attendant on such activity suggests that the primary concern is that of enough meat and tubers to feed family and kinsmen to whom one is obligated *before selling any available surplus.* The proletarian perspective focuses on the *potential cash value* of any activity for *purchase of subsistence goods* and for investment in other aspects beyond subsistence in the political economy.

Only when cash gain for subsistence goods represents a *clear alternative* for aggregates of people with equal access to basic resources can we contrast the two perspectives as strategies. It should be obvious that, in the absence of external hindrances (such as those based on racist limitation), proletarian strategies of adaptation can evolve through investment and uneven exchange tactics into entrepreneurial strategies, provided that there is sufficient capital available for uneven distribution.

I regard this Afro-Hispanic social and economic system as revolving around a proletarian strategy when cash gain is available. The Indians in the area—the Cayapa in Ecuador, Coaiquer, Chocó, and Cuna in Colombia—are more clearly understandable in terms of a continuing peasant strategy, whether or not the national and international economy would seem to allow for proletarianization. This means that Indians pay greater attention than the blacks to first meeting their subsistence needs with direct natural resource allocation, and then convert such surplus as may exist from peasant strategy into cash to supplement such a subsistence life.

Of course, peasant and proletarian strategies are not uniform in all environmental zones of the wet littoral. Furthermore, the concentration of factors in the political economy also imposes limitations and opens opportunities to various forms of coping behavior. I shall be directly concerned in this book with the 450 year old adaptation of Afro-Hispanic culture. Because of this concern more concepts are introduced from chapter to chapter as they are needed to give us a continuing perspective on the adaptive dimension of the phenomena under consideration.

BLACK CULTURE

Black men and women today in the wet littoral are *mobile*. Scarcely can one ascend a river, move a few miles along the coast, follow the estuary pathways of giant tidal swamps, or even slog along a trail without meeting single men, groups of men, or whole families from three to a dozen or more people traveling to some other place. Travel is extremely hard, often necessitating great physical power to move a heavily loaded canoe against a current by pole or paddle. Even when moving with a current, the action of waves, or river rapids, together with ubiquitous flotsam, keep people constantly alert. Sometimes, though, in the estuaries, the tide and currents are favorable to easy movement, and then the rise of work and travel songs resound through the trees, or across the water. The music itself may follow the lines and melody of national music, but more often it takes on a leader-response pattern where one male or female leader maintains continuity of expression, while others answer and respond to the leader in stylized West African patterns.

The energy expended in travel creates a certain vibrancy of river, estuary, and sea life not often found in villages and towns, except on festive occasions. Black men and women call to one another, using terms such as *"primo,"* "cousin," and yodel back and forth in a variety of stylized falsettos. Such noisy awakening of the otherwise drab scenery is not the Colombian or Ecuadorian way, and many nationals find it jarring, and fear the loud strength of black people, attributing to them tendencies to violence which do exist, but seldom break out.

Black people customarily talk much louder, and use "loud" or "obscene" expressions not normally heard in daily life among "mestizos" (people of stipulated Euro-Indian descent). They work tremendously hard; sometimes, when traveling, they are on the move for as many as 24 hours with scant rest. They work and yell when they feel good. If illness overtakes them, energy is conserved through rest, and rest is normally regarded to be a private affair. Black people in this zone quite reasonably believe that to work and exert strength when feeling "weak" is to invite still greater weakness by draining remaining strength.

Afro-Hispanic culture is flanked and penetrated by cordilleran mestizos and highland Indians with elaborate hot-cold concepts, generally asserting that a person's inner "heat" and inner "coldness" must stay in some state of balance, such balance often demanding subtle attention to specific foods and spices. Not so in Afro-Hispanic culture, which scorns such subtleties. If a man is too "hot" (angry, overly excited) then he must be isolated, or physically restrained, to prevent his doing damage to another. If he is too cold, a shot of rum should do; if one shot doesn't warm up the taker, then several ounces or more may be necessary.

When a black man "is hot," *tiene calor,* he tends to provoke a fight, and in such a fight may kill, or die. Black men, when forced, fight with the only weapons at their disposal. They fight with machete and muzzle loading shotgun, or with their bare hands, feet, teeth, and nails. The strength that can be hurled against a fellow is often spoken of and feared in this region, and black people take pains to prevent their men from fighting, whenever possible. This is not the case with women, however, who are not regarded as strong enough to kill, under ordinary circumstances. They are allowed to "cool off" by engaging in actual combat with one another from time to time. When a man is beating a women he is not normally interfered with, though there are occasions, not too rare, when a man in his zeal becomes too hot and kills his women.

Strength, a preference for peaceful interpersonal relations between men, great physical power overtly manifest through travel and through work, and the counter tendency toward complete rest when one does not feel well—or does not *need* to travel or work—all of these traits characterize the black people. All contrast to some extent with *blanco,* "white," or "National" inland culture. On the rivers, estuaries, and sea, black people thrust against the natural elements—willfully and consciously pitting their strength *against* nature. Theirs is a black centered environment, and they regard the environment as theirs to exploit, whenever they want to, for as much gain as they can get out of it.

Material poverty is clearly obvious in Afro-Hispanic culture. Homemade apparatus is sparse compared to Indian cultures. Rectangular, thatched pile houses with carved *burros,* top posts, to hold thatch are sparsely furnished. The area around the house contains scattered dugout canoes, platform gardens, flowers such as hibiscus, flanking palm trees, and some subsistence plants. This is the case, if space permits, whether the settlement is part of an urban *barrio* in a large town, or a rural hamlet of only a few houses. In the mangrove swamp, of course, such vegetation is non-existent except on high points of ground, and the various paraphernalia of fishing dominate the material appearance. Village life moves slowly, in contrast to "traveling" life, except during a fiesta. People are home to rest, to play with children and talk with friends, to prepare for a fiesta, or to engage in politics; otherwise the strength and vibrancy of life is conserved for work or adult play. In towns people adopt a lazy-like atmosphere, except for those women with actual in-town work tasks such as washing and ironing. Outsiders, unaware of the relationship between town and work-travel zones, often incorrectly perceive the people as lazy.

Men are a bit more spatially mobile than women. Consequently, every river and estuary has more men on the move than women, and every town has more women who have recently been "left" than men without women. Marriage, a Catholic rite, is regarded by most men as a bit too binding, and few take part in the ceremony. Women, on the other hand, are often a bit closer to the church and the advantages (economic and social) which the local or visiting priest may confer, and tend to favor a church ceremony, though again, few find time, opportunity, or the right man with whom to undertake "marriage." Some men travel to and from villages and towns, and may have two or more "common law" wives, who remain more or less sexually faithful and work within the framework of his enterprise. Some particularly strong and clever men are able to muster the sexual and economic wherewithall, together with the psychological powers of maneuver, to have two, and occasionally three, women as *mujeres,* "wives," in the same town and occasionally in the same house. More often, the existence of two or more wives signals the attenuation of one consensual bond, and the intensification of another. For this reason, I use the term "serial polygyny" as a marriage pattern characteristic of Afro-Hispanic culture.

Men work together in pairs, and shun the lone endeavor more characteristic of mestizo colonists. The overlapping of pairs of men can define chains of individuals loosely united for some tasks (usually for cash gain) which can melt away in other situations. The ability of large numbers of men to cooperate with one another when there is cash gain, but to return to their basic work habits of pairs of cooperating men in the absence of such gain, is a particular characteristic of the wet littoral social system. Not infrequently, a large group of men clusters around one particular man. Such a man is the locus for many work parties and is regarded as an equal. But he is particularly *responsible* to someone from the outside, to a white or mestizo who will actually *pay* for work done. It also usually results that such a man takes most of the earnings of a cooperative endeavor, such as collecting lumber, but pays back each worker through time.

We shall say much more about such work habits later in this book, in Chapter IV and Chapter VII. Also, let us note that work and co-operative habits in this zone puzzle outsiders, who see black people as atomistic at one moment and cooperative at another. Outsiders also often see that some men make all the money, but never seem to have any to spend. We shall examine such labor and cooperative habits in terms of adaptation to the cash and subsistence economy, and try to show the inherent organizational flexibility in Afro-Hispanic culture.

Ritual life in the Pacific Lowlands is dominated by contexts of musical expression ranging from quite African-sounding music in the *currulao,* or marimba dance, to national songs and dances. There is a sacred, or at least respected, pantheon of saints which are Catholic in derivation, but perhaps parochialized by syncretisms of 16th-18th century Spanish and West African customs so that they appear "different" today. This difference provokes some nationals to refer to them as "African," a referent not appreciated by black people in this region. Saints and men compete for power in daily life, and women turn to both living and mystical patrons (but not "ancestors") when they need help. Ghosts, spirits, and demons are thought to exist, and indeed some of the sights and sounds of swamp, jungle, and sea make more sense if one accepts folk-explanations. For the most part, na-tional ghosts and demons are readily incorporated into the fear-systems of black people, but aboriginal spirits and ghosts are primarily ignored, or thought to bedevil only Indians. More work by historians on 14th and 15th century Spanish and African ritual, medical and procreative life is needed to establish cultural base–lines in these areas. When this is done my guess is that a number of customs sur-rounding birth and death will appear quite Spanish. A number of the customs reported by George Foster (1960:112-123), for example, are found here and there in the Pacific Lowlands. Yet, the style by which such customs are enacted seems Black African.

Body gestures, patterns of carrying children (on the hip and back) and some loads (on the heads of women), patterns of eye avoidance when asking for a favor, together with musical patterns, the role of certain saints such as San Antonio, and some themes from folklore are perhaps as African as anywhere in the New World. But it is not an African culture that seems to endure; rather, we have what I have chosen to loosely call "Afro-Hispanic culture." Whatever the con-figuration of events and statuses, whatever the particular relationships between material, social, and mental cultural apparatus, the general sense one gets is of a vibrant society with strong roots in Africa and Europe, but of the New World.

In Chapter II, *The Wet Pacific Littoral,* I define more carefully the actual geographical area which the book is about, and discuss three environmental zones within it: the sea-edge, the forest, and the mangrove swamp. On matters of geography I rely heavily on the earlier observations made by Robert C. Murphy (1939a) and particularly on the work of Robert C. West (1957). West is the only scholar to date to publish a comprehensive monograph on man and nature in the area of our central concern. The title of this work is *The Pacific Lowlands of Colombia: A Negroid Area of the American Tropics.*

Chapter III, *Blackness in Northern South America: Historical Dimensions,* gives some background information on the entry of Africans into the wet littoral and the subsequent history of slavery and freedom. The chapter is frankly interpretive, and argues a perspective for seeing the basis of continuing black cultural adaptation lying in the relationship between non-black exploitation of the Pacific Lowlands for profit, and the need of outside exploiters to cope with the strength and human needs of the black labor force. Toward the end of this chapter I outline the idea of a "purchase society" which refers to "rural participants in the wider economic network formed either by industrializing nations searching for raw materials for their growing industries, or by trade with agrarian states." (Helms 1969:329) The concept, developed by the anthropologist Mary W. Helms, allows us to consider the general cultural ecological experience of black people to be a "frontier" one.

Chapter IV, *Exploiting Nature and Man,* is designed to portray certain relationships between continuity through subsistence exploitation of three environmental zones, and constant change and fluctuation through creative adaptation to the externally imposed money economy. The concepts of "boom" and "bust" in the money economy are considered, and a concept of expanding national infrastructure is introduced. I then turn to an examination of "niches." These are black activity patterns which play particular roles in the political economy according to four settlement patterns: the dispersed rural scattered dwelling, rural settlement, town, and large urbanized town. Particular attention is given to the town niche, for we return to a specific town niche—San Lorenzo, northwest Ecuador—later on.

The discussion in these first four chapters is designed to explore *Afro-Hispanic adaptation* to a frontier cultural ecology. Part II focuses directly on the ritual, social, and ethnic dimensions of *Afro-Hispanic culture.* The approach in this second part is contextual, and designed to let the reader understand how an anthropologist may sort out the textual and behavioral material going on around him in order to say something meaningful about the lifeways and life chances of a people.

In Chapter V, *Secular Rituals,* I begin to elaborate on forms of ritual expression in secular contexts. A context is a community setting where stylized behavior takes place. Three such secular contexts are discussed: the *cantina* context, the "saloon" context, and the *currulao* context. Here we get into cultural orientations, and ritual styles, not characteristic of non-black peoples in Colombia and Ecuador. In the relationships between the contexts we see an underlying structure of Afro-Hispanic culture emerging.

Chapter VI, *Sacred Rituals and Social Structure,* probes more deeply into Afro-Hispanic culture by first noting the relationship between independence, mobility and responsibility of the living, and the wandering souls of the dead. Having demonstrated this relationship I discuss sacred musical contexts, and the relationship of these contexts to the Afro-Hispanic universe, spirits, and saints. Specifically, I discuss the contexts of the *alabado-novenario-la tumba* ceremonies for deceased adults, the *chigualo* ceremony for deceased children, and the *arrullos* (spirituals) offered to saints. I discuss not only the ceremonies themselves, but also those aspects of the ceremonies which enact such social structural components as sex roles and kinship criteria. We find a rich integration in Afro-Hispanic culture, and uncover a set of coded material used by black frontiersmen to cooperate with each other in a variety of economic pursuits.

Chapter VII, *Adaptive Strategies,* focuses directly on the survival plan of black frontiersmen. This is not a conscious plan which people describe to the anthropologist, but rather a model of social organization constructed by the anthropologist. The model is based on first hand observation and participation. But it is nonetheless a model. Reciprocity is dealt with in several ways. I first set forth the concept of the "dyad"—an interpersonal relationship transacted by two actors, where each actor becomes indebted to the other—and then discuss two crucial dyads from which families and households expand and contract; these are the mother-child dyad, and the mother-husband dyad. This discussion leads us into the maximal kinship grouping upon which both dyads depend for a sustaining group of kinsmen: the kindred. I then discuss outwardly ramifying chains of dyadic ties—networks—and specifically note the position of "network brokers," "action-sets," and "stem kindreds" in the social organization. This is followed by a summary model of "strategies of adaptive mobility: peasant-proletariat-entrepreneur," which helps us see the social dynamics of cultural adaptation among black frontiersmen in the wet littoral.

By the end of this chapter the basic adaptive strategies of Afro-

Hispanic culture emerge. These are seen in the processes of "spatial mobility" where black frontiersmen move their residence in response to cash and subsistence economies; "horizontal mobility" where people rally around a traditional work group head, support his drive to higher social status, while eroding his economic position; and "vertical mobility" through which individuals and groups move upward within a community by consolidating mutually exploitative dyadic ties in order to take advantage of economic and political opportunities. The adaptive strategies form on the complementarity of network and group bases upon which some individuals maneuver successfully toward goal-oriented action when it is economically or politically advantageous to do so.

Chapter VIII, *Blackness in Northern South America: Ethnic Dimensions,* returns to the theme of "blackness" in an Hispanic (or Iberian, or "Latin") cultural milieu. Access to basic and sociopolitical resources in the wet littoral is related to the ethnic position of black people in a wider social order. I first sketch general concepts of "race" and "race mixture" in Ecuador and Colombia and then discuss the various viewpoints in one area. I use northwest Ecuador here, because I know this area best from participant field work. My own field work in other towns and settlements in western Colombia, and that of other anthropologists such as Thomas J. Price, Aquiles Escalante, and David Pavy indicates that although the terms and specific ethnic relationships vary from place to place, the general sense of contrasting and complementary terms and positions are comparable to the northwest Ecuadorian system.

This final chapter is an attempt to bring the reader to a deeper sense of what is happening today to black people in the wet littoral. By various means I try to establish black disenfranchisement as a concomitant of economic development. An altered social demography works to black material advantage, but at the expense of social advantage. People nationally classed as being "non-black" have more access to resources in the political economy than do people classed as black.

The first seven chapters describe and analyze aspects of a particular Afro-Hispanic culture in its relatively unique dimensions, and the last chapter describes and analyzes the position of black people in the wet littoral in terms which suggest a common, hemisphere wide, perspective.

NOTES

[1] This brief discussion owes a great deal to John J. Honigmann's (1959:121-135) more extensive summary. Combining the concept of "culture" with that of "adaptation" reflects a shifting anthropological emphasis in the study of man away from concern with social or cultural rules, to an interest in adaptive strategies of human aggregates. The general theoretical basis for such work seems to lie in multilinear evolutionary theory, especially as set forth by Steward (1953, 1955), and discussed as "specific evolution" by Sahlins and Service (1960). Concepts and definitions reflecting this emphasis on a cultural adaptational perspective owe much to the works of Firth (1951), Lévi-Strauss (1953, 1967), Barth (1956, 1959, 1966). Service (1962), Sahlins (1964, 1965), Alland (1967, 1970) and Wolf (1969). This and other comparable literature is reviewed in Whitten and Whitten (1972).

CHAPTER TWO

The Wet Pacific Littoral

I think of the sea as an outer shell affecting the web and hustle of life within the confines of littoral forests and swamps. The inland forest itself provides a subsistence base, and contains most of the raw materials sought after by nations. It is the swampy mangrove delta with its myriad of navigable channels, high-ground areas for habitation, excellent fishing and large towns that seem most "alive" to me. In the mangrove delta we have the real hum and buzz of conjunctive relationships where western cultural currents wash through the small and large-scale transactions involving Indians, Blacks, *mestizos, zambos,* mulattoes and foreign whites; where the forces which demand adjustive response are most clearly perceptible.

THE SEA

Beyond the resounding breakers far off the coast lies one of the world's busy streams of international shipping. It is the occasional ship slipping out of the main waterways between continents and threading through some difficult passage into a rain or sun-drenched swampy, hot port that constitutes a major environing feature, not only in today's industrial economy, but back through the colonial era to the possibilities of Pacific Basin (Asian-New World) and Atlantic Basin (Africa-New World) diffusion, as well.

This discussion considers the Pacific Ocean as it touches the low alluvial coast and outlying islands, either on the Pacific rim of the lush mangrove swamps (among the world's largest), or on the broad sandy beaches. It also considers the dominant effect of the ocean in conditioning the natural and sociopolitical environment. We reserve

19

discussion of the tidal areas of mangrove delta until the effects of both sea and forest have been discussed.

The rise and ebb of the eight to thirteen foot tidal flow effects entry and exit of large ships, and also imposes limitations and provides advantages to smaller craft.[1] The tidal flow also creates a warm, north flowing coastal current which facilitates movement *abajo,* "down the stream," for a variety of small craft, but presents some hindrance to *arriba,* "up stream," or southward navigation. Occasionally, according to Murphy (1939a:18), reversals of relative force in the interplay of coastal currents take place:

> Only at intervals of years, during full-fledged counter-current or Niño episodes, do cargoes of palms, *camelotes,* mangrove fragments, alligators, and forest snakes from Chocó or Guayas drainage drift southward along the desert coast of Peru.

The warm, inshore currents contrast in all respects with the qualities of the Humbolt current which swings westward toward Ecuador's Galápagos Islands off her south central coast. Beyond and counter to the northward current flows the Japanese current. Whether or not it might have been a major vehicle of diffusion in ancient times is still vigorously discussed in anthropology while evidence continues to amass that, via one current or another, the Pacific rim prior to the coming of European and African, can indeed be considered as an Asiatic-New World diffusion sphere.[2]

But to return to the environing qualities of the sea, exclusive of their function in uniting widely dispersed cultures, West (1957:53) gives the general picture from ocean toward Andes as consisting of five sorts of zones: (1) offshore sand bars or mud flats, (2) sandy beaches interrupted by estuaries, inlets and mud flats, (3) mangrove forest, (4) fresh water tidal swamps behind the mangroves, and (5) rain forest on *tierra firma.* Although the waves battering the broken, alluvial, current-ravished outer shore line at high tide tend to range from one to eight feet, giant "tidal" waves sporadically occur, and are frequently attributed to the whimsy of Christian deities or saints. Local names for them include *El Divino Patriarco* (heavenly father), and *La Visita* (the [supernatural] visit). Old people up and down the coast recall the destruction of whole villages during a tidal wave. As beaches and their villages are destroyed—suddenly, or by more gradual action of wind, rain, tides, and currents—surviving inhabitants create new ones, often on new beaches. For example, where a large fishing settlement on one side of a channel mouth or island exists during one decade, a comparable unit may exist on the other side when one makes a return visit, a decade later.

The Pacific littoral is one of the world's rainiest areas. Between February and May, and October and December, particularly spectacular torrents, driven by brisk winds and accompanied by brilliant electric displays, occur. The prevailing winds are generally coastwise and more or less southerly most of the year (except in the north, where more northerly breezes prevail). The slight northerly shift in July and August ushers in a dryish season in southern Esmeraldas province of Ecuador (where rainfall averages 120-180 inches a year), which is not noticeable at the Colombian border. By the time the north winds reach the central west coast of Colombia they are as rainbearing as the southerly; here, in the Chocó, and in parts of the west-northwest sectors of the Department of Valle, annual precipitation may average over an inch a day. The temperature is high, in the 80's and 90's all year round, and the humidity near saturation all of the time.

Interesting, perhaps, is the fact that the wet-onshore winds of the Pacific littoral closely resemble the dry winds blowing over the arid coast of Peru. The difference between the two is primarily conditioned by the temperature of the sea surface. One of the world's dryest deserts and wettest forests lie within a few hundred miles of each other; both are a product of the sea, its temperature, and resulting winds and precipitation.

Regular commercial fishing is yet undeveloped off the wet Pacific littoral. Attempts have failed due to inadequate and insecure shore facilities, notably a lack of predictable electric power, and therefore a critical uncertainty about ice. Small scale commercial activities center around the ports of Esmeraldas, Ecuador, and Tumaco and Buenaventura, Colombia, although none approach those characteristic of Manta, on Ecuador's central dry coast, or Ecuador's Guayaquil fishing industry. Some people do engage in sea fishing, drying and selling their catch of albacore, sea bass, occasional sea turtles, and even sometimes large sharks. Such sea fishermen may supplement their work by smuggling between Colombia and Ecuador near that border, and also by raising coconuts, mangoes, bananas, or pineapples when the particular coastal soils are favorable, or cattle where the grasses are adequate.

Coconuts, plantains, bananas and taro-like tubers are generally grown on or just behind the beaches, and people utilizing the sea maintain continuous interaction with those for whom the primary adaptation is found within the mangrove swamp and riparian forest zones.

The sea creates the dominant feature in the natural environment: the rainfall. This, in turn, produces one of the wettest forests in the world. This wetness generates products, the quest for which gives us the dominant feature of the political economy: *sporadic contact with world traders,* and their local suppliers—the people who exploit natural resources on the basis of world demand for marketable goods.

THE FOREST

The forest zone, *el monte,* most clearly delimits the entire Pacific Lowland culture area of northwest Ecuador, western Colombia and southeast Panama, ". . . a strip 600 miles long and from 50 to 100 miles wide. Excepting Darién, the area lies between the Pacific Ocean and the western versant of the Andean Cordillera Occidental" (West 1957:1). Ranging north to south this area traverses the Province of Darién, Panama, the northeastern corner of Antioquia, all of the Department of Chocó, the western sectors of Valle, Cauca, and Nariño, Colombia, and almost all of Esmeraldas Province, Ecuador. West (1957:3) adequately portrays the area, so I shall use his words:

> Seen from the air the canopy formed by the giant trees resembles a sea of green, overlapping umbrellas, broken only by streams and occasional clearings. Hundreds of rivers, often in flood, run through the forest from hill and mountain slope to sea. They are the pathways for human travel and their banks are the main sites of human habitation.

To this areal description I should add that, in order to *see* the canopy (from the air) it is almost always necessary to "find a hole" in the dense layer of clouds overhanging it, and plunge downward, often to within a few feet of the canopy itself, thence to skim along the riverway, following by air the ground routes of riparian man in a search for the proper intersection, for some natural beacon to guide the flier into this forest.

The forest itself is made up of two major botanical strata, the enormous one of evergreen broadleaf species ranging from sixty to one hundred feet high, and the other one of slender, shorter palms ranging up to twenty or thirty feet. On the ground itself, meeting the traveler at or above face level is a cover of giant ferns, shrubs, vines, and where the sunlight gets through the canopy there is an impenetrable wall of second-growth soft wood, bushes, palms, etc.

To drive home the "feel" of this forest a bit, let us consider a well-known discussion by Marsten Bates (1960:80) who says:

> "Rain forest" and "jungle" are frequently taken to mean the same thing. But I have never liked the word jungle. It has all the wrong connotations. You hack your way painfully through the lush vegetation of the jungle,

dripping sweat in the steam-bath atmosphere; snakes hang from trees and lurk under foot; leopards crouch on almost every branch and there is always a tiger just beyond the impenetrable screen of foliage. There are hordes of biting, stinging and burning things. The jungle is green hell.

Bates (1960:81) prefers another view reminiscent of Hudson's famous *Green Mansions:*

> . . . the cool, dim light, the utter stillness, the massive grandeur of the trunks of forest giants, often supported by great buttresses and interspersed with the straight, clean columns of palms and smaller trees; the Gothic detail of the thick, richly carved, woody lianas plastered against the trunks or looping down from the canopy above.

Unfortunately, for our image-building, I choose Bates' first "negative" characterization to suggest a "feel" for the Pacific rain forest. The littoral is a *jungle;* and it *is* green. The colorful orchids, bromeliads, and other brilliant flowers which give such beauty to the forests east of the Andes are scarce in the Pacific Lowlands. A deep green color prevails, except on the river banks where lighter green and brown combine with it.

Bates' serene, silent beauty does exist; but one is hard-pressed to enter the areas which feature it, for the journey is rugged across hundrds of streams, rapid and near-still rivers and swamps, up and down over broken terrain which includes muddy, slippery climbs, embankments, and the near ubiquity of scratching plants, and biting and stinging insects (including ants with a wasp-like stinger, and six inch centipedes with lobster-like claws). Those who reach the virgin stands most frequently are not philosophers or artists, or even adventurous anthropologists and ecologists, but lumber buyers with a view toward destruction, a view to making the forest even more a man-centered, green hellish morass of second growth forest which itself becomes *the* forest as it effects man's adaptation to it.

Penetration of the Pacific Lowlands forest is normally by waterway, following the routes of large rivers, of which the north-flowing Atrato and west-flowing San Juan of Colombia are the most prominent of the region. Colombian developers hope to some day dam the two rivers to create a lake over what is now a small land strip between the Atrato and San Juan, thereby making an east-west sealevel waterway through Colombia. North American developers are more grandiose: they conceive of a sea-level canal to replace the Panama Canal. This would be created by blowing out the "low" (one to two thousand foot) continental divide in southern Panama or northern Colombia with nuclear or conventional explosives, subsequently altering the coastal ecologies of Atlantic and Pacific Basins. Other ranges, not yet designated for damming, flooding, or exploding, include the smaller Serranía del Sapo south of the "canal-proposed" zone, and the larger Serranía de Baudó which defines the boundary between inland and coastal Chocó, the inland being the better known because of the ease of travel along the Atrato River and its tributaries. Otherwise, the ground rises and falls from sea-level, or below, to several hundred feet, increasing in altitude eastward to about 3,000 feet (with 1,000 foot depressions) before the rain forest environment begins to change.

Some of the more alluring resources which have spurred exploration of this forest include drugs such as quinine, spices such as sarsaparilla, and gold, platinum, ivory nut (*tagua*), wood such as mahogany and balsa, furs, and rubber. The nations of Ecuador and Colombia, with aid from England, France, Germany, and the United States, have managed to open some of the forests to internal use and quite recently the ports of the Pacific have at last become a part of their respective provinces and departments within the nations "owning" them, rather than simply a gateway to forest products for foreign exploitation. Ranging north to south there is now a roadway from Turbo in the Gulf of Urubá to Medellín, the capital of Antioquia, and another from Quibdó, capital of the Chocó to the Medellín-Cali highway. Road and rail link Cali to one of the finest and least developed natural deep-water harbors in the world—Buenaventura—following the old trail where first Indians and later Black Africans back-packed cargo and passengers over the western cordillera (life expectancy under such labor: 3 years). Another road connects Tumaco and Barbacoas with Pasto (on the Pan American Highway), and moves on east to Puerto Asís, while still another road is planned to the town of Guapi from Popayán. When this last road is completed the Department of Cauca will have an outlet to the sea, joining Antioquia, Chocó, Valle, and Nariño, Colombia. In Ecuador the Quito-Ibarra-San Lorenzo railway is the only overland link of highland Ecuador with its northern deep-water port, though a road from Quito-Santo Domingo-Esmeraldas connects this latter port (which does not have a harbor) to other national centers.

Five roads and two narrow gauge railroads form the only overland links to the Andean interior in a 600 mile long stretch of dense rain forest of Colombia and Ecuador. Only the road to Esmeraldas is "all weather." The others must be constantly repaired, and some are out of service as often as they are "passable."

In Colombia, air service into remote areas and to Buenaventura by single engine "Beavers" and occasionally DC3s is quite good, and DC3s fly regularly to Tumaco, Quibdó, Turbo, Condoto, and recently to Guapi. Esmeraldas, Ecuador, has the only usable airport in the Ecuadorian wet littoral, though single engine planes may occasionally land on a beach near San Lorenzo, a town which in 1968 had a large, unopened airstrip of mud and clay ruts replacing another tiny unusable one.

The Atrato is travelled by sturdy river ships out of Cartagena to Quibdó, the last upriver deep water river port, and sturdy vessels ply the coast and mouths of rivers such as the Cayapas and Santiago in Ecuador, and the Patía, Iscuandé, Micay, Docampadó and Baudó of Colombia. Otherwise, travel is by dugout canoe, with or without a motor. Floating downstream on rafts is common on the Atrato, but is not common on other rivers as a means of transportation. Walking trails which are well maintained are common, and form their own network between tiny settlements in the forest. Those near the Colombian-Ecuadorian border are particularly well maintained with corduroy construction over perpetually damp areas and small bridges over many streams. Most trails either give evidence of regular foot-travel, or are rapidly and completely overgrown with "the bush."

As the forest gives way in places to allow thin communication links inland it does so reluctantly. The tremendous rainfall washes away roadbeds, streams appear to cross roads, which then must be altered, and even waterfalls gush forth out of the cordilleran hills to utterly alter a passage through slopes and depressions. Landslides are common on the Andean slopes, where young mountains are still cracking and moving, and where water percolates through earth and rock causing various kinds of physical disruption, even where the forest forms a formidable buttress. Airstrips are subject to disuse due to perpetually spongy ground in many places, and often deteriorate beyond repair in a short time. But others are built, following the dictates of exploitable and needed raw materials from the forest.

The forest and its rivers provide many resources for human survival, including various animals, birds, medicinal and food plants, native and introduced cultigens, fish, and building materials. With proximity of the Andes, the Caribbean, and the Central American forests providing a bridge to the North American continent, the Pacific littoral is perhaps one of the most complex ecosystems in the world. Classification of plants has scarcely begun, and the specific species within a given genus of fauna are not established in many cases.

How can we study cultural adaptation in such an area, if we still lack adequate data on the "natural ecology?" This is easy if we accept a growing position in botany and biology, recently articulated for Panama by Charles F. Bennett (1962, 1968). Writing about the Bayano Cuna Indians of eastern Panama Bennett (1962:47-48) states:

> It appears safe to assume that exploitation of plant and animal species by man is certain to result in changes in the ecological conditions that existed prior to human intervention. (1962:47) . . . The long-term exploitation of selected plant species for fuel and construction materials may have resulted in alteration of the floral composition of the forest. (1962-47-48) . . . virgin forest in the New World humid tropics may not exist except perhaps for some remote non-riverine tracts in the Amazon basin. (1962: 48) . . . Man becomes a selective force of some consequence through his hunting and fishing activities. By extrapolation from the Cuna area we may deduce that most terrestial fauna have been genetically modified to some extent by man and that in extreme cases some wild animal species may possess such degrees of variation that we should perhaps refer to them as "domesticated" animals.

Bennett's position makes sense to me, and it brings those of us who work in today's jungles to a parting of the ways: we either sit back and wait for the "natural ecology" to be worked out before stating man's place in this environment; or, we begin now, with a concept of man-centered environment and describe this dominant animal's behavior patterns, as they relate to environing political economies of industrialized nations, leaving it to botanists and biologists to follow Bennett's lead in then placing the flora and fauna in proper adaptive perspective. I shall endeavor in ensuing discussions to demonstrate to the reader what man is *doing* in (and to) *his* natural environment.

Large animals including species of tapir, agouti, peccary, paca, and deer are all important sources of meat. The jaguar, ocelot, margay and jaguarundi provide marketable furs. The mountain lion is occasionally found, and his fur sold, while a number of less savory or less marketable animals such as sloths, ant-eaters, armadillos, grey foxes, bushdogs, otters, kinkajous, coatimundis, exist—all of which are killed and often eaten when encountered, unless they are sold to a tourist or to an inland buyer. A wild black guinea pig, cotton tail rabbits, and squirrels are also eaten when caught, but not much effort is made to secure them. Monkeys are rare, except in the northern Chocó. Native muscovy ducks and their eggs are eaten, as are a variety of large birds and turtles. Species of toucans, parrots and macaws are kept as pets or sold; occasionally, they are eaten. Crocodiles and caiman are now rare, though both exist in swampy areas and in the inland lakes. Manatee also once inhabitated the river backwash zones and swampy regions, but are rapidly becoming extinct (as is obvious by the overabundance of water hyacinths in most of the calm waters). Capybara seem to have disappeared.

Wild palms such as the *chontaduro* (peach palm) provide considerable subsistence nourishment through nuts, pulp, and young shoots, in many areas, and in some (particularly on the Río Raposo near Buenaventura, Colombia), the chontaduro is harvested in large amounts and sold. During "chontaduro season" in Cali, Colombia, the roasted "fruit" is sold on the streets and regarded as a delicacy. Many palms are of lesser food and commercial value, but do provide *some* food value, as well as thatch for roofs, and the trunk is frequently used for the pilings of houses. I shall mention the coconut palm below, while discussing the mangrove swamp, and analyze its significance when we consider socioeconomic adaptation (Chapter VII). Many species of soft and hard woods grow in the forest and supply building materials, while *balsa* is also bountiful for making balsa sides for cargo canoes. Wild rubber trees, once so sought after, also exist here but only in a very few areas do people collect rubber for sale; now it is used for such purposes as making heads for marimba mallets.

Bamboo is found in large stands along the rivers where the altitude begins to rise, and provides an excellent source for house floors and walls. There are plenty of grasses and reeds for making mats and hammocks, and tree bark is used to make mats (and hats). A bark sleeping mat lends a pleasant aroma to the generally dank smell of wettish-dried grass and bamboo.

River fishing is now poor, but a number of species still inhabit the rivers; unlike sister rivers in Amazonia, the famous piranha does not exist west of the Andes. Nor are there any gigantic fish such as those justifiably famous to the east. I shall say more about fishing when I discuss the mangrove swamp. About the only creatures not eaten are the snakes, which include boas, anacondas and many poisonous varieties such as the coral snake, fer de lance, and bushmaster.

Staple crops of the area include plantains, maize, bananas, cocoa, coffee, rice, sugar cane, manioc, sweet potato, taro-like tubers, tomatoes, peppers, and a variety of tropical fruits. Breadfruit is grown around houses for the aesthetic appearance of its magnificent tree, but it is not usually regarded as an important food.

One final class of forest denizens must be mentioned to suggest a real sense of the jungle—the diseases carried, or associated with, insects and parasites. Malaria is carried by the anopheles mosquito, which is endemic to the region. Although under control during the past ten years, malaria is again rampant in parts of the littoral, effecting migration patterns as well as conditioning population sizes in various areas. Yellow fever is carried by the domestic aedes mosquito, which is surprisingly absent, or nearly absent, in the littoral. Fleas bearing bubonic plague must not be in large abundance, or if so then the expanding rat population must keep them satisfied near the coast, for thus far plague outbreaks (known to Manta and Guayaquil) have not touched the wet littoral and its forests. Various species of amoebas, paramecia, protozoa, and worms thrive in the human hosts, conditioning them or killing them early of dehydration caused by chronic dysentery. Hook worm, whip worm, various round worms, filarial worms (though probably not the one causing elephantiasis) abound. Schistosomiasis seems absent from the entire area. A type of botfly which lays eggs in a human host is particularly repugnant and dangerous.

Tuberculosis is quite common in the jungle, as are lung fungi and various venereal infections including syphillis, gonorrhea, and lymphogranuloma in its venereal form. Yaws is nearly under control, but various forms of "tropical ulcers" which resemble it exist and are spread by either venereal, or other forms of close contact. Tetanus and typhoid are common, as is hepatitis, and other bacillary and viral infections. Vampire bats spread rabies, as well as other diseases.

The human body in the Pacific littoral is continuously beset by debilitating deadly forces which cause oozing sores, infected sputum, vile colored stools, and pain. A restricted life cycle, and late maturity are an expected part of the human condition.

THE MANGROVE SWAMP

Convenient though portrayals of the "sea and the jungle" might be in describing the environment of the wet littoral, we must temper any tendency to conjure up images of jungle meeting ocean, with South-Sea-like idyllic beaches lined with coconut palms being the only line of demarcation between ocean and forest. Such situations most certainly do exist, one of them near the area which I shall presently focus upon in greater detail.

Sea and jungle combine in much of the littoral to which black adaptation has become dominant to form gigantic swamps where fresh and salt water grade into one another, and where forces generated by land and sea merge, swirling and synergizing into a specific adaptation, which is the subject to which we now turn our attention. Murphy (1939a:14) wrote about this zone:

This is the maritime Chocó [again, in this context, read Chocó as "wet littoral"], a flooded lowland of perpetual rain, of selva and morasses, of hundreds of streams which pour into the Pacific through multiple mouths. The line between earth and ocean becomes tenuous, for the greater part of the shore is fringed with a maze of mangrove-covered flats and islands, separated by a network of *esteros,* and grading into shifting bars and shallows, which in many places extend for miles offshore.

Let us consider the action of warm, sheltered sea and rivers meeting on a one to fifteen mile wide delta, which is completely above water at low tide. The perpetually rain-fed streams carry fertile silt, the steady warmth of the sea pushing and grading such fertile silt into ever-wider plains. Where proper shoals and shore line allowing for wind and high-wave protection occur, the parameters for adaptation of botanically unrelated species of land trees restrict and encourage the mangrove. Tropical trees of various species began through the willy-nillyness of adaptive response (a process which began long ago in Africa and Asia) to lace themselves more firmly out over the wind-sheltered high tide. The evolution of a tremendous system of aerial roots, which encompass most space around the mother trunk, is one striking characteristic of the mangrove adaptation. During low tide the curious viviparous seeds (which germinate inside the fruit before separation from the plant) plop into the knee to waist-deep oozing mud and quickly gain a root-hold if they sink deeply enough so as to avoid being washed away at high tide. With equal frequency they splash into the swelling or ebbing tide, beginning a process of migration that may perhaps span an ocean.

The two most notable species of mangrove tree in the wet littoral are the "red mangrove," *Rhizophora,* with great trucks supported by a wide aerial buttress-like root system, and "black mangrove," *Avicennia,* which send up bamboo-like sprouts all over a given mud bank, and then grow rapidly upward into massive interlaced stands of vine-like appendages. (See West 1957:61-75 and Acosta-Solis 1959 for a full, technical discussion, and for photographs).

Where the land rises a bit within the mangrove swamp, preventing high tide from moving over the soil, and directly behind the mangrove plain for a narrow stretch of up to a mile, there is a belt of brackish to fresh water. This belt will be regarded as part of the mangrove ecosystem in this book because, from a man-centered exploitative perspective, saline mangrove, freshwater mangrove, and the slightly higher brackish-fresh water swamp zones are utilized through the same complex system of human activity.

The fresh to brackish water zone contains some very large trees of one hundred feet or more in height, and some ferns and palms. One of the currently important of these big trees is the *Cuángare,* and related species such as *Tángare* and *Amarillo,* which are now in demand in the United States for making veneers. Unlike the salt-water mangrove zone, the fresh water swampy adjoining area is an extraordinarily fertile milieu for the propagation of insects, including the malarial-carrying anopheles.

The rise and fall of tides which define a *"lunar day"* govern most of the activities of people in the mangrove swamps, and since the swamps in many cases provide major access to and from the jungle and the outside world (via the sea) they are doubly important. As the tide (which averages about 11 feet) rises, it moves in through the mangrove trees, flooding all, and making the "fresh water zone" brackish in many areas. Thick mucky areas that were impassable by foot during low tide become waterways for canoe at high tide. Some *esteros,* estuaries, of low tide become impassable at high tide as canoes rise to the level of the interlaced mangrove roots. In the broad channels between the mangrove stands the flow of tides allows for floating of large rafts of wood, or cargoes going to and from market. Earlier (Whitten 1965:86), I wrote:

> It would be foolhardy, to say the least, to try to bring in several tons of timber against the tide, with no more than large oars for propulsion. Nor can a canoe be moved easily against the flow;- even a canoe with a motor can enter many areas of the mangrove swamp only when the tide is flowing in (at low tide the channel is dry) or flowing out (at high tide the mangrove roots form a solid wall at water level).

Since the mangrove trees themselves form protection from sea-wind and heavy waves, while allowing fresh breezes to prevail through the deep tree-free channels, they form boundaries for acceptable human habitation sites where the land rises sharply. Also, since large channels, cutting through the mangrove stands, are suitable for navigation of seacraft, shipping and commerce are possible to a degree not realized in the forest itself, except on large rivers such as the Atrato.

The estero and channel together provide for networks of waterways connecting coastal towns. Travel can be effective over a hundred miles or more in some places without entering the sea itself for more than, perhaps, a 20 mile stretch. Although some have claimed otherwise, walking trails do extend for a mile or two in the mangrove swamp; such a "trail" is usually established about 5 feet above the low-tide flat, at a level usually submerged at high tide. People literally scramble over the slippery, bent, and sometimes barnacled mangrove roots, ducking those over their heads, and clearing a minimum of roots from the space around which they wish to walk. Such a "walking" trail—like a high tunnel—frequently presages the completion of more efficient canoe trails, which involve removing many of the roots of the mangrove tree to allow a canoe to slide freely in the low-tide muck, or move with the tide during its flow in or out of the swamp. Sliding along in such a channel, one may find species of crab peering down on him from above, or scrambling along at shoulder level.

Habitation in the mangrove swamp ranges from single houses built on high points of land, or on stilts in the swamp itself, to large towns such as Buenaventura, Colombia, with a population approaching 100,000, or San Lorenzo, Ecuador, with a population which has grown from a little over 2,000 in 1961 to 6,000 in 1968. Prehistorically, too, some of the largest settlements in all of the New World lowland tropics probably occurred in and near these mangrove stands, many of them on the very sites of presently growing towns.[3]

The resource potential of the mangrove swamp is considerable, both for subsistence life, and also for expansion of international economies. Let us begin with the mangrove tree itself, which is one of the world's densest woods, virtually "indestructible" when used for pilings, though difficult to transport because it sinks, even in salt water. The bark is a principal source of tannic acid, and is stripped and sold. Bark stripping, however, kills the tree. Many of the stands in northern Ecuador have been startlingly decimated during the last few years. Such decimation, always critical in altering an ecosystem, takes on crucial significance in the mangrove swamp. According to ecologist Rachel Carson (1955:210): "The mangrove may be the only kind of tree, or the only seed plant growing there [in the sea]; *all the associated plants and animals are bound to it by biological ties.*" (emphasis added).

Small black mollusks, called *conchas* (large black ones regarded as *hembra*, "female," small lighter ones being *macho*, "male,") are abundant in the mangrove swamp, and of considerable commercial value since they constitute the basis for famous *"ceviche de concha."* They also provide an important local food source. Other shellfish include shrimp, crab (six edible varieties), oysters, abalones, clams, and mussels of several varieties and varied commercial value. There are a few crayfish in this area and prawns are limited in their distribution. Dozens of species of fish inhabit the swamps and channels, ranging from more than a dozen locally named small fish such as mullet, pompano, perch, bonito species, to medium size croakers and sea bass, to large manta rays, sharks, sawfish, and albacore. All are caught by a variety of techniques. They are locally eaten everywhere, and sold fresh, or dried. Iguana are commonly found in the brackish fringes, as are a variety of turtles and tortoises. Now and then one still encounters a sea snake and crocodile. Birds, and especially their eggs, provide food.

Lumber operations to secure the large softwoods are quite important to the cash economy; the wood comes from the fresh-brackish water zone, and is moved through the esteros and channels between forest stands. There are sawmills in the swamps and near the ports. Timber from the interior must be floated down to the mangrove delta, in most instances. Where logging operations are completed in the high-ground areas surrounded by swamp land, this land is sometimes cleared and cash plantations as well as small farms (both called *fincas*) are formed. Principal crops from them are bananas, plantains, pine-apples, sugar cane, rice in some areas, manioc, and the very important coconut. I shall say more about fishing and farming in Chapter IV.

Towns themselves represent different adjustments to the broad ecosystem, reflecting different forms of environmental exploitation. For example, there are villages given over completely to fishing, with as many as 50 houses built entirely over the water, where even the pigs and chickens learn to move up a notched log into the dwellings during high tide. Many small houses, or clusters of houses, exist for the sole purpose of maintaining a farm or series of farms in fertile areas. Towns such as Limones, northwest Ecuador, are primarily commercial, while one town near the Colombian-Ecuadorian border is almost exclusively given over to smuggling operations between the two countries. Towns rise and fall in size and importance according to the vicissitudes of external world markets. Towns were "made" during world *tagua,* rubber, and banana booms, only to decline again as the apparently inevitable depression of "boom-bust" economies appeared.

We shall have to examine with some care the manner by which the people in the wet Pacific littoral adjust their lives to such boom-bust economies. It will not be enough to understand their exploitation of the mangrove swamp zone in terms of fish, coconuts, mussels, and the like, though an entire volume could be written on this intriguing ex-ploitation of micro-environmental zones alone. It is essential that we understand that the mangrove swamp itself provides the major contact point for a good many international transactions, ranging from lumber booms to possible international political intrigue. *Such transactions are a crucial part of the socio-economic environment of Afro-Hispanic*

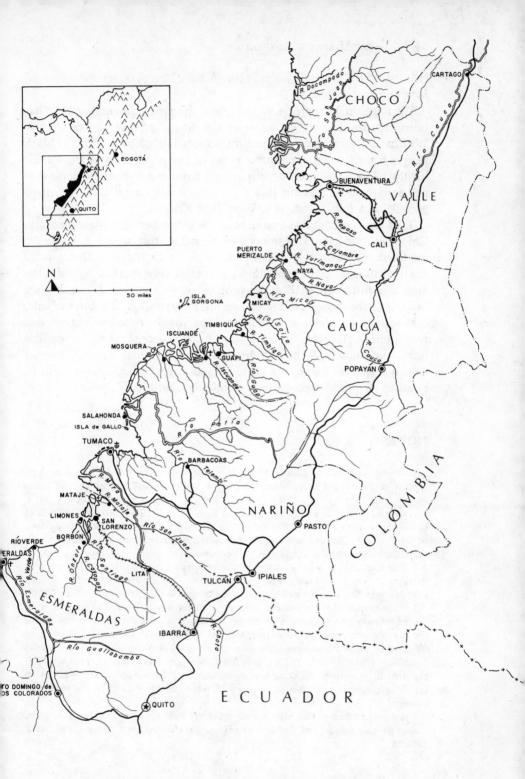

Map II: The Wet Littoral of The Pacific Lowlands

culture, which is caught up in, though not altogether dependent upon, international economy.

We have now reached a point where the environmental setting has been broadly sketched in terms of sea, forest, and mangrove swamp. Within this setting an expanding population of over 500,000 black people constitute 90 per cent or more of the population of the Pacific littoral. The population density ranges from one to over forty persons per square mile, making this the most densely populated region of New World rain forests (see West 1957:82).

This environmental sketch depicts the sector between Buenaventura, Colombia and central Esmeraldas, Ecuador, but would have to be modified to adequately portray the zone from the Río Docampadó north, where a more mountainous coastal zone occurs. Within the area to which we shall restrict ourselves[4]—"the wet Littoral" (see Map II)—the mangrove swamp seems to crystallize the buzz of life, conditioned by the sea and backed by jungle resources. From this point on "wet littoral" refers to the area between the Esmeraldas River, Ecuador, and the San Juan River, Colombia. The Colombian Chocó is *excluded* from the patterns and characterizations set forth in ensuing chapters, except where explicitly mentioned.

NOTES

[1] The rise and fall of tides is, to say the least, a quite complicated process. This process in the natural environment, like many others already alluded to, and many more which I shall need to introduce, can scarcely be dealt with here in any but a cursory and literary manner. The reader is directed to West's (1957) work as well as to that of Murphy (1939a, 1939b) for a more detailed examination of specific sections of the Pacific Lowlands coast, and the winds, rains, currents, and other forces which shape the ecosystem in which man is forever coping.

[2] This statement reflects my own conclusions drawn from reading of the relevant literature. Should the reader wish to delve into this fascinating subject he should read Meggers, Evans, and Estrada (1965), Reichel-Dolmatoff (1965) and Lathrap (1970).

[3] Much more archaeology needs to be done in the Pacific littoral to unravel what is undoubtedly the fascinating prehistory of the area of northwest Ecuador where the greatest concentration of sites called "La Tolita" (and known in Colombia as "Tumaco") styles come from. Preliminary references include Uhle (1927), Costales Samaniego (1957), Estrada and Meggers (1961), Meggers (1966). Pizarro (Prescott 1874) reported huge settlements along this coast, and his pilot Ruiz was nearly killed on several occasions upon entering apparently fortified villages within the mangrove swamps.

[4] Such restriction to the area between Esmeraldas, Ecuador and Buenaventura, Colombia also follows the division of prehistoric culture areas (Reichel-Dolmatoff 1965:38).

CHAPTER THREE

Blackness In Northern South America: Historical Dimensions

In the fifteenth century—the age of exploration—the measure of power of European nations was found in their access to precious metals, particularly gold, and "the hot, humid rain forest of Colombia's Pacific lowlands has been one of the outstanding sources of gold in Latin America . . ." (West 1952:14, see also 15). The search for means of expanding national wealth led to rediscovery of the Americas some 20,000 or more years after human adaptation to a variety of natural and sociocultural surroundings had taken place. The searchers and culture carriers from Europe smashed head on into vibrant, evolving bands, tribes, states, and empires and in a short time created a whole new series of "colonial tribes."[1]

Native peoples in the land of El Dorado were working gold at the time of the conquest, wearing the results of their advanced craftsmanship as ornaments and as symbols of political and religious authority. At first it was sufficient for the conquering Spaniards to simply take the riches of native craft; Professor Gerardo Reichel-Dolmatoff (1965:18-19) puts it well:

> They took it from the living and from the dead, by torture and violence, and by looting shrines and graves. The search for gold soon became a decisive factor in determining the routes of the conquering troops and in the choice of sites for the establishment of the first Spanish settlements.

Indians fought back fiercely, for El Dorado was a land of native warfare, bloodshed, and terrible atrocities long before the coming of new conquerers. Looting and chicanery to acquire native gold soon proved to have limits, and the Spanish turned to the source of gold itself, using native slaves as miners and as beasts of burden. By the middle

35

of the 16th century not only was the magnificence of Chibcha and Quimbaya (for example) gone, but the culture carriers themselves, the native Indians, were in danger of physical extinction. Yellow gold from the Americas and black manpower from Africa were about to merge on a large scale, for slaves had been arriving in northern Colombia since at least the early 1500's (cf. Jaramillo Uribe 1963).

Early in the 16th century the Spanish Friar Bartolomé de Las Casas issued his famous proclamation on the humanity of the Indians. So taken was he with his firsthand experiences, and so moved to compassion at his observations of the destruction of the Indians, yet himself such a part of the culture of his time which asserted a biological racism as one of the foundations of western thought, that he inadvertently opened the doors of Latin America to one of the world's great horrors. Las Casas argued that humanity of the Indians had to be protected, that in order to protect them large scale labor forces would have to replace them; he recommended the massive importation of Black Africans to take over the animal tasks heretofore largely relegated to native Americans.

Thomas J. Price (1955:1), the first anthropologist to undertake serious ethnographic field work in the Pacific littoral, is explicit:

> They [African slaves] were brought through the main port of entry, Cartagena, sold there, and either transported by river to one of the provinces of Chocó, Popayán, and Antioquia, the three major mining areas, or remained in the region of Cartagena for work on the plantations. The middle of the sixteenth century found them engaged in mining in many parts of Colombia, and by 1544 they were being used in the mines near Popayán . . . It is estimated that, by 1590, approximately one thousand slaves were imported annually through Cartagena.

This information takes on even greater significance in terms of the white, Euro-American folk-history of our time, when we consider how many textbooks on slavery date black arrival in the "New World" as 1619, and proceed as though the Yankee way was dominant. Over one hundred years before any Dutch ship brought "Negars" to Jamestown, Virginia, Black Africans were entering South America (and Central America, Mexico, and the Caribbean) as slaves; almost immediately on their arrival they began to revolt, to fight back, to enjoin the New World in series upon series of self assertive freedom and self liberation revolts and movements.

For example, an entire black state emerged in the very area of our concern. Esmeraldas Province, Ecuador, was dominated by "zambos" —people of stipulated African-Indian descent—who apparently established hegemony over native Indians, and began to negotiate with emissaries of the Spanish Crown before the end of the 16th century (Phelan 1967). The state perhaps resembled the black state of Palmares on the opposite side of the South American continent. There, in what is now the state of Alagôas, Brazil, Africans stood off the colonial armies for nearly a century (Chapman 1918, Ramos 1939:25-26, 42-53). How many new Afro-American chiefdoms and states arose in the New World before the slave trade with Africa really got underway, and remained until destroyed by colonists, is not known. The question remains one of the more crucial subjects for historical inquiry. Whether Africans were in the New World prior to the European conquest is still not clear, but recent evidence (Jeffreys 1971) does indicate a pre-15th century African-European-Caribbean-South American trading sphere. Historians, ethnohistorians, botanists and archaeologists have much to contribute to this awakening controversy.

THE AFRICAN BACKGROUND

Africa is a large continent, with many civilizations. Where did the Africans who wound up in the Pacific littoral after 1492 come from? Using data which he found in the Archivo Nacional de Bogotá, and drawing from a prominent Colombian ethnohistorian, José Arboleda, Price (1955:2) firmly establishes that the majority of slaves were brought from West Africa.

> The names which appear most frequently in the documents are the Angolas, the designation given to the people taken from the territory between the Dande and Cuango Rivers in north central Angola; the Lucumi, or Yoruba, from Nigeria; the Mina, people brought from San Jorge da Mina, factory of the Fanti territory in the Gold Coast; The Chamba, from Nigeria; the Carabalí, the designation given to people taken from the Calabar Coast in Nigeria; Bambara, sub-group of the Mande-Tan of the Upper Senegal River in French Guinea; Guaguí, people from the Niger River, Nigeria; the Mondongo from the Congo; the Mandinga, a tribe in the French Sudan; and the Dahomeans. Of these the Carabalí and Mandinga are mentioned as being particularly intractable and therefore undesirable as slaves. For the most part these Negroes were brought directly from Africa for sale, though a small number consisted of those who had been brought to Jamaica and then reshipped to the mainland.

Price (1955:2-3) is again explicit when writing about the area of our greatest concern:

> With regard to the significance of slavery for the regions of Colombia . . .

it is known that the Negro population of Tumaco is descended from slaves who were originally brought to Popayán and Barbacoas, plus a few isolated spots on the coast, to work in the gold mines. With the end of slavery, large numbers filtered down to the coast and formed small fishing and agricultural communities, many of which still exist today. The tribal groups represented follow the list of names already mentioned, with the Yoruba particularly numerous.

David Pavy (1967) in a recent article draws heavily from the Cuban historian José Antonio Saco (1938), the Colombian historians Jaime Jaramillo Uribe (1963) and Aquiles Escalante (1964), from Reichel-Dolmatoff, and others, and from his "discovery" of the Jesuit scholar Alonso de Sandoval (a contemporary of Pedro Claver, who worked in Cartagena in the early 17th century) to reinforce the material presented by Price. Breaking down the African slaving zones into three areas: "Senegambia, central coast, and southern region," Pavy (1967:56) writes:

> The Senegambian area . . . was the first to be exploited. It probably was the principal source of supply of slaves to Colombia until the middle of the seventeenth century. . . .
>
> The acquisition of slaves from the central coastal area involved trading of the Europeans with the large independent African states emerging in this region. The introduction of arms by the Portuguese and later Europeans contributed to the expansion of the states of the Fanti, Ashanti, Yoruba, and the Dahomeans . . . It is likely that during the whole of the slave trade to Colombia the central coastal area contributed most slaves. It was the most densely populated of the three areas and dominated the trade at its height. . . .
>
> Angola is something of a problem . . . A steady flow of slaves from Angola entered the Spanish Main throughout the years of slavery, but it is doubtful that they were ever the most numerous group. [Pavy should be consulted for more detail, including a methodological argument. See also Velásquez 1962, Escalante 1964, 1971, Curtin 1969:15-49].

Historian James King (1939, 1945), among many others, notes that a large number of Black Africans arriving in the Pacific Lowlands through the northern port of Cartagena were classed as *"bozal,"* a term that came to mean "fresh from Africa." "Bozal" actually derives from ". . . the Spanish word for the crude halter used on bronco horses before the use of the bit." (Bastien 1959:79) For a slave, "fresh from Africa" must be understood in terms of Euro-African imprisonment prior to departure, the horrible "middle passage," and above all adaptation to New World settings.

The natural environment of the Pacific littoral with its lodes of gold and a mercantile political economy exploiting labor through concepts of biological racism coincided in the 16th and 17th centuries to place Black Africans in new settings in a new world. The massive reshuffling of cultural elements, and the subsequent adaptations, must be understood in terms of the dynamics of African maneuver in the face of European exploitation. We must understand the growth and spread of Afro-Hispanic culture in the Pacific Lowlands by first developing a sense of social adjustment and then seeing Afro-Hispanic culture as it contributes to the maintenance of dynamic adaptive strategies. I do not deny resilience and persistence of African ways in the New World.[2] I simply give more attention to creative, adaptive aspects of such lifeways, seen as forever unfolding in response to new environmental challenges.

SLAVERY, SLAVE REVOLTS, AND "FREEDOM"

El Dorado is the early and romantic name for the Spanish Main, which I previously used because of its crucial referent to gold. *Nueva (new) Granada* is the colonial name of the Colombian-Ecuadorian region of which the Pacific littoral is a part. In slavery, and subsequent freedom, historian King's (1945:296) statement is crucial for those who seek to understand the evolution of Afro-Hispanic culture: "Only in New Granada were Negroes consistently used in large numbers during a long period of time as the chief source of labor in the mines. There the *señor de cuadrilla* [slave master, overlord] and his gang of black, half naked gold washers constituted a major foundation of colonial society." To this Jaramillo Uribe (1963:14) adds that of the six bases of colonial society—mining, agriculture, cattle raising, handicrafts, commerce, and domestic work—slaves were destined for only a few tasks beyond mining. By the 18th century they worked on cattle haciendas, produced sugar beet and transportable brown sugar loaves on hand–run sugar mills, and transported cargo, including slaves, on the major rivers. But mining was predominant (see also Escalante 1971). A section of this chapter will be devoted to the organization of labor in the mines, and I shall also discuss the probable impact of missionaries, pirates, and generals in wars of liberation before attempting to sketch broad parameters of black adaptation.

Hispanicized Slaves

Long before the beginning of the African slave trade to the New World, there was a trade across the Sahara into the Circum-Mediterranean in general, and for our interests, into Spain and Portugal in particular. The years preceding the trade to the New World saw a maritime expansion of slavery from Africa into Europe (Curtin 1969:17-21). Historian Magnus Mörner (1967:16) tells us, "The first Negro slaves, already speaking Spanish (*ladinos*), were servants recruited among the many Negro slaves who at the time were kept in Spain as well as in Portugal." Such *ladinos* (the word also means deceitful person, or a tricky person in coastal Ecuador and in Spain, but simply stands for *"mestizo"* [mixed blood] in Guatemala) sailed with Columbus, with Vasco Balboa, with Francisco Pizzaro, to name only three well known explorers and conquerers.

> Perturbed by the possibility that the Negroes, by their demoralizing example, might jeopardize the conversion and submission of its new American subjects, the crown at first forbade any but blacks born into slavery among Christians to be taken to the West Indies. But experience having demonstrated that *bozal* Negroes — those fresh from Africa — were much more tractable than the sophisticated and "mischievous" *ladinos* from the Peninsula, the law was reversed in 1526 (King 1945:300).

According to a traveler (Miguel Cabello Balboa, reprinted 1945) who visited Esmeraldas province, Ecuador, in the late 16th century, a slaving ship ran aground near the present town of Esmeraldas sometime in the mid-16th century. There a group of some 20-23 Africans (17 men, 3-6 women) from the Guinea coast, led by a *ladino* named Alonso de Illescas, fled their captors and proceeded somehow to gain dominance in the area and, by intermixture with various Indian groups, came to propagate a new race. By the end of the 16th century the Province of Esmeraldas was considered a *"zambo* republic" (Phelan 1967:8), *zambo* being the term for "African-Indian mixture."

> The potential threat that this zambo republic posed was not lost on the Spaniards in Quito. An *oidor* of the Audiencia . . . traveled in and around San Mateo from 1597 to 1600 and claimed to have persuaded five thousand zambos to recognize the overlordship of Spain.

A group of "zambos" did journey to Quito in the late 1500's, and there recognized the sovereignty of Spain. A painting of these early Black Americans now hangs in the *Museo de América* in Madrid, depicting them in princely robes, with gold ornaments in their noses and ears and around their necks (photograph of painting in Phelan 1967:224-225). *Ladinos* they began, *zambos* they became. Whatever the actual history of the as yet unexplained explosion of zambo dominance in Esmeraldas province, this information is indicative of a very early hispanicized "black" population, free and slave, coinciding with the growth and expansion of African slavery.

Phenomena such as the domination of Afro-Hispanic culture in Esmeraldas province, and the freedom to negotiate with new, expanding centralized systems, distintegrated by the 18th century, when successive dominance of the *audiencias,* and later nations, came into being. Slavery, for example, expands in the zambo state of Esmeraldas, and as late as the mid-19th century we learn of a slave revolt in the little town of Río Verde, today symbolized by a statue there erected to honor a self liberated black man.

Slaves Fresh from Africa

West (1952:85-86), basing his statements on considerable archival work in Colombia, writes:

> Slaves destined for the mines of western Colombia entered through the port of Cartagena, one of the largest colonial slave marts of the Spanish mainland. Mine owners obtained slaves chiefly through itinerant merchants, who purchased Negroes in Cartagena and, together with other types of merchandise, shipped them up the Magdalena and Cauca rivers in canoes. Rarely did a merchant carry more than 25 to 30 slaves at one time. During the eighteenth century *bozales,* or young bucks newly arrived from Africa, were valued at 300 pesos, whereas *criollos* [Negroes born in the New World] brought from 400 to 500 pesos. Young females were often valued as highly as males, for women were used not only for breeding and as household servants but also as agricultural workers and mine laborers, particularly in the placers.

Regarding the economics of this trade, as it effected the slave buyers, we learn from West (1952:86-89) that the buyers often went into debt, and complained about the high prices and unpredictable supply of slaves. One of the reasons for unpredictability was the growing numbers of *palenques* (fortified villages of free blacks) from which marauding guerrillas attacked slave canoes on major transport rivers. Only a glimpse can be given here to the growth of the slave trade from Africa through the Colombian port of Cartagena. As a convenience, let us again quote the historian James King (1945:302, 303, 304):

> The increasing need for slaves resulted in the development of the *asiento* system . . . a formal contract . . . in Spanish public administration the term was by no means restricted to the slave trade. But because of the outstanding importance of the Negro contracts, an unqualified word *asiento,* particularly among foreigners concerned in the trade, came to mean the monopolistic right to provide the Spanish Indies, or some part thereof, with slaves . . . The essential characteristic of the system was strict regulation, in the interest of controlling, first, the revenue which could be drawn from the traffic, and second, the quantity and quality of the Negroes imported into the Indies . . .

The trade was facilitated by the union of the crowns of Spain and Portugal from 1580 to 1640; for the latter nation, at least until the mid-seventeenth century, remained chiefly in control of the African sources of supply. (See also Curtin 1969:21-22).

King does a masterful job in a brief article, tracing the relationships between European states competing over access to the slave trade from Spanish-Portuguese domination, to brief French ascendancy, to British advantage around 1713 won at the Utrecht settlement. He then describes how the British forced the establishment of the viceroyalty of New Granada, which then became the unit for administration of the slave trade. His conclusion, after unraveling many diplomatic and legal threads, allows us to return to the problem of understanding black adaptation without undue reference to the enormous legal and diplomatic framework governing the flow of slaves into the Spanish Main:

> The history of Negro slavery in New Granada cannot be told entirely in terms of *asientos* and changing importation policies. The Negro traffic, which tends to bulk unduly large in accounts of colonial American slavery because its regular evolution provides a convenient chronological framework, is chiefly important because *it provided human raw material for a complex social process which has by no means reached its end even at the present day.* (King 1945:307, emphasis added.)

Slaves (men and women) from Africa were landed at Cartagena in wretched condition, naked or near naked, and carrying a number of contagious diseases, including leprosy, yaws, malaria, smallpox and tuberculosis. Immediately upon arrival they were measured and branded and reduced as human beings to their status as *"Piezas de Indias."* This was a *measure of labor,* sometimes translated as "prime Negroes" for only the strongest male individuals would equal one such measure (see Curtin 1969:22). For others, not so prime, stockades called *barracones* (after the English term barracoon) provided meagre or no shelter, until a buyer, or death, released them.

Early in the 17th century the Jesuit order of Catholic Priests took a strong interest in the spiritual and, in some cases, material, well-being of the slaves. It should also be noted that Jesuits themselves held slaves. The most famous of the Jesuit soul savers was Saint Pedro Claver, who today is known as the patron saint of Colombian Negroes. San Pedro is said to have learned an Angolan language in order to communicate with new bozales, and to have baptized over 300,000 black men and women during his life time. According to Pavy (1967:45) he had interpreters in African languages, among whom were "two

Angolas, one Biáfara and a Congo." Another such Jesuit, Alonso de Sandoval, is the scholar from whom much of the available material on ethnohistory of the Africans entering through Cartagena evidently derives. San Pedro Claver and other Jesuits also treated the sick and attempted to make life a bit more comfortable in the stockades prior to their purchase.

West (1952:18-19) tells us a good deal about slavery in the area of the wet Pacific littoral. Not until after the Zambo Republic of Esmeraldas was incorporated into the *Audiencia* of Quito did the Spanish reach what is now Barbacoas, on the northern fringe of that area. There, at Santa María del Puerto, military engagement with the Barbacoas Indian chiefdom commenced at the beginning of the 17th century. And by the end of that century we learn that black and Indian mining gangs were at work from Barbacoas north to Buenaventura. The continuation and expansion of mining activity near the beginning of the 18th century mark the near total obliteration of native cultures in this area and the rapid expansion of Afro-Hispanic culture. Throughout this one hundred year period mines were periodically closed by Indian and African revolt—and black people undoubtedly went free—but, "By the mid-18th century every major river of the coastal plains . . . contained gangs of Negro slaves" (West 1957:100). And, ". . . . by the end of the eighteenth century Iscuandé, Santa Bárbara Timbiquí, and San Francisco Naya were among the largest towns along the west coast of New Granada." (West 1952:19)

On the placers, as in the highland mines, disease was rampant, and constant supplies of fresh slaves were required. The movement of people transporting the coffles from Cartagena into the wet littoral stimulated other trade, and maintained and expanded economic relationships between the mining towns and growing pre-industrial cities such as Cartagena, Bogotá, and Quito, as well as intermediate administrative towns such as Cali, Popayán, Pasto, and Ibarra.

The mines of the wet Pacific littoral seem to have been instrumental in stimulating the economics of New Granada. Critical in the mining complex were the black men and women, slave and free. We must not, however, assume that the economic importance of an aggregate of people (in this case black people) implies social and political power; the very institution of slavery itself belies the notion. Social and political power must be won and held; and it is often found in inverse relationship to the value of a given aggregate in the labor force.

Freedom

Black freedom and strife toward social and political power began with the Spanish Conquest. For example, in 1529 the pioneer city of the Spanish Main, Santa Marta, was burned to the ground by rebellious African slaves (King 1945:301). Throughout Colombia, in every single place where slaves were imported, there are records of rebellion, of escape, and innumerable instances of the establishment of successful fortified villages, known as *palenques*. Not only did *cimarrones* (as escaped slaves were called) revolt and resist, they also initiated counter attacks on mines, plantations, and shipping routes, acquiring capital, goods, skill, and more manpower.

According to Jaramillo Uribe (1963:43), rebellion, *"cimarronismo"* and the proliferation of palenques constituted a major threat to non-Afro-Hispanic society by the second half of the 18th century. The palenques are described as democratic, with elected leaders, and containing well organized religious and social life based on an amalgamation of Afro-Hispanic traditions (see Jaramillo Uribe 1963:42-50). Some of these palenques expanded into small kingdoms, like that of Palmares of Brazil, forever threatening the established society until destroyed by military strength, or by trickery.

Since the international scene through the years of slavery involved many rivalries between foreign powers such as Spain and Britain, and since rivalries between legitimate gold seekers and illegitimate ones (pirates and buccaneers) also existed, self-liberated slaves could sometimes find powerful external allies. King (1945:311) tells us that, "So great a threat to colonial society did the runaways become, in fact, that *the Spanish authorities were often forced to recognize their freedom* in an effort to pacify and bring them once more under civil government." (emphasis added)

Slave revolts beginning in the 16th century continued right up into the 19th (cf. King 1939, Jaramillo Uribe 1963), this time stimulated and aided by the rising wars of independence, the wars of self-liberation of emerging nation states:

> When Bolívar's armies passed through [plantation areas and mining areas] thousands of the mining slaves were recruited, often forcibly . . . Another result of these proclamations [of immediate manumission] was a series of Negro rebellions in various parts of the Colombian lowlands. In 1821, a serious revolt . . . took place on the Río Saíja. The slaves burned the mining camps and fled to the Pacific coastal lowlands (Hudson 1964:231).

In 1821 Colombia passed a law freeing all slaves born after July 21, 1821, when they reached their 18th birthday. (cf. Sharp 1968) The revolts continued. An illustrative case occurred in Barbacoas. Hudson (1964:237) writes:

A typical example of a political explanation for racial unrest was the attack of the *guerrillero* Agualongo on the town of Barbacoas in 1824. Most Colombian historians characterized this attack as a royalist raid to gain supplies and disrupt the independence movement in that area. On the other hand, an English traveler reported that Agualongo's troops were Negro slaves who had run away from the gold mines, and Tomás Cipriano Mosquera, the commander of the troops at Barbacoas, stated in a letter to Bolívar soon after that attack that, "[Agualongo's] project was to revolutionize the four thousand slaves of [Buenaventura] province and even those of the Chocó."

Finally, in response to unrelenting black pressure through guerrilla warfare, the nation of Colombia freed all slaves in 1852. Further south, in Ecuador, black people played an important role in the fight not only for liberation from Spanish rule, but also in the separation of Ecuador from Gran Colombia in 1830.

> The Negro distinguished himself as a leader and soldier in practically all campaigns for independence in the New World. He brought his talent and aptitude for warfare to the campaigns of both Simón Bolívar and San Martin, in which there were well-organized and well-disciplined troops of Negro soldiers (Herring 1961:113).

I have previously noted (Whitten 1965) that "some of these soldiers remained in Ecuador. According to Dozer (1962:320), Vicente Rocafuerte, a liberal reformer and President of Ecuador from 1834 to 1849, 'opposed and sought to reduce the power of the Negro troops whom Juan José Flores (military leader under Simón Bolívar and later responsible for Ecuador's separation from Gran Colombia) imported from Venezuela."

Let us briefly recapitulate what has been learned. Slaves first entering the Pacific Lowlands were both hispanicized and African. They were followed by a 350 year continuous flow of Black Africans. But escape, revolt, manumission, birth (the offspring of a free white and black slave was legally free), and even the purchase of freedom began almost immediately. Both free and enslaved black aggregates are present from the early 16th century into the mid-19th century. In order to understand 450 years of black adaptation, we must consider a base line consisting of both slavery and freedom, with African and European influences. Such influences are carried to direct contact with indigenous Indian people. What, then, was the nature of life among the slave and the free? Hudson (1964:226-227) gives a good summary:

> The general consensus of travelers and historians appears to be that Negro slaves in Spanish America were better treated than elsewhere and freedom

was comparatively easy to secure. Consequently, a large free Negro population arose prior to 1810. Under the Spanish colonial government these Negroes formed the lowest stratum of free society. *The free Negroes, as well as mulattoes and zambos . . . were hemmed in very tightly by restrictions.* They could not travel freely, leave their homes at night, carry arms except in separate colonial militia units, hold public office, join craft guilds, or even wear fancy jewelry. (emphasis added)

Well-treated slaves—but *hemmed in, aggressive, black freemen*—this seems an apt summary for a dynamic base-line of black adaptation. Returning to the wet Pacific littoral we once again find the research of Robert C. West (1952:89) to be most helpful:

> By the end of the Colonial period a sizeable group of free Negroes *(libres)* had evolved in the mining areas of New Granada. The free element was composed mainly of Negroes who had been able to buy freedom, the runaways, the mulattoes . . . and the few individuals who had been emancipated by compassionate masters. Almost invariably the *libres* continued in the mining profession, usually working either as independent gold washers or as free laborers in Spanish mines; some even acquired ownership of small placers and one or two slaves . . . when general emancipation of the New Granadan slaves took place in 1851, *an occupational precedent had been long established, and most of the freed blacks continued as miners, forming the labor base of the present industry in the lowlands of western Colombia.* (emphasis added).

Labor Organization and Trade

Let us turn now to the work situation in the Pacific Lowlands, our assumption being that the organization of labor (slave and free) in relation to the money economy is crucial in establishing certain parameters for continuing elaboration of Afro-Hispanic culture. Our source for the organization of slave and freemen in the placer mining system is Robert C. West's (1952) work, entitled *Colonial Placer Mining in Colombia*. His discussion will be utilized extensively. After describing basic techniques of panning, sluicing, and working banks for deposits, West (1952:86) turns to a discussion of the slave gang.

The apical figure in the chain of command from master to slave, or from owner to worker, was known as the *señor de cuadrilla,* "master, overlord." Normally, this señor was the colonial mineowner. If the señor were sufficiently wealthy he would assume the role of absentee boss, residing in a large town, such as Popayán. Under such a señor was a white or mulatto overseer, known as *administrador de minas,* "administrator, overseer." Such an overseer would reside in the major mining towns or settlements, and would probably be one of the most important persons, if not *the* most important person, in the town.

Since West specifically mentions that this overseer may be "white" or "mulatto," a digression into white master-black slave social-sexual life is instructive. According to Price (1955:5):

> The Spanish conquerors seem to have freely taken Negro women from the very beginning, a common practice being for an owner to have one or more of his female slaves as mistresses. With some frequency liberty was given to the half-caste children, and *even to their mother as well*. (Emphasis added, see also Jaramillo Uribe 1963:35).

Returning to the *cuadrilla,* West (1952:86) tells us that the slave gang contained from a half dozen or less up to one hundred black people. The gang was often divided in half: "mine workers," *piezas de minas,* brought in the gold, and "field hands," *piezas de roza,* raised food for the camp. Men and women were employed in both mining and farming. In the placers women dived and panned with the men, but when a sluice was used some division of labor by sex took place, ". . . it was usually the task of women to scrape the sluice with the *almocafre* [adze-like tool] and to pan with the *batea* [shallow wooden bowl], while the heavy work with the iron bar was assigned to the men." (West 1952:86) Although the free administrators included a white overlord and light or mulatto overseer, the *immediate boss* of the work crew was a black slave. This *capitán de cuadrilla,* "captain, boss," was charged with ". . . the disciplining of his gang, the distribution of food, and the collection of weekly take of gold for his administrator." (West 1952:86) In other words, *responsibility ranking* within the black work gang was instituted in the Pacific littoral with slave labor. Within each work crew, whether engaging in agriculture, or in panning gold, a fellow slave was charged with great responsibility and given considerable authority.

> The Negro *capitán* was an important person; he was something of a chief, and held the respect of his gang. He was likewise respected by his master, who often gave him special rations to induce him to keep his people working. Occasionally a female *capitana* had charge of the women of the gang. (West 1952:86-87)

There were also free blacks working the placer gravels but we know less about their social organization. West (1952:89-90) tells us about all that is really known: they were called *"mazamorrero"* which is derived from *mazamorra*—tail sluice—and that they re-worked areas abandoned by slave holders and their cuadrillas. Such mazamorreros still exist in the Pacific littoral.[3] The typical mazamorrero family contains a man, or "jefe," sometimes a single brother or cousin of the jefe, and two or more women of the jefe, together with their children. The man clears land, builds a house, and does much of the heavy labor in the sluiceways, while his women and children harvest crops, care for land, pan gold, dive, wash gold, and attend to cooking and housework. On the most productive lodes the mazamorrero may work a deal with one or two young men to help him, offering equal shares in the earnings, but he usually takes the larger share for himself, regarding a disproportionate amount for himself as legitimate in his role of "chief" or "head."

In colonial times it was probable that both slave and free *worked* within the same system in which high rank and responsibility were assigned to one particular figure, usually (but not necessarily) a man. The slaves took the most gold out, but got little for themselves, while the free blacks, and Indians, did clean-up work, gaining all of the meager remains for themselves. Although the *jefe role* was defined as masculine, women could, and did, assume such a role in the absence of a capable *hombre*.

Whether slave or free the miners had to eat, and whatever specific organization might have characterized the early cuadrillas, provision had to be made for a steady food supply. Food was locally grown, and it was brought from outside as a source of trade. West (1952:87) lists "plantains, maize, salt and fresh or salted meat" as the staple food rations, to which I think we must add manioc, taro-like tubers, and fish. All of these products can come from within a given mining area in the wet littoral, all can be sent outward as trade goods to other mining areas, and all can be purchased from other areas. We have already noted that the slave trade and movement of men and women themselves stimulated trading ventures between the Pacific Lowlands, and growing pre-industrial colonial cities. Such trade was further stimulated due to the *buying power* of blacks in the Pacific Lowlands. *Both slave and free* had some direct access to strategic tokens of mercantilism and capitalism—gold. According to West (1952:88) mine owners allowed black slaves to work the mines *for themselves* during their Sunday "rest" period, and on religious holidays. Apparently, this custom began in the 1500's and continued until slavery ended in the 19th century. The slaves earned enough to make merchants come all the way from Quito, Bogotá, and Cartagena to sell them things. West (1952:88) said that meat and other food, tobacco, and cloth were the most common commodities. Apparently, then, the black slaves were linked directly to colonial trade networks, as well as to their local work situation, from the 16th century.

All slaves did not have equal access to the results of Sunday panning. The *Capitán* of the *cuadrilla*, the black man with the greatest responsibility to the white or mulatto administrator, had differential access to the gold. According to West (1952:88), he was the only one likely to accumulate enough gold to buy his own freedom. The first evidence we have of mobility within the black labor force appears to have worked as follows: one individual of high rank, the slave gang boss, became particularly *responsible* to the white, or "light" (mulatto) overseer, who was in turn responsible to the overlord, a white "señor" who was absent if sufficiently wealthy. The black boss was a slave, presumably equal to his fellow-slaves, but his responsibility was greater. He could use his higher rank to gain differential capital on "free days," thereby turning his responsibility into cash and using the cash to buy a new status, that of *libre*, "free."

The expanding free black labor force continued similar work habits, it would appear, though perhaps the income from working the tail sluices was no greater than it was in the richer lodes through Sunday work. It is not clear who bought the gold from the free blacks, but it was probably often sold to the same merchants to whom slave-produced gold was sold. Also, and this is still apparently hedged in obscurity, competition between Britain and Spain over control of the flow of gold directly affected black people in the Pacific Lowlands. While Spain controlled the labor, Britain (by the late 16th century) "ruled the waves," and pirates, buccaneers, and other adventurers and soldiers of fortune from many nations made direct contact from time to time with blacks from the rain forest and mangrove coast. Goods such as muskets, shot, and gunpowder were exchanged for gold and some forest products. Stories abound in the wet littoral about the secret places of past pirate caches.

Missionaries, too, exerted European forces upon the black people of the Pacific littoral from early times, including Jesuits' concern with soul-saving in Cartagena. Price (1965:6-7) sums up the attitudes and strategies of Catholic missionary work, appropriately setting his discussion against the actual ecological and demographic aspects of black expansion.

> . . . the gradual dispersal of slaves, plus the chronic shortage of priests, created serious problems with regard to their continued education and ministration. Large numbers of Negroes, as runaways and freemen, deserted the major centers where churches were likely to be located, forming many new and frequently uncharted settlements. A number of priests then dedicated themselves to establishing missions which they could visit periodically, and to exploring the bush in search for unknown communities . . .

It has remained the practice through the years of sending "missionaries" to settlements which were known to continue various "barbaric" rites, *even though many of these in actuality are basically Catholic ceremonies to which were added various practices and beliefs of unofficial Spanish Catholicism and some African usages.* (emphasis added)

The strategy to seek out and destroy "barbaric" customs is well documented by the Catholic Father Bernardo Merizalde del Carmen (1921) who lists many of the customs which contemporary priests are *still* seeking, ferreting, and attempting to subvert. This mission pressure becomes important later when we consider the sacred domains of Afro-Hispanic culture, for we shall have to deal with the "hidden," the "secret," and covert, as well as the overt and manifest.

The effect of mobility strategies (buying freedom, and establishing free settlements away from the centers of Spanish economic and mission power) in the face of mission activity is interesting. Apparently, free black communities established their sacred domains as the *true Catholic ones,* and resisted all priestly attempts to redefine their God, saints, spirits, and other worlds. They came to regard themselves *not* as lost, or misplaced, Africans, but as veritable Spaniards.

> Today there is an evident identification with Spanish culture in all parts of Colombia save in Palenque [a community in northern Colombia famous for its self-identification as "African"] . . . Even in areas characterized by a general antipathy toward whites, the priest is the object of great respect and a great deal of fear; it was not uncommon for a priest to enter a hostile village, demand, and cause the people to desist from the practice of a particular custom . . . there developed an integrated complex of Spanish Catholic and African usage, believed by the people themselves to be completely Catholic and therefore particularly immune to the efforts of priests who desire to banish "pagan" elements. This complex is a fundamental, functional aspect of their total way of life, and the adjustment they have made to their spiritual and practical needs, an adjustment unshakeable by Catholic and Protestant missionaries alike. (Price 1955:6-7)

RACIAL SUCCESSION

As white dominance spread insidiously into village after village, following the dispersal of black men and women into forests and swamps, black survival strategies themselves had a profound effect on aboriginal Indian cultures. As these Black South Americans expanded, native Indians became hemmed in. Intertribal contacts were everywhere buffered by expanding black settlements, and in some areas black households were built between aboriginal houses.

Colombia and Ecuador today have no "Black Indian" settlements analogous to the "Black Carib" of Central America (González 1969). Nor have blacks acquired facility with aboriginal languages, in spite of their enduring and continuing contact. In the Chocó of Colombia Cuna culture is nearly gone, and the inland Chocó, or Emperá, are to be found mainly in small settements far from the rivers of trade, where their attempts to maintain subsistence life are of necessity supplemented with minor sales of baskets and sleeping mats in the larger towns. The money gained from such endeavor, however, is normally used to increase personal and group prestige through the purchase of silver ornaments such as nose rings and ear plugs. The coastal Chocó, or Noanamá, are also to be found near the head-waters of major streams, above the commercially valuable sector which is inhabited completely by blacks. The Yurimanguí, who may have spoken a Hokan-Siouian language, have not been seen for a century. But as late as the early 1930's they were still reputed to be sending little model boats down-river, and current tales of their existence far up the Yurimanguí River are carried today. The Coaiquer have maintained an ethnic awareness on the slopes of the western Cordillera of Colombia by keeping their overt identity obscure, by keeping their language and aboriginal customs "secret" from travelers, explorers, and the like. In Ecuador, the Cayapa dispersed settlements are filled in their interstices by black people who are ever-more encroaching on their territory (see, for a recent analysis, Altschuler n.d.).

In the context of purely subsistence life, i.e., back on the rivers where sizeable numbers of Indians live, they are looked up to by the ordinarily dominant black people. But at the same time, the Indian, though proud of his ethnicity *vis-à-vis* blacks, is not unafraid of the louder, more sizeable black aggregates forever spreading into his territory. Whether simply by upstream retreat, or by becoming surrounded, aggregates of Indians are dominated by aggregates of black settlers. But on a one-to-one basis the black man shows considerable deference to the Indian, provided that money does not enter the situation. Black men feel that they have achieved a most desirable marriage should they win an Indian woman's hand, though the black man moving to town might leave his Indian wife in the forest. Such unions are quite rare, and there is considerable anti-black sentiment among Indians in terms of black man-red women sexual relationships. Indian men, on the other hand, readily sleep with black women, and take them as wives now and then. The children of mixed black-Indian unions are called "zambo;" they always fall into a non-Indian category, from the Indians' standpoint.

The Cayapa call the black man *juyungo*, "black devil," "howler monkey," and warn their women to shun him. Black men and women fear areas known to be in cultivation or use by Chocó or Cayapa, and also are wary when approaching an Indian house. This fear and caution stem from the Indians' abilities with animal traps, and their knowledge and use of blowguns and poison-tipped darts or pellets.

In spite of respect manifested by blacks toward Indians, they also reverse their respect role from time to time and actively deride or are deliberately rude to the Indians. For example, when drinking, a large number of black men (10-20) may "invade" a Cayapa house, or on hearing marimba music (which is African in style) being played by the Cayapa, black men and women may take over both the playing and dancing. Among the Chocó, black men are more reluctant to manifest role reversal in a Chocó settlement, though they readily display contempt *vis-à-vis* the Chocó in the towns.

When traveling, many Indians seek ritual kinsmen (co-parents) among black townsmen in order to have a household in which to stay. They stick to the outskirts of town, and actively avoid contact with most black residents, especially when the residents are themselves in the presence of whites or mestizos. Such "white presence" seems to work as a remarkable social catalyst on black ethnic demeanor *vis-à-vis* Indians, for black people go to considerable length to embarrass Indians when they have a mestizo or white audience. The only exception to this catalytic function occurs in an Indian settlement, where the reverse may take place; there Indians may be more threatening to blacks when a mestizo or a white is present.

A way of perhaps summarizing the nature of Indian-black relationships would be to say that Indians are precariously equal to or even dominant over blacks in strictly subsistence life. But, the subsistence economy itself is subject to variation according to the nature of the cash economy. Black people dominate Indians in the cash economy, but are in turn dominated by external white interests (sometimes represented by mestizos from the interior of the countries of Ecuador and Colombia). Ethnic relationships seem to reflect the degree of reliance on cash, the degree of access to money sources, and the ethnic mix of Indian, black, and white or mestizo in given settings.

It is crucial to understand that in the eyes of Indians and blacks the offspring of an Indian-black union is *zambo*. But this may be true in a specific area only if parentage is known. So we must also understand that, from the standpoint of all ethnic perspectives in the wet littoral, the offspring of an Indian with a black or zambo or mulatto is *non-Indian*. What he *is*, or what he *may be regarded as being*, we will discuss in the final chapter. Suffice it to say here that, from a non-black national perspective, such a person falls into a general category politely called *"moreno,"* "dark," or rudely *"negro,"* "black."

The expanding black population (Curtin 1969:30, 92-93)—including zambo-mulatto expansion—has gathered genes from all parts of the New and Old Worlds. Writing about Panama, Colombia and Ecuador Philip Curtin (1969:93), in the most comprehensive census of Africans in the New World ever undertaken, says: "That region of northwestern South America appears to have imported only about 2 per cent of the total slave trade. Yet it emerged in 1950 with 7 per cent of the Afro-American population."

Indians, by contrast, were early decimated by disease. Survival strategies for aboriginal populations with rapidly dwindling numbers came to involve a more tangential relation to the uncertain and fluctuating money economy thrust into the wet Pacific littoral from time to time. Strategic withdrawal from the money economy and heavy reliance on subsistence pursuits plus increased dependency on some products of the industrial economy (machete, axe, and beads) has characterized Indian adaptation. Milton Altschuler (n.d.) has this to say:

> If we think of the Cayapa and the Negro approaches as different risk assessment strategies vis-à-vis a fluctuating money economy it is clear that the Cayapa have, for the most part, hedged their bets in favor of subsistence while the Negroes'risk loss of subsistence life in favor of greater participation in the money economy.

The notion of peasant-proletarian adjustive activities in the face of a fluctuating money economy will provide a theme running through successive chapters. It seems that the contemporary black advantage lies precisely in the ability of aggregates of black people to maintain a series of complementary mobility strategies that allows them to exploit cash gain during economic boom periods, but to also maintain subsistence skills for a peasant adaptation during times of depression. Maintenance of a strategy sequence itself is undoubtedly dependent on the larger *numbers* and greater *rate of expansion* of black people (relative to the Indians). What the absolute demographic basis for proletarian strategies may be, I do not know, but such a basis within environmental parameters undoubtedly exists.

BLACK FRONTIERSMEN

Early decimation of Indian populations through disease, warfare with the Spaniards, and slavery produced a need for the continuous im-

ETHNICITY AND MARKETING.

Left. *A Chocó Indian on the Rió Capá, Chocó, Colombia.*
Above. *His House*

Market day in Quibdó, capital of the Chocó. A black family (above, center) and a Chocó family (front, right) bring goods to sell. Those of Afro-Hispanic culture bring chairs, a table, and firewood. The Chocó Indians bring subsistence food stuff and woven baskets.

Indians and Blacks in the wet littoral are part of a purchase society.

Above. *Chocó man dons trousers at the edge of Quibdó before entering town to shop for goods.*
Right. *A black highlander on the way to a new market in San Lorenzo, Ecuador.*

San Lorenzo, Ecuador. The rail terminus provides a new market area. Here, in 1961, highland and lowland Afro-Ecuadorians mingle.

portation of Black Africans. Afro-Americans in this zone actively expanded their territory and customary ways of doing things at the expense of surviving Indian groups. Both black and Indian aggregates developed survival strategies linked both to subsistence agriculture, hunting, and fishing, and to trade networks within the confines of a boom-bust economy. Black expansion at the expense of the Indians seems to lie in the *relative* black success within the wider political economy, supported by an expanding, mobile population.

The historical material and this mode of analysis suggest that both Indians and blacks in the wet littoral make up what Mary Helms (1969a:329) calls a *"purchase society."*

> Members of purchase societies appear as rural participants within the wider *economic* network formed either by industrializing nations searching for raw materials for their growing industries, or by trade with agrarian states. Geographically, purchase societies can be found on economic frontiers of states, in territory that is beyond de facto state political control (although often falling within the official de jure boundaries claimed by the state), but lying within economic reach of state activities. From the point of view of the local society, the over-riding factor, the channel that directs and influences all other activities, is the need small at first but constantly growing, for items of foreign manufacture. These goods quickly become cultural necessities, either because traditional crafts are forgotten, or because they become necessary for the psychological well-being of the group.

The idea of a purchase society suggests that black people in this zone are *frontiersmen*—veritable *pioneers*—men and women beyond the effective national boundaries (though within the formal confines of two nations) who cope with nature in a manner at least partly prescribed by the dictates of world demand for commercial products. Here, and subsequently, the term *"frontiersmen" is used in the sense of people facing a particular type of cultural ecological experience.* Self reliance and the ability to sustain, and expand, a population and a culture in the absence of "outside" support is crucial to frontier life, even within the purchase society. We turn now to the material apparatus of the black frontiersman adaptation, and then set this in the political economy of the wet littoral frontier zone.

NOTES
1 For concepts pertaining to "Colonial Tribes" see Mary W. Helms (1969b, 1971).
2 For the reader particularly interested in lists of Africanisms, or potential Africanisms, there are available materials. For example, see Price (1955), Escalante (1964), Velásquez (1961a, 1961b, 1962), Pavy (1967).
3 For a recent study of a contemporary Afro-Hispanic mining settlement near Barbacoas see Friedemann and Morales Gómez (1966-1969).

CHAPTER FOUR

Exploiting Nature and Man

EXPLOITING NATURE

Afro-Hispanic culture in the Pacific littoral contains considerable capacity for the exploitation of forest, river, swamp and sea. Black frontiersmen regard the environment as theirs to exploit. They do not see themselves as merely "fitting into" the environment—they seek to conquer it. In all three environmental zones—riverine-forest, sea edge, and mangrove swamp—the mobility necessary for survival must be complemented by a flexible, but relatively durable, system of shelter. Shelter does not merely refer to the houses themselves, which are the most obvious sign of human habitation. Shelter is a dynamic concept with an ideal model which is not always realized. Let us consider the frontier shelter system, and then turn our attention to exploitation of nature in the three environmental zones.

Shelter in the Pacific littoral may be thought of in terms of a sequence of increasingly permanent forms. At the start is the *rancho*—a hastily, but well–constructed sleeping structure made by bending limbs or stems of small pliable bushes into an archform, and arranging thatch over them. Binding by lianas completes the temporary shelter used in the forest (usually about 10-15 feet off the ground with a hurriedly constructed platform underneath for sleeping). When a sleeping structure is attached to the stern of a canoe, the canoe becomes known as a *canoa ranchera*. The canoa ranchera, in turn, symbolizes long trips, or change of primary residence. Some people who frequently make overnight canoe trips keep one or two portable ranchos around home.

The first movement toward settlement is the construction of a *cocina,* "kitchen," which also serves as first sleeping room, *"cuarto."* The

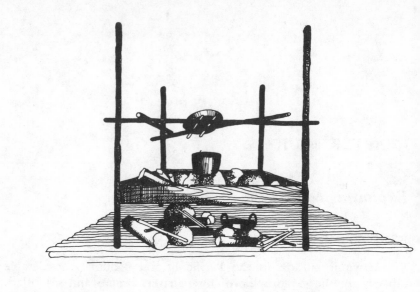

Figure IV-1, La cocina *and the* fogón.

kitchen is like a lean-to on piles, with a low sloping roof about 4-5 feet high in the back, and 8-10 feet high in front. The floor is split bamboo, or split palm, and extends out beyond the lower side from 5 to 10 feet. The sides are made of split bamboo, and the roof consists of cross poles, bound by lianas, and thatched.

A *fogón,* "hearth," is built, consisting of a raised platform with split palm or wood base, lined with clay and salted with rocks. (See Figure IV-1). Into this fogón (and sometimes under it, on a bed of clay) charcoal is placed, and kept burning if possible. Fire fans, *abanicos,* are woven from split reeds and used to tease charcoal into a blaze when new charcoal, or even fresh wood, is added. The charcoal is produced outdoors by starting a fire of wood and mounding dirt over the fire. A broom made from a simple pole and grassy fibers, calabash dishes, *"calabazos,"* shallow wooden bowls, *"bateas,"* and hexagonal loose weave baskets of various sizes make up the minimal equipment used in the early cocina. Meat and fish may be hung over the fogón to dry; other foods are stored in the cocina. At this stage of house construction there is little or no surplus, and people may go without meals to get the cocina built.

The platform extending out back is used by women as a work space. Only the machete is absolutely essential for the construction of the cocina, though an adze is needed for making bateas and in squaring the pilings. Tin pots and pans are preferable to calabash shells, both for cooking, and for providing a pot for children (and sometimes women) to eliminate into. Waste is normally thrown off the kitchen platform, as are the sweepings from the floor.

The batea is used to wash clothes and children, carry loads, shuck beans and cacao and to wash gravel in placer gold mining. The batea and fogón are as basic to intra-household life as the canoe, paddle and pole to life on the river and sea.

The cocina may or may not be elaborated upon. If housing is temporary, or to be sporadically used during occasional work in forest, or near a small farm, additions will not be made. The next addition will only be made to a particular house if it becomes central to regular economic endeavor. We might note in passing that any house that is *regarded as temporary* is known by the term *rancho.* Hence, even a completed house, if provided by a mining company, might be called a "rancho" *if the occupants did not expect to spend much time there.* Indians frequently call the typical, completed black dwelling, "rancho."

The second phase of settlement consists in extending the floor of the kitchen outward through the higher side from 10 to 50 feet, with more or less equal breadth. The most difficult job during this process is the felling, hewing to shape, and insertion of heavy hardwood pilings, which are frequently the nearly indestructible guayacán, but may be mangrove. Boards are used for floors and sides, when available. Otherwise, a floor is built of split palm or bamboo, arranged over bamboo poles, themselves supported by cross beams. This construction is more time-consuming than the work going into the cocina, and in fact the work itself may be destructive of the particular cocina (though it usually is not). A notched log or bamboo ladder provides access to the platform. An axe and an adze are necessary, in addition to the machete, for building this part of the house. People continue to sleep in the cocina, but eat on the *sala* platform.

Figure IV-2, Cocina *plus* sala *platform and roof.   Azotea *is in background.*

Step 3, though entirely logical in sequence, may not take place for some time, for reasons discussed below. It consists of building sides of bamboo or wood, cutting windows, and a front door, erecting cross beams and bamboo supports. Onto these supports more supports are laced by lianas or rope woven from plant fibers to form a rectangular roof structure, which is thatched with palm fronds, and capped by a crown held in place by *burros*. Sometimes the burros are carved, and sometimes a plank over the front door is carved into curving forms. One partition may be built separating the sleeping quarters from the rest of the sala; the sleeping quarters then become known as the *cuarto*. But people use the word *cuarto* for wherever they sleep, and *sala* for whatever room (outside of the cocina) they gather in. Often, cuarto and sala are the same room.

Smoke from the kitchen passes up through the crest of the main roof, and on out through coarse areas in the thatch. Storage platforms may be built on the roof supports. Sleeping mats, musical instruments, fish spears, and other paraphernalia are hung from exposed beams.

The front of the house may be on the far side from the cocina, or it may be on a side adjacent to the cocina. The silhouette looks like this:

Figure IV-3, *Rural dwelling of black frontiersman.*

Although one or two stools might have been fashioned prior to the completion of sides and a roof, little elaboration of material culture is evident in the houses in the first couple of phases. With the completion of the house, though, other apparatus such as stools, perhaps a table, more baskets, sleeping platforms in the cuarto, bark cloth called *damajagua* made into a sleeping mat by pounding it with a wooden mallet, and woven *petates* (sleeping mats) are added. Lighting consists of adding more beeswax candles, or purchased candles, kerosene lanterns, or even electric lights in some towns. The final step (in logical sequence) is totally dependent on the developmental sequence of the particular people coalescing in and around the household. This consists of adding sections to the house, either by building a second story, or adding more rooms onto the sides. Sometimes adjacent houses are built, and when this occurs the occupants may, with sufficient help from kinsmen and neighbors, forego the sequence just described, and go directly into construction of a stage 3 house; but, again, such building is a function of the coalescence of people engaged in economic activities through mutual cooperation.

It must never be thought that house building is the only labor expenditure which settlers have. Quite the contrary is the case. The cocina provides shelter and warmth, and the platform of the sala-cuarto assures an aggregating area in the household. Many things must be done before full attention can be turned to the construction of the desirable stage 3-4 house. Unless one is fortunate enough to be building adjacent to relatives who are already established, the house builders must turn their attention to a number of vital activities. People must always maintain a food supply, and this means farming, fishing, and hunting-gathering as a vital subsistence backdrop to the exploitation of cash opportunities. The carrying through of the latter activities is often predicated on successful understanding of the former basis and, for that reason, we continue to develop the concept of black exploitation of nature, prior to introduction of black exploitation of the capitalistic political economy.

The household itself is a context for certain forms of interaction. Men and women who know someone in a given household are expected to immediately exchange information with that person about something of mutual concern. Such exchange may, or may not, be preceded by standard greetings—*buenos días, como está, que hay de bueno*, etc. In such exchanges voices are kept loud so that everyone within the house can hear. If there is no one in the house whom a given participant in Afro-Hispanic culture knows, then the "traveling demeanor," described below, is supposed to be used.

When traveling-men approach a strange household, or one without close relatives, they must walk straightforwardly up the ladder into the sala, if it has been constructed. A standard greeting is given by each man entering the room, as each removes his hat. Men who wish to greet the newcomer step forward and shake hands. Women normally wait for a man of the house to pull them forward, or for the visiting man to directly address them. They then return the greeting, drawling it, particularly in the initial part of the phrase; they extend a limp hand and turn the head either left or right and slightly downward. If a man approaches a relative he first issues an exclamation followed by the appropriate kinship or ritual kinship term: *"aaaaaiiii primo," "aaaaa comadre!"* before moving to the behavior described above.

When greetings have been made, whether or not an overt response takes place, met sit down, and they may put their hats back on. It is normally up to the women to initiate further dialogue thereby setting the tone of intra-household interaction. However, if the man entering the house wants something, he is expected to directly, simply, and loudly voice his purpose, which might range from a request for a meal, to a place to sleep, to even a desire for a woman (I am hungry [*tengo hambre*], I am horny [*estoy arrecho; tengo arrechura*]). Voices are always kept loud so that everyone in the household can easily hear everyone else. The purpose of a visit may be made the subject of jest, or the visitor may simply give a generality—"we are traveling on this river."

Women traveling with their men, or only with children, approach a strange house directly, and sometimes use the same approach described for men. But they may also approach with turned head and averted eyes, looking away from everyone in giving their initial greeting, and wait for a woman of the house to jest with before speaking further. Some loud joke from any woman in the household normally breaks the ice and usually the visiting woman retires to the cocina with one or another of the household female occupants. Again, though, conversation is pitched so that all can hear. When men adopt the approach and stance of women, they symbolize deference to a clearly different status position; e.g., to a rich patron, or to a powerful white, mulatto, or mestizo.

Meals within the household are prepared in the cocina and back platform, and served in the sala. Generally, one large meal a day is expected together with snacks at two other times. It is during snacking that body humors are regulated, if necessary, by the addition of "hot" substances. For example, a man who feels a bit ill at dawn will readily take a shot or two of *aguardiente,* rum, or guzzle a calabash full of *guarapo,* sugar beer. He is not imbibing or nipping, just warming up through his morning snack. The major meal is normally taken at night; but more significantly, it is eaten at the end of a work period.

Men are served food by women, and they eat from either dishes (which are purchased) or from banana leaf or common pot. They usually sit on the floor or stools, and sit at a table if there is one. Women may eat with the men, or by themselves in the cocina. Material apparatus in the kitchen includes the grinding stone and pestle, wooden spoons, and a wash-board like wooden grater. These make up the minimal utensils used in preparing the various meals.

Hammocks are woven and hung in the sala for day time rests, but people sleep on the floor. All adults normally sleep in the same room, together with the children. The former may build a sleeping platform, and purchase a mosquito net, but such luxuries are not provided for children. Internal partitioning within a sala (beyond the simple division of cuarto and sala) normally symbolizes household division, or expansion, into two separate social units, united temporarily by spatial proximity within the same physical structure.

Let us briefly consider the material apparatus used to exploit forest, sea-mangrove edge, and mangrove interior.

Riverine-Forest

Houses in the riparian-forest zone (exclusive of towns which grow in response to the money economy) are usually strung along a river. Clustering and expansion from a river often indicate the existence of cash gain, or the site of a local market. Pigs are penned under or adjacent to the house in a bamboo enclosure. Native muscovey ducks and chickens often wander the banks, but they too may be penned. Tomatoes, peppers, and a little sugar cane and manioc are grown near each house. Right behind the cocina platform is a garden with taro-like tubers called *rascadera* and *papachina*—"itcher" and "chinese potato."[1] Women use this garden as an occasional place in which to urinate, as do men urinating from the platform. Water from washing and cooking is also thrown into this garden of tropical aroids. Adjoining most houses is an *azotea*, or platform garden (the usual Spanish meaning of azotea is "verandah"), used for starting onions, growing herbs, and in some places starting rice. Rice is also begun in large new canoes, which can simply be paddled to the cleared flood ground with 4-8 inch seedlings intact, to be quickly transplanted. The usual azotea is a bamboo or split palm platform, but sometimes an old rotting canoe is used. If rice is grown in the area one finds the wooden *pilón*, deep mortar, with pestle, together with calabash shells for winnowing, scattered among the households, sometimes one per house. Also, where the rivers wind into the hills, bamboo troughs are fixed with crotched sticks to run from sources of fresh water to households. A round frame, called *aro*, is made to dry and stretch animal skins.

Virtually every settlement of ten houses or more has one clay-domed baking oven, called *payón*, where corn bread is regularly made, and where bread made from purchased wheat and flavored with salt and sugar is sold when it is profitable to do so. Sometimes, where there is sufficient cane, a *trapiche*, sugar mill, is built for grinding the cane into *agua surumba*, sugar water; this is boiled into *panela*, which may also be called *surumba*, brown sugar, or fermented into beer, called *guarapo*. Clay stills sometimes are used to produce raw rum, *aguardiente*, called *trago*, or *puro*.

Every settlement has one house with a marimba *(casa de la marimba)*. It, and other houses, contain *bombos* (double headed base drums made from a tree trunk) and *cununos* (hollowed logs in the form of a "conga drum" with one head), as well as two types of rattle: the well-known maraca, and the tube-shaped *quasá*, the latter of which has hardwood nails driven laterally through the bamboo segment to arrest and give resonance to the flow of maize and small black seeds. An occasional shrine to a saint is found in the settlements.

Fishing paraphernalia in the riverine settlement reflects the importance of the waterway. Shrimp pots, *catangas*, are used for shrimp and crayfish, and fish baskets called *pando* are used for small river fish. The shores of rivers, frequently below the town, manifest many *corrales*, which are baited sliding door traps designed to exploit fish runs, but also trap a number of river fish and crayfish. Fish screens, *esterados*, may be used, and also the *atajada*, which consists of poles with net stretched between—but such apparatus is more common near the mangrove swamp where fishing is of greater importance. Pavy (1968) and Altschuler (n.d.) both report the use of fish poisons on the Raposo River in Colombia and Camarones River in Ecuador. Black riverine residents also fish with hook and line, spear day and night, and cast the *atarraya*, circular net, when fish schooling calls for it. Dynamite is commonly used on many rivers. But in spite of the intensive exploitation of the riparian resources, rivers beyond the tidal zone are best thought of as roadways through the forest; fishing, though important, today must take a second place to farming, animal husbandry, and hunting.

A wide variety of food staples is grown as close to the household as possible. These common staples include plantains, taro-like tubers, manioc, sugar cane, sweet potatoes, yams, avocadoes, cocoa, coffee, tomatoes, peppers, and tobacco, all of which are for intrahousehold use. A few bananas (called *guineo* or *mampora*) are grown for hog fodder and trap bait. When bananas are grown commercially they are usually called *bananos*.

Depending on the place, some households have palms such as the important *chontaduro*, "peach palm," and coconut near the household for internal use, or a bit of cash gain. Other palms such as the royal palm provide nuts and oils, while tagua is sporadically collected depending on demands from the cash economy. Mangoes, oranges, limes, *zapotes, papayas, chirimoyas, guanábanas, guamas,* guava (*guayaba*), and many other fruits are grown near the homes and readily eaten as they ripen. The beautiful breadfruit tree is used primarily to provide decoration—its great leaves lending grace to combine with the colorful hibiscus and other variegated leaves planted around the houses. Color seems to synergize particularly well with the breadfruit form to signify man's presence against the otherwise drab contrasts of forest green and river brown.

Further from the homes are the principal gardens or small farms of Indians and black settlers. These consist of plantains, corn, taro-like tubers and manioc as main subsistence crops, with pineapple, bananas and rice as prominent cash crops. The first and most productive plots are planted on natural levees.

Early in the construction of the house the major garden itself, called *rastrojo,* "stubble," or *finca,* "farm," is begun by men while women tend home plots and gather various wild foods. The major garden may be on the levee of a river, on a side hill, or in the bottom area, *quebrada,* of broken ground away from a major river. Even where fortune permits good gardens in the natural levees, or quebradas, however, the ever present danger of flooding forces the riparian settler to maintain smaller and less desirable sites away from the river. Consolidation of one good spot for his household necessitates the beginning of back-up gardens in more predictable, but poorer, soils. Mobility remains a major factor in black frontiersman adaptation to the subsistence economy. If women are to tend a distant garden, a house or rancho must be built near that garden. Such dispersal of work requirements may leave undertaken work in the settlement unfinished. Some settlements that seemed to be just on the verge of sustained growth when the levee gardens were first being planted still have an "incomplete" cast as unpredictable actions of the river interfere with the frontiersmen's plans, and as frontiersmen endeavor to maintain a back-up supply of food against anticipated flooding.

To move to and from the farm plots which are away from the river, canoes are used to get to a jumping off point. Men then trek to their gardens from the river. The black traveler-settler, leaving his canoe, characteristically carries a minimal number of necessities. On his back is a large woven basket fixed with two bark shoulder straps to which will be added a tump line to aid in transporting a heavy load of game or produce. He may carry over 200 pounds with a tump line. In Ecuador he normally carries both machete and muzzle loading 20-gauge shotgun, but Colombian prohibition on arms leads him to either hide his gun, or to do without. Some dried fish or meat and perhaps a hot coal or two wrapped in a plantain leaf make up his minimal necessities—he will get new line, as well as food, and build his shelter with machete and hands from forest materials. His clothing is ragged western khaki or white trousers and shirt (a change is scarcely ever taken), usually without underclothing, and barefoot. Occasionally he sheds the whole thing for breech cloth, though this is increasingly rare. He moves rapidly, almost at a dog trot, until fatigue overtakes him. When quite tired, he plods at a moderate, ground-eating walk, scarcely stopping to rest until a spot for productive work has been found. Then, he searches for food, and rests before undertaking his tasks.

Slash-Mulch Cultivation. *Roza* in Spanish means "clearing," and the notion of a "clearing" is relative to the normal inpenetrability of second growth or the dark corridors of pristine rain forest growth in the wet littoral. In the Pacific Lowlands it refers to the *cutting of bush* which is done *after planting*. *Rastrojo* means "stubble" (what is left after the roza), and is also descriptive of the planted field of the wet littoral. A clearing on a side hill is called *peña molida*, literally a worn out big stone, but figuratively a stripped side hill. Subsistence agriculture in the wet littoral forest is what anthropologists call a "diagnostic trait"—a particular relationship between economy and environment which manifests itself in this region of South America (and in some very wet areas of southeast Asia and Oceania). This diagnostic trait is called "slash-mulch cultivation" by geographer Robert C. West (1957:129):

> . . . a peculiar system, which might be called "slash-mulch" cultivation, of probable Indian origin, has evolved. Seeds are broadcast and rhizomes and cuttings are planted in an uncleared plot; then the bush is cut: decay of cut vegetable matter is rapid, forming a thick mulch through which the sprouts from the seeds and cuttings appear within a week or ten days. Weeds are surprisingly few, and the crops grow rapidly, the decaying mulch affording sufficient fertilizer even on infertile hillside soils.

As the shoots come up, and the bush and even large trees are felled on top, the result is quite a mess of rotting wood and vegetation. One must take care in walking through such a garden so as not to fall through a rotting trunk and break a limb! Using Miguel Cabello Balboa (1945:I:16) as his source, West traces this method of farming to the late 16th century in Esmeraldas province, Ecuador. Occasional burning does occur, but is uncommon and may be as infrequent as from five to ten years (Altschuler n.d.).

West (1957:127) identifies three principal land types: natural levee subject to sporadic flooding, swamp, and hill side. His characterization of the risks involved in choosing the *best land to grow things,* versus the *risk involved due to flooding* tells a good deal about the complex decisions effecting black frontiersmen:

> The natural levees and the low terraces, whose top soil is periodically enriched by deposition of new alluvium during floods, are the best farm lands . . . On such soils fields . . . are often cultivated for five or six years

before they are abandoned; if planted in maize, levee or terrace plots are farmed every other year. The alluvium best suited to primitive farming is usually located not on the low levees that border the large rivers, but along the smaller streams and *quebradas,* where rich soil is less subject to long periods of inundation. Unfortunately, these fertile strips of alluvium are extremely limited in area and comprise a small percentage of the total surface of the lowlands. Furthermore, flood waters erode the cut banks of rivers and *quebradas,* causing large quantities of good soil and crops to topple into the water.

The machete is *the* instrument used in clearing, planting, and harvesting, though axes are necessary to fell the large trees. Neither plow nor hoe is used in the wet littoral.

West (1957:130-135) elaborates to some extent on the maize grown in this zone, and on the various techniques employed, while Pavy (1968:148-151) talks about a "cultural emphasis on corn," implying elaboration in a focal sort of way in the planting and harvesting of this staple. The area in which I have worked most extensively has no such focus; corn is simply another of the staple crops to be used, and it is definitely subordinate to plantains and root crops. It is clear, however, that much more work needs to be done on the time-energy-caloric production of the subsistence agriculture of the Pacific littoral riparian zones if we are to get a realistic picture of the parameters imposed by this pioneer agriculture on population expansion and maneuverability within the subsistence economy.

Agriculture and hunting go hand in hand, for not only is the rastrojo a good place to find game, particularly agouti and deer, but travel between home and farm allows men to hunt for white lipped peccary, collared peccary and occasional tapir. Hunting is a usual adjunct to farming. Every mammal and reptile is killed, skinned, and (except snakes) eaten. Pelts, dried on the *aro,* are sold. Most large jungle birds are also killed and eaten when opportunity presents itself, small birds are sometimes used for food, and all bird and turtle eggs are gathered for food. Snakes are normally killed, but never eaten, as far as I know. Small crocodiles and caimans are killed and eaten, and their fat used for cooking, and as lamp fuel. Manatee are also used for meat and fat, but they are no longer common.

Sea-Mangrove Edge

What I am calling the *sea-mangrove edge* includes the sandy beaches opening onto sea or inlet, as well as the outer fringes of mangrove swamp facing the open sea, or channels leading directly to the sea. Here agriculture and animal husbandry is dominated by the scarce availability of soil where the human staples of plantains, manioc, taro-like tubers, sweet potatoes, and maize can be grown, and where animal fodder can be obtained. The coconut palm is the characteristic agricultural feature of this zone. It forms the first line of evidence of human habitation; houses are right behind the palms, and back behind the houses lie the rastrojos.

The material apparatus around the sea-mangrove edge is designed to maximally exploit fish and shellfish. Houses themselves are either on a stretch of beach about 30 feet beyond the normal reaches of high tide, or are on a point of land which may be periodically inundated by the rising tide. The platform on which the house sits is usually wider than in the forest, extending out in front of the house. Catwalks sometimes connect houses so that inhabitants can move between them at high tide without moving into the canoes—this is even more common within the mangrove swamp itself.

Canoes are larger than in the riparian sectors, and often have balsa logs attached to one or two sides. The dominant canoe style is identical with that used in the forest, but another type, variously called *potro, panga, imbabura* is found with increasing frequency as one travels northward in Colombia. This has higher sides, a square back with keel, and is readily adapted to a larger sail. A small sprit sail is used in both types of canoe.

Deep sea and estuary fishing involves bottom fishing with hook and line for a savory croaker, sea bass, and salt water catfish, sawfish and rays. The latter two are also harpooned either after they have been hooked, or as they drift in sight of a canoe. Albacore, yellowtail, bonito, barracuda, snook, and sharks are also caught on hook and line in the open sea. Tuna are sometimes speared, as well. Small fish such as mullet, pompano and many others are caught on hook and line, but are more frequently netted in a variety of ways. Sea turtles are harpooned or just grabbed. Large nets involving the cooperation of from 5 to 20 men are used for fishing. They are the *trasmayo* and *chinchorro*. Screens, *esterados,* across estuaries or within small bay zones on the beach are used. The atarraya or one man casting net is regularly used on schooling fish (though dynamite is preferred). Lobster and shrimp pots are regularly set. A trot line, *calandra,* is also run across channels. The variety of nets, anchors (which are rocks within a wooden frame bound with lianas), balsa floats of various sizes, fish drying platforms, *"barbacoas,"* shellfish pens, sails, harpoons, and ropes suggest an unforgettable visual background to the pungent smell of fish and salt in the sea-mangrove edge.

Coconuts themselves provide the principal source of fresh water to those who live in these areas. Both the common *coco* and less common *coco manila* are planted in low levees on sandy beaches or high points of land in the mangrove swamp (and on rivers). Channels are dug amongst the roots to allow an equitable rise and flow of salt water to the roots. The important thing is that tidal waters reach the roots of the coconut, but that they not flood the entire base. The *pipa,* or green nut, is used for drinking water, and the coco itself—the drier, mature nut, for cooking. Dozens of *seco,* "dry," dishes are made in the sea-mangrove zone, and in the interior. Each combines some sea or forest food with grated coconut meat. Coconuts from the coast, together with dried fish, are traded with people in the forest for plantains, and fresh or dried meat. The role of coconut production in the money economy will be discussed a bit later, along with other cash crops.

The fisherman of sea-mangrove edge spends a great deal of time in his canoe, and it is in this zone that we find a number of permanent portable ranchos built on four short (3-4 inch) posts which are quickly put into the canoa ranchera, together with the sprit sail and fire pot. Women in the area also spend a good part of the day in canoes as they travel to and from nearby gardens (within an hour or two paddling time), and seek crabs, mussels, clams and oysters by wading and diving, and by scraping various crustaceans from the rocks and mangrove roots. But women typically return home at night, while men may continue their work, staying the night under the rancho. Cooking is commonly done in a metal pot carried in the canoe. Burning sticks are stuck into some coals in the pot, and the smudge also repels mosquitoes. Transporting barter goods, or sale goods, by canoe also keeps the people of this zone quite mobile, and in touch with events in the swamp and forest. Baskets and other paraphernalia are identical to those described above for the forest-riparian zone. Men tend to travel in pairs, both paddling in a standing position, while women more often work in groups of from 3 to 8 per canoe, and paddle from a sitting position.

Obviously, work routines are governed by the rise and fall of tides. The lunar day is *the* measure of life in the sea-mangrove edge, regardless of specific tasks.

Mangrove Swamp

If we combine *all* of the material apparatus of sea-mangrove edge together with that of the forest, we will have a picture of the material culture of the mangrove swamp. Within the sea channels the same fish are caught (except albacore which are rarely caught in the channels), and the same methods employed depending upon the specific micro-setting, and the specific run of fish. I recall fishermen near Limones, Ecuador, who in the period of one hour used hand lines to catch small fish, then changed rapidly to dynamite as a school of bonito swept through. In the ensuing mellee which resembled a small scale bombing of a submarine with hand-thrown depth charges, the men suddenly switched to harpoons to gather the floundering larger fish. Into the semi-circle created by a dozen or so canoes aiming at the bonitos, swept a number of sharks, creating a froth-filled climax of carnage around the tippy bobbing dugouts. As smaller fish began to school a few minutes later in the now peaceful sea-channel the atarrayas were cast. Finally, some men began setting a calandra across the channel, while others began making preparations to unfold and drag the large chinchorro. Still others during this time took out hooks and lines and began to hand fish for croakers and sea bass.

The houses themselves in the mangrove swamp have characteristically large platforms and are commonly laced together with catwalks. Pigs and chickens are kept, and they often must move up the notched ladder into the house as the tide rises underneath. The settlement is often just outside of the mangrove trees themselves, the cocina sometimes virtually touching the outermost glossy leaves.

A small mussel, called *concha,* abounds in the mangrove swamp, and women, called *concheras,* devote considerable time to gathering it. In some areas large concha pens are built, often under the houses. No particular material apparatus is used in the concha industry beyond the ubiquitous hexoganal woven basket and knife. Children join the women in this work. We shall say more about the concha industry in northwest Ecuador later in this chapter.

The cultivation system, together with intensive exploitation of the marine environment with the addition of abundant crustaceans and some swamp birds, creates a rich subsistence base in the mangrove swamp. The lunar day prevails, and undoubtedly influences a number of forest activities, because those wishing to maximize both mangrove and inland riparian environments must govern time according to the rise and fall of tides.

EXPLOITING MAN

Black frontiersmen adapt not only through exploitation of their natural environment; they also adapt to shifting emphases in national and international demand for specific products. Until now I have used the word "exploit" in the first sense of Webster's Third International

FISHING.

Dynamiting a school of mullet in the mangrove swamp.

Scrambling after some stunned fish blown into the mangrove roots.

The concheras *(concha gatherers) return with a day's catch of mussels. The mussels live in symbiotic relationship with the mangrove trees.*

Fishing in the mangrove estuaries provides considerable food for both subsistence and money economies.

Waiting for fish to school in a tidal estuary near Limones, Ecuador

A guacapa, *sawfish, is brought to the* canoe . . .

. . . *and the coup de grace delivered.*

Dictionary: "to make use of: utilize; turn to account." To understand black adaptation to a money economy we must expand the usage to include a broader meaning, "to make a profit from the labor of others."

International demand for certain products periodically effects the wet littoral. The demand brings with it people who are not black, but rather associated with some variant of the non-black world. By making use of resident labor such "outsiders" exploit the frontier through the frontiersmen. Whenever they see the frontiersmen as black they "color code" their labor force. It is necessary then to consider people making up such a labor force as "color coded" in relation to the "color coders," the outside exploiters who "make use" of black labor. At the same time, we should consider the ways by which black people in the wet littoral devise techniques to wrest an income *from* outsiders—the ways and means by which they "make use" of cash inputs. "Exploiting man," then, refers to the ways by which black people are used *for* profit, *and* to black people as exploiters—people who attempt to maximize the advantages and minimize the disadvantages coming into the littoral according to the resources available to them, and to their concepts of resource. We view black people in the wet littoral as pawns of external exploitation. But they are not passive pawns who play by imposed rules. They are active, organized people who move according to *their own* strategies and rules in response to inevitable external pressures. We shall begin to build a perspective of black adaptation to the boom-bust economy, and reserve a discussion of "color coding" itself for the final chapter.

THE POLITICAL ECONOMY

The insatiable European demand for gold established, so to speak, the primary conditioning economic domain for black frontiersmen. Black Africans came in large numbers as slaves to mine placers; they revolted; and they adjusted to hemmed-in-freedom through a labor system represented by the slave and free *cuadrillas*. Today cuadrillas still work various gravels, and small groups of women may pan gold nearly anywhere, selling by the ounce to resident buyers in various towns. In some places, platinum is found in with the gold. Large-scale mining financed by foreign concerns has taken place in the Chocó (see West 1957:179-182, Escalante 1971). Recently, large-scale dredging has been attempted here and there by foreign speculators.

Medicinal herbs, roots and barks such as sarsaparilla, epicac, and quinine were historically purchased in various centers in the wet littoral, along with sandalwood, tagua, kapok from the ceiba tree, balsa and furs. All were gathered by Indians and blacks and sold in centers established primarily to provide an outlet for gold. On the whole, men and women gathered the products in the forest, selling them individually in the respective centers.

"Ivory nut" (*tagua*) enjoyed a boom just prior to World War II. At one time this wild palm product, which looks sort of like a potato, was in demand because all of our buttons were made from it. The advent of plastics changed this, and tagua today is used primarily to carve "ivory" chess pieces, tops, and other toys. Gathering tagua involved individuals (both men and women), who spotted the trees in the forest, stripped them of their nuts, either by climbing them, or cutting the palm down, and delivered them to a center of distribution, or way station on a river. Tagua buyers were generally from Ecuador or Colombia and they sold to foreign buyers in other port cities. World demand for wild rubber caused booms from the mid-19th century through World War II. Individuals gathered the latex and sold it to local buyers at stations on rivers, or bypassed the local buyers and went directly to the centralized towns, where they made contact with foreign buyers.

Right after World War II a banana boom hit the Province of Esmeraldas, Ecuador, and black people began to put in special crops of this fruit (which they despise as a food, regarding it only as pig fodder, or starvation fare). Plantations grew near large towns (such as Esmeraldas) run by highland and south-coast lowland whites and mestizos. The fruit was sold on various rivers to buyers who announced the day of purchase in advance. (For a full account of the process on the Cayapas River see Altschuler n.d., Erasmus 1961:151-153). The banana boom effected the ecology in a new way, for the crop had to be planted in land which otherwise could have been used in the subsistence economy. It affected the agricultural round, as well as travel and work habits. The introduction of this cash crop encouraged expansion of the cultivation complex, and often forced sellers to turn around and pay cash for subsistence goods that otherwise could have been raised for home consumption or barter. Banana buyers came from within the nation, and were also foreign entrepreneurs. In parts of the Colombian Pacifiic lowlands, including the mouth of the Atrato which empties into the Atlantic, wet rice cultivation is now growing in commercial importance. In such areas the impact on subsistence crops is comparable to that discussed for bananas (for more detail see West 1957:149-151).

Timber exploitation of the soft and hard woods of the Pacific littoral has been going on since World War II. At first sawmills were established in distribution centers, or near a road or railroad. Timber was floated to the mill and sold there, the sellers often working to bring the timber in on credit relationships with buyers. More recently, new types of timber operations are creating an economic boom in some zones. These new adjustments will be discussed in some detail shortly. Timber buyers are predominantly foreign middle-men—including North Americans, Europeans, and other Latin Americans.

Shellfish, notably the *conchas,* are in demand in Ecuador, and the demand is manifest in mangrove zones where the mussels live in symbiotic relationship with the mangrove trees. The conchas are purchased by the sack in distribution centers and either sent to the highlands by rail, or to coastal towns by ship. Buyers are national Ecuadorians, usually from the highlands or southern coast.

Mangrove bark contains about 50-60 per cent tannic acid and so is in some demand in tanneries, in Ecuador, Colombia, and in the United States. Mangrove bark is purchased in bundles in distribution towns, and either freighted to the interior of the country by rail or truck, or shipped to other port towns for export or subsequent distribution. Buyers and sellers are usually highland nationals or hail from large coastal towns.

Dried fish and coconuts are in constant demand. Bales of dried fish and bundles of coconuts are purchased in distribution centers by middlemen in shellfish, mangrove bark, gold and fur businesses, as well as by captains of ships or other shippers. They are often sold to small shops in poor areas, where they make up an important source of protein and minerals. Local people do their own trading of these items, sometimes traveling to a market to sell directly to buyers, but they more often sell to distributing middlemen in various towns. The cash value, however, is a function of the boom-bust economy because of the dependence on towns and money.

The means by which inputs of money are made are generally the same: 1. a center of operations is established where access to supply, and access to the shipping lanes, is advantageous; 2. white and mestizo outsiders take up residence at the center, and purchase the desired product which is gathered by blacks, zambos, mulattoes and Indians. The same outsiders sell to shippers or manage the transference of the product to the outside world. As the demand for goods waxes and wanes, and as sources are discovered and depleted, sellers and shippers move, and the entire system arising in response to external demands is forced to readjust. The bases for such major readjustments lie in *spatial mobility* just as in the subsistence economy. In any area where the center is developing or expanding we can think in terms of an economic "boom"—a rapid influx of cash—and where centers are exiting, or declining, we may talk of a "bust"—a rapid decrease in money and consequent dependence on nature. The characteristic economic picture then is that of "boom-bust" economy imposed on a subsistence economy.

In the purchase society, a creation of international capitalism, goods and labor have cash value. I shall give all figures in the Ecuadorian *sucre*, which was worth about five U.S. cents in 1965. The Colombian unit is the *peso* worth about one and a half sucres in 1965. The normal day wage of dock worker, sawmill worker, lumberjack, railroad worker, helper on a farm or in moving produce to market, and other comparable laboring jobs is from 12 to 20 sucres per day, either in cash, or in credit redeemable in the towns. Day labor for women is not yet possible in most of the littoral, although preparing and serving food and washing other people's clothes brings in 7-12 sucres per day. For the most part, though, the only reliable paying jobs are concha gathering, and prostitution. In a previous work (Whitten 1965:84) I argue that:

> Averaged over a month, the daily net income of a lower-class family may amount to 15 sucres. The significant point here is that by marketing essentially subsistence products, a lower-class household may earn as much money as it could by working regularly for wages.

I do not propose to recapitulate the calculations leading to this conclusion here, for the reader may re-think them for himself by consulting the original source. I do think that this point is accurate: *people giving proportionately more time to wage labor make choices invariably costing them more money when they go to buy subsistence goods; while those choosing to produce subsistence crops, to fish, or to hunt may also make the same amount of money which allows them to purchase goods.* Wage labor in the Pacific littoral does not provide any measure of security for black frontiersmen. Money is a basic necessity but there is no institutionalized means within the purchase society to guarantee a worker a subsistence income. Even regular wage workers cannot *rely* on cash return for their labor; they must have other social and political supports, and these supports themselves demand outlays of money and time. The manner by which man exploits man in the Pacific littoral is in itself dependent on external exploitation strategies, and on the degree of penetration of national infrastructure which creates a series of niches within which adaptive strategies take place.

Black settlers in the wet littoral are in partial control of natural resources. But they are *not* in control of the money economy which

WORKING IN THE WET LITTORAL.

Washing clothes in a batea at Salahonda, Colombia.

A woman and her two children bring coconuts to San Lorenzo.

Grinding sugar cane to make guarapo, sugar beer, in a trapiche.

Women and men contribute to survival and mobility strategies by hard work.

Sewing clothes is a man's occupation in the wet littoral.

On the way to a small farm in the forest.

A modest shop in San Lorenzo.

so effects them. They must deal both with the impressors—outsiders who pay for goods—and with one another. Black people in this setting must deal in *social and political capital*—with human beings as potentially exchangeable tokens. To do this they generate a cultural code based on the concept of *reciprocity*. We will now examine the expanding infrastructure and the niches of the environment, and then return to culture and adaptive strategy.

EXPANDING INFRASTRUCTURE

An infrastructure is the network of transportation facilities enabling economic expansion, together with the administrative and educational apparatus which establishes a bureaucratic-information system facilitating the expansion based on transportation networks. The expanding infrastructure in the wet littoral consists of roads and rails, outlined in Chapter II, together with shipping systems—which include port construction and canoe tentacles to the interior. The expansion of infrastructure itself produces various booms in various places from time to time, sometimes in direct response to the international need for a particular product, and sometimes due to internal need to "open" a given area.

Usually infrastructure expansion brings a number of laborers from the interior of a nation (mestizos, highland Indians) together with a bevy of bosses, speculators, managers, engineers, politicians, and others, representing various economic class sectors of the respective nation. Completion of work frequently marks a "bust" in the local economy, even though natural resources should be more accessible to local exploitation for cash gain.

NICHES

With the notion of an expanding infrastructure, conceived of as an environing feature, we can introduce the notion of *niche*, a concept establishing the local parameters for adaptive strategies. The concept of niche refers to not only where the particular human aggregate lives (its *environment*—sea edge, mangrove swamp, or forest) but what it *does* within this environment. It is convenient to classify human activity in the wet littoral by relating it to four settlement patterns: rural scattered dwellings, rural settlements, towns, and large urbanized towns. This suggests that human activity, and the organization of human activity into describable roles and statuses, is a function of residential advantage and population concentration. Residential advantage and the accompanying social demography in the wet littoral vary according to the demands imposed by international markets, and the expanding national infrastructure.

The crucial difference in behavior adjustments in the four niches are defined as follows.

A. Rural Scattered Dwellings

The activities defining this niche, in any of the three environmental zones, are oriented toward providing for household subsistence by clear division of labor by sex and age. The orientation of men's work is toward establishing a *rastrojo*, where possible, providing meat and/or fish by hunting, fishing, or barter, and finding some means of exploiting something of value to the money economy. Women and children work the rastrojo, gather foods, prepare foods, wash clothing, and engage in almost unending subsistence tasks. Only by freeing the men of the household for gathering, planting, harvesting and marketing cash crops (e.g., bananas, pineapples), or fishing, mangrove stripping, *and* bundling and marketing the fish or bark, is there hope for more than a day-to-day, hand-to-mouth existence.

Households in this rural niche tend to be large, averaging eight to ten people. Within the household there tend to be interlaced kinship ties, such as we find when first cousins marry one another, and the subsequent children themselves marry their cousins and bring some into the household to live, work and cooperate. As the household expands, through the natural processes of reproduction and mating, one of two things must occur: either the majority of children move on out of the immediate area, or they do not. If they stay, and continue the process of consolidation and physical expansion, we enter niche B, the rural settlement, and other activities define people's relationships to one another.

In niche A an *egalitarian* pattern of human interaction pertains. There are no *positions* of prestige beyond those of physical strength, mental wit, or particular conviviality. Differential interaction based on race or ethnic affiliation is non-existent. People owe one another the same sorts of things: food for food, work time given for work time accepted, a tool (axe, adze), for a tool (machete, net), and so forth. Cooperation by people in other dispersed households is repaid in kind, and/or by festive exchange. For example, sometimes several people (usually "cousins") will come for a week to help a family build a house; when possible they are rewarded by large meals, aguardiente, music, and a general festive spirit. But more often the sheer expense involved in festive exchange demands the more common agreement

EXPANDING INFRASTRUCTURE.

Ibarra, Ecuador. People from this Andean town control sectors of the wet littoral economy.

The autocarril *prepares to leave Ibarra for the coast.*

Highland Ecuadorians of both African and Indian background serve food to travelers as the autocarril *descends the Andean slopes.*

Extension of rail and road expands opportunities in the money economy, and facilitates interaction of people of various backgrounds.

San Lorenzo, Ecuador, 1963. This is the terminus of the Ibarra-San Lorenzo railroad line. In 1968 most of these buildings in the center of town were occupied by highlanders.

Barbacoas, Colombia. A center of gold mining during colonial days, the community is presently tangential to expansion of the Colombian infrastructure.

SETTLEMENT.

Dispersed dwelling at sea-mangrove edge.

Beginning of a settlement in a mangrove-flanked estuary.

Settlement in a sea channel in the mangrove swamp, Machetajero, Ecuador. This Afro-Hispanic hamlet is built on the remains of an old Indian archaeological site.

Black frontiersmen expand in mangrove, sea-edge, and riparian-forest environments.

Beginning of a settlement on the Mataje River, Ecuador.

A river town, Maldonado, on the Santiago River, Ecuador.

to simply reciprocate the same sort of task, and dispense with the festive repayment. Such reciprocity is "symmetrical." Sometimes a group of people aligned by repeated requests and answers for aid move into the vicinity of one another, or elect to move to a sector of a town as a group. But again, such behavior generates niche B.

Niche A is a lonesome place for the inhabitants. Life is grim, hard, and oriented towards settlement activity—towards creating niche B. But the general adaptive strategy of the littoral—balance subsistence based survival activities with those bringing in a cash gain—necessitates such movement ever outward from the growing settlements where money is more available to the upward mobile, but where it is also necessary to buy more subsistence goods.

B. Rural Settlements

Activities in this niche allow for hamlet or village specialization in addition to the patterns described for niche A. For example, a group of men may fish daily together, and cooperate in drying and transporting bales of fish to a market, while others in the settlement carry on the intra-household cooperative activities making for subsistence. Also, family specialization is possible, as occurs when one family builds a little sugar mill, *trapiche,* and specializes in making *guarapo* which others buy or trade goods to obtain. The settlement itself is usually definable in terms of its particular mode of articulation to the money economy.

Households tend to remain about the same size, though some expansion by mating causes a few splinter families to begin building their own homes. Cousin marriages are common, and the notion that one ought to marry a cousin, or kinsman, is prevalent. Within the household individuals have acknowledged obligations to close family and kinsmen in other local households (often adjacent), and these obligations serve to unite people through chains of reciprocities. The clever man or woman who can become central to a series of obligations may occasionally "pull" these ties together, and get a number of people to help him in some activity. A man known to be able to so manipulate his kinsmen and neighbors for economic gain gets the label *"jefe,"* chief, attached to him. The *jefe de la minga,* cooperative group head, or *jefe de la madera,* lumber chief, for example, is a man who is known to be able to mobilize people for short run gain—such as the cutting and transporting of timber to a sawmill or export center. The jefe has high *rank,* but his obligations in return to all those who help him *drain him of differential wealth.*

The rural settlement, then, has the *criterion of ranking* built into its structure. Some positions within this community are regarded as carrying higher prestige than other positions, but the prestige position itself does not insure the holder of differential economic power over his neighbors, kinsmen, and friends. Rather, higher rank confers greater responsibility to reciprocate, and thereby serves as a leveling, egalitarian mechanism. (For a full theoretical discussion of ranking in relation to egalitarian and stratified societies see Fried 1967).

Relationships between people in the rural settlement are symmetrical, as in the rural dispersed dwelling niche, and they are also asymmetrical. In the latter type of reciprocity, partners owe one another different sorts of things. For example, the jefe de la minga owes all who help him aid in *cash* or *goods* when *they are in need,* while those who make up his party owe him *labor.*

Non-black visitors to the rural settlement are not treated as equals, for whatever the potential exchange may eventually come to be, the partners in that exchange will come to owe different sorts of things. The white or mestizo outsider entering the rural settlement should not expect deference, though. People in the rural settlement are aware that asymmetric contracts with absentee whites are useless, and in this sense are far more demanding for hard cash for services rendered than townsmen who may opt for long term patronage relationships with resident whites.

Black visitors are not treated as whites, but rather as potential future resources, as well as potential dangers. As a future resource, a visiting black man or woman may later be called on for comparable service. As a potential danger, the visitor may steal with impunity since he is not as yet bound by residence or kinship to settlement members.

Ritual life is rich in the settlement, in striking contrast to the rural scattered dwellings. Special days to saints are observed by women, weekly marimba dances, *currulaos,* are held in the *casa de la marimba* (almost all settlements are characterized by *one* such house), and, it seems, the demons and frightening spirits, as well as the various protective and supportive saints, find the settlement and bedevil or help inhabitants. Black frontiersmen in the settlements fight back, booming the child snatching ghost *Tunda* away with the *bombo,* base drum, setting candles to ward off *El Riviel,* a ghostly cannibal, soliciting the help of saints in their struggle with human and non-human adversaries.

Sorcery and witchcraft too are prevalent in the settlement. Fears of soul theft while dreaming and fear of those who walk trails in other worlds and visit ancestors best long-forgotten lead to defensive personal ritual, to the wearing of amulets, and to the burying of roots in strategic places where those walking mystic and real trails will step over them, and be injured in their malign activities.

Because the rural settlements are dependent on the vicissitudes of the money economy for their structure, growth, and continued vitality, and because they are nonetheless removed from the town niche, where money defines most human relationships, they are often loci for fugitives. People who have stolen money or goods flee to settlement niches. One might think that the dispersed rural dwelling would be safer, but this is only true when one carries goods necessary for survival. The settlement can provide enough surplus for refuge, particularly in exchange for needed cash or goods, and the cash and goods support the growth of the settlement. Perhaps because of this refuge function the settlement is also the locus of powerful diviners, called *brujos,* who are able to "find" lost money, or a motor, or supply of goods.

Niche B is a vibrant place, precariously balanced between subsistence and cash pursuits. Its social relationships are symmetrical and asymmetrical, with ranking defining high prestige-obligation roles for big men. The settlement, *qua* niche B, lacks formal administrative apparatus, lacks differential access to cash except as discussed, and is usually built on a foundation of kinship and affinity. Introduction of stratification and administrative apparatus moves us into niche C, the town.

C. The Town

Today the littoral town falls in the path of the expanding national infrastructure. In earlier times the town occurred as a center for the outward dispersal of some goods demanded by world markets. Activities defining this niche revolve around what black people in the United States refer to as "the man." Administrators with legitimate authority and external power over black townsmen, together with capitalists with economic advantage and differential access to goods and services, impose new organizational imperatives. People must adjust their activities not only to the egalitarian and ranked behavior of fellow men and women, but also to the activity and organizational patterns of people with differential administrative, political, and economic power. The town is *stratified.* Those of high rank hold differential power over their life chances due to their differential purchasing power. Most people holding differential advantages are called *"blanco,"* white. The concept of "whiteness" in the town niche becomes a "categorical," or "stereotypic" social relationship, through which access to money is channeled. The town then is defined by white over black asymmetry, whether or not there are people of color standing in the category "white."

Formal town offices include that of *teniente político* (political lieutenant), or his secretary or designee (depending on the size and national importance of the town—in large administrative canton seats a *jefe político* coordinates the tenientes; see Whitten 1965 for a full discussion of the town niche).[2] In the larger towns there is a *comisario nacional de policía,* appointee of the supreme and regional courts of justice, who oversees the *policía rural.* Police live in the town niche, and very seldom visit the settlements, unless murder has taken place. Political parties oriented toward influencing public policy are also here, including those with international as well as national affiliation.

There are also Catholic clergy and nuns, and sometimes Protestant missionaries, and occasionally local fundamental Protestants. School teachers (government and mission) provide instruction through about the fifth grade, and public health officials administer campaigns against malaria and yaws. There is normally a physician and perhaps a dentist when the town passes 3,000 in population. Saloons, cantinas, shops, hostels and small "restaurants" exist as permanent edifices. Carpentry and masonry workshops have sporadic business, and *motoristas* working the various rivers and estuaries have permanent bases in the towns. Sawmills provide boards and planks so that the frontier dwellings can evolve into western houses.

A town is not specialized. Sawmills, resident buyers and shippers, and owners of cash crop farms all provide some employment on a wage labor basis. They also buy products from people organizing their own labor force to make money from forest and sea products. Resources provided by legal-juridical and political office are used by people to advance themselves and to compete with others also seeking advancement in this niche. The paperwork necessary to the carrying through of any economic activity gives the literate manipulator in the jural political domain asymmetrical control over economic activity.

Activities in the town niche are oriented toward the acquisition of money, or toward alliances with people known to have access to the goods and services which money can buy. Role positions that I label "rural contact," and "ethnic-cultural broker" are important. The rural contact is a man or woman able to mobilize people outside of the town for gainful economic activity (farming, logging). He is the town analog to the settlement *jefe*. A cultural or ethnic broker is a man or woman able to translate demands and needs of controlling outsiders into activity patterns of black frontiersmen. It is through brokerage roles that black people have transformed their activity patterns from settlement to town, from subsistent peasant adaptation, to proletarian participation during boom periods. The broker himself may best be regarded as an entrepreneurial role finding new goals to which to apply Afro-Hispanic organizational patterns.

Division of labor within households (which vary greatly in size from one or two individuals to more than 20 persons) is frequently in terms of balanced activity in many different economic pursuits. Because national and regional politics impinge on so many activities in the town niche some men in every household, or kinship grouping, must maintain awareness of events effecting the town economy, and must also maintain some viable contact with those who are able to manipulate the political economy to personal advantage.

In the town niche the household is not the basic economic unit, and first cousin marriage is not favored, and rarely found. The basic economic unit is somewhat larger and may be termed a "kindred." It includes all those consanguineal and affinal relatives upon which a given person can depend, for a particular purpose, at a particular time, under particular conditions. Some of the small rural settlements in the wet littoral consist of one kindred (usually focused on the first settlers, or their resident children); some include many. In similar manner, some town *barrios,* "neighborhoods" or "sections," contain one or two kindreds, again focused on the resident children of successful settlers.

Since the town is a place where people compete with one another for economic advantage and since such competition may involve either success (upward mobility) or failure, individuals' affiliations to kinsmen also involve the factor of economic advantage-disadvantage. The manners by which successful individuals maintain a network of cooperating kinsmen, without owing so much that success levels their economic gain through expected obligation fulfillment, defines a particular kind of social organization. The adaptive strategies within the town niche effect people in the settlements and scattered dwellings, too, as we shall see later on.

All of the activities described for niches A and B go on in the town niche, *among those who fall into the lower economic class.* But these activities themselves are caught up by the various organizations and alliances defined by mobility processes *out of* the lower class. Hence a class-oriented frame of reference helps us understand even subsistence activities.

Saints, spirits, and attendant ritual behavior to solicit help and exorcise evil go on in the town niche, side by side with scoffing saloon-goers and damning clergy. From town to town the particular mix varies, but careful observers find no difficulty in perceiving the basic complex of settlement life intertwined with the ritual life prescribed for town. As towns become larger than 500-1000 people, barrio formation tends to take on increased ritual significance and sacred rituals are performed in relative secrecy. It is within the barrio that particular spirits tend to visit, or particular demons tend to haunt. As the town grows, and the center of administrative activity becomes lighter and lighter, barrios get their own marimba houses, their own specialists, and characterize their lifeways as increasingly "traditional." Town sections resemble rural settlements as the town grows larger. As this process expands and barrios spread from the center, the secrecy of sacred rituals declines.

The town is a wild, exciting place when a boom is on—when there is actually cash to sustain the mobility strategies of black frontiersmen. It is a place where ethnicity sharpens, but also where inter-ethnic relationships become intertwined in class defined interests which would seem at first to negate the ethnic categories. I will discuss this process at some length in Chapter VIII.

When the demand for a product declines, or the nation is unable to sustain its infrastructure in a particular area, the town becomes a terribly depressing place. The shell of activity rapidly decays, leaving precariously wobbling docks, green mold-covered foundations of older frame houses, and some remnants of previous size and importance. Most such towns become settlements again. Many maintain some national facade of previous importance: a priest visits occasionally, a school teacher comes for a few months every few years, a political appointment is made; but without anything to exploit administration is at best nominal. The bust town is common in the wet littoral, and all too often travelers see life in the bust town as slow and "lazy," and blame local inhabitants for letting "their" town go. The concept of the purchase society teaches us that we cannot blame those caught up in international capitalism for the effect of decreasing product demand on the expansion of administrative units, the towns.

D. Large Towns: Consequences of Urbanism

Buenaventura and Tumaco in Colombia, and Esmeraldas, Ecuador range from over 100,000 down to 40-50,000 people. I shall call these "large towns," though the reader might prefer "small cities." However we label them, we refer to changes which occur with demographic growth due to increased cash opportunities, and greater stratification and division of labor—these are the processes of urbanization. The attendant culture of cities, or large towns, is called *urbanism*.

Urbanism, of course, extends throughout a region, far beyond the city or large town, but an expanding infrastructure is necessary to realize goals of urbanization.

All the activities sketched in niche C continue in niche D. I would not even bother discussing niche D as separate, were it not for three interrelated phenomena: 1. the appearance of labor unions as a political and economic organization; 2. increased ethnicity separating "white" from "black" with a concomitant *expanding* set of middle range concepts (*mulato, zambo, claro,* etc.); and 3. concentration of black people in outlying barrios which resemble in activity pattern the rural settlement.

As a result of these three patterns there is a tendency to identify black behavior with country-bumpkin life, and lighter behavior with union-political (urban-national) orientation. De facto exclusion of black people—a sort of social circumscription of black frontiersmen—forces them back into a settlement niche, though the settlement itself now is in, or on the edge of, a large town rather than swamp or jungle. The relevant environment for black frontiersmen in *this* settlement niche becomes the large town, rather than the natural environmental zone.

All three of these large towns are ports. Through these ports pass products of the respective nations. There are markets, stores, hotels, restaurants, bars, houses for amusement and sexual outlet, and movie theaters. All three are connected by road and air to the national centers, and all three are totally immersed in the money economy. Political apparatus is that of the national urban type, with elected mayor, resident governor in the case of Esmeraldas, urban police (as opposed to rural police), courts, public health centers, Protestant and Catholic churches. Strangers are constantly in the large towns, and the number of goods to buy (watches, souveniers, jewelry, etc.) reflect this. Each of the three large towns also has a nationally known tourist resort nearby.

Yet much of Afro-Hispanic culture is as settlement oriented as back on the rivers, or in the mangrove delta. Black people play their marimbas, beat the drums, light candles to saints, and perform rituals of death and veneration as they do in the rural areas. In fact, in the large towns one finds a rural-areal focus of the majority of poor black people. Such people name their barrio after the river or area of the founder, and discuss inter-barrio differences in terms of differences reputed to exist between people of various zones in the hinterland.

In fact, many rural people, including tribal Indians, by-pass the smaller towns and head directly for the three large towns. Such people give two reasons for this: 1. there is more likely to be a ready, immediate market for their products in the largest towns; 2. they are more comfortable in the larger towns for *they are more likely to have relatives there.*

San Lorenzo in northwest Ecuador is growing, and many of the processes alluded to for Esmeraldas, Tumaco, and Buenaventura seem to be emerging there. For this reason I shall frequently allude to San Lorenzo when discussing effects of urbanism and alterations in social demography. In subsequent chapters we shall return to the notions of social demography, ruralization of black barrios, urbanism and its effects on ethnicity, and other subjects raised by our discussion of four relevant niches in the Pacific Lowland environments.

But before we close this chapter a word of caution is perhaps warranted. Niches refer to activity patterns of definable aggregates within particular environments. Actual people come and go from the different niches, and the different environments. We are not classifying people, but activity patterns. The activity patterns are contextual, subject to the immediate environing features, as well as a product of the specific cultural styles and adaptive strategies which have evolved through past generations. In fact, in Chapter VII, we shall come to see that people must maintain series of complementary strategies played in the various niches, if they are to find ways to survive in the total environment of the wet littoral purchase society.

NOTES

1 I am being deliberately vague on exactly what sorts of manioc exist, and on what the tubers are which resemble taro in the Pacific Lowlands. Manioc is boiled and its flavor ranges from quite sweet to not very sweet (and not very tasty). Manioc which is simply no good is known, and black frontiersmen keep watch over the progress of the manioc clones to get the "best" tubers. But what "best" means depends on what they want to do with them — eat them right away, leave them in the ground, dig them up, store them for awhile, take them on a long trip, etc. Since I do not *know* that all the manioc is "sweet manioc" as opposed to "bitter manioc" I prefer to just let the matter simmer. No manioc flour is produced in the Pacific littoral, so if the reader wants to think that the people raise only "sweet manioc" then he may do so. But a recent symposium on manioc at the American Anthropological Association 70th annual meeting in New York City in November, 1971, cautions us all not to do any labeling of manioc type until botanists and chemists tell us what it is that the black frontiersmen are planting and eating.

The taro-like tubers probably range from "true" taro (Colocasia species) to various aroids with their homelands in both Old and New Worlds, including varieties of the "South American taro" — *Yautia* (Xanthosoma species) — to other edible tubers with plant form similar to taro. From river to river I find that the terms "rascadera" and "papachina" are applied to tubers which look similar, but are not identical. The only distinction made among the edible varieties refers to the degree to which the plant irritates one's skin when he breaks the stem or tuber skin. The contrast between relatively high skin irritant (rascadera) and relatively low skin irritant (papachina) is only one aspect of the classification system. I would guess that there are a half dozen or more taro-like aroids, the leaves and roots of which resemble Old World and New World taro.

2 For convenience I am describing only the Ecuadorian jural-political system, and omitting the Colombian. Although much more of the wet littoral falls within Colombia, I am more familiar with the Ecuadorian system, and choose to write on the more familiar of the two systems.

PART II:

Afro-Hispanic Culture

CHAPTER FIVE

Secular Rituals[1]

As the anthropologist learns to become a black frontiersman in the Pacific Lowlands it becomes increasingly apparent to him that proper ritual behavior is as important to his teachers—those who adapt through Afro-Hispanic culture—as is the economic and political system to which he is beginning to adjust his own life style. Long before he has figured out the social structure he will have learned how to behave in a number of ritual settings. In this chapter I change modes of analysis to begin to build an awareness of social roles and norms as seen through a variety of ritual contexts.

How do we go about determining which contexts to examine? As an anthropologist moves about in his increasingly familiar surroundings he quickly finds that his friends' and neighbors' behavior varies from setting to setting, from context to context. In time, it becomes increasingly apparent that patterned behavior in a given context remains essentially the same, in contrast to patterned behavior in other contexts. Such patterned, stylized behavior is called *ritual*. The context of ritual behavior may be either "secular" or "sacred." I regard a context as secular if no saints, spirits, or non-worldly beings are seen by cultural participants as *part of* the social interaction. But even in secular contexts information is passed about other non-human actors.

In this chapter I shall discuss three sorts of secular contexts—the cantina, saloon, and *currulao*. I will then indicate the manners by which certain basic human relationships are signalled, expressed, formed, and broken in the respective contexts.

SECULAR CONTEXTS

Cantina behavior involves only men, and neither local nor regional music is played. Common male-male non-musical ritualized behavior

may begin in someone's home. It becomes a public event when moved
to a little hut, perhaps a particular room in someone's house, called
a *kiosko* (dialectially *kioko*), or *cantina*. When men are engaging in
cantina behavior they may begin to sing national songs, and when
they do, after an hour or so, they often go and look for women with
whom to dance. Usually, they move to a new location where there is
national music, and engage in what I call *saloon behavior*. The sort of
music played in the male-female saloon setting is a form of national
popular music, associated in Colombia and Ecuador with dance bands,
juke boxes, gramophones, and saloons. The vibrant pulse of *cumbia,
guaracha, merengue, merecumbea,* or *gaita* rhythms dominate. Certain
associated behavior occurs with saloon going by lower class black
people, in *contrast* to cantina behavior. Sometimes, in a particular
cantina, it becomes more usual for men to bring women in, or for
women to begin hanging around outside. In all such cases known to
me, the cantina simply becomes a saloon within a few months. So I
say that the cantina and saloon contexts are mutually exclusive, but
recognize the everyday fuzziness between the actual edifice in which
saloon and cantina contexts are enacted.

Both cantina and saloon contexts contrast with another secular
event, the *currulao*. The currulao is also a male-female musical event,
with dancing and singing, but the entire style of song, dance, body
carriage, and the symbolic portrayals of male and female action initiative contrast with the other two contexts, even though the *same people*
may be involved in each context and even though the *same house* may
be used for the different contexts. I shall discuss these three ritual
contexts in this chapter.

The Cantina Context

The cantina context may find a man playing a guitar, or may be established without any music whatsoever. In spite of the fact that inex-
pensive blaring transistor radios have made considerable impression in
the last few years in the wet littoral, they are not used in the cantina.
The cantina context is a male setting. Aguardiente is drunk, and from
two to eight men gather to engage in ritual exchanges of songs, riddles,
décimas, stories, or information about demons, ghosts, phantom ships,
spirits, and souls of the deceased. Children may sit on the steps listening, and other men and women may loiter nearby, also listening to
the stylized conversation within.

Music does not dominate this setting. When it is played it is almost
always either a Mexican *ranchero,* or a ballad from the highlands of
Ecuador (in Ecuador) or in a style of a non-coastal area of Colombia

(in Colombia). The musical aspect of the setting seems to signal national or international identification. But the non-musical *content* expressed is, on the whole, a characteristic of Afro-Hispanic culture. It consists of traits either not found in the interior of Colombia and Ecuador, or found in different forms, with quite different sets of meanings.

Cuentos, or stylized stories, are a favorite means of ritual communication in the cantina setting. One man relates a tale, usually one that the others have heard, and tries to build in *his own* elaboration, working in bits of other stories that he has heard, and exaggerating experiences that he has either had, or dreamed. The speaker endeavors to establish deep emotional tone through onomatopoia; he imitates animals, demons, spirits, and human sounds of agony, ecstasy, fear, and violence. While the speaker is relating his text others listen in silence, interrupting only to laugh uproariously at the jokes and at the sexual and political innuendoes. Three themes dominate most cuentos: extensive travel, great bouts of interpersonal combat, and amazing feats of sexual intercourse. In all cases elaborate intrigue characterizes the plot, and the speaker continuously affirms ways by which he learned to turn someone else's strategy to his own use. Animals from the area (even *Tío Conejo,* "Brer rabbit," and *muñeca de brea,* "Tarbaby"), animals from other areas (elephants), saints, and highly elaborate social orders (with kings, queens, counts, dukes, slaves, etc.) all figure into most cuentos. When the speaker has finished he makes up a stylized limmerick, a common one of which is this:

Contando, contando, que se me acabó mi cuento.
Periquito al viento, que esta de mi lado eche otro.
(My long tale has ended. It flies [as a parakeet]
to the wind; this fellow next to me casts another).

Political discussions in this context are also highly ritualized, and the speaker may go on and on about the structure of a government (of Ecuador, Colombia, Russia, China, Cuba, the United States) and of political parties. The attempt in such settings is to create a mood of successful, individual male endeavor, and to express one's personality. The elaborate structures of tale-telling seem to me to assert the complexity of an individual, including in that complexity all the social, political, religious and mystical systems that his mind is capable of conceiving.

Fear of the unknown is also communicated, together with means of combating the manifestations which the unknown may take at a particular time. For example, there are a number of fear creatures in the wet littoral called *visiones*. They have various names and characteristics from place to place, and from one time to another, but their general qualities are the same. Let me briefly indicate the ones most prominent in San Lorenzo between 1964 and 1968.

Figure V-1, Visiones *of San Lorenzo*

La Mula
(In Spanish, "the mule," but no relation whatsoever exists between La Mula as visión, and a mule).

A masked flying female spirit, usually in the form of a great bird. She may be invisible, and in that form may enter a woman sleeping with her husband, stealing her soul and entering her body. Her child will be born with the power of foresight.

La Tunda

A terror specialist that seeks bad children and frightens them to the point of death or total debilitation. Lurks about dead children and tries to snatch the body, but is frightened by the *bombo*. Also appears to adults working in the sun without hat, or who are weak from hunger or fatigue. Few recover from an actual sighting of Tunda.

La Viuda
(the widow)

A flying masked witch. Can turn herself into many human and animal forms. Sometimes takes the form of a saint, but can be detected since she returns to the cemetery. A ghoul who lives in the cemetery.

El hombre sin cabeza
(the headless man)

A particularly dangerous phantom, which seeks to kill, rather than to terrify. Attacks strong men by first growing larger than the man, and then physically assaults him. Has greater power than the others to resist the power of exorcism of Catholic priests.

El Riviel

A particularly dangerous ghost-ghoul; a "Living dead." Before his death he went to the cemetery and cooked and ate a corpse. He saved ashes from the corpse and drank them just before he died, thereby avoiding God's punishment. He is able to move freely in the world, on the sea, in Hell, and in all parts of the sky and in other worlds. He is afraid of guns, the atarraya, and the bombo and tries to trick the living into giving these to him. He takes the form of a man at work, but gives himself away by slips of the tongue. One must fight him with a shotgun or rifle. Associated with *La Candela*.

Figure V-1 *(continued)*, Visiones *of San Lorenzo*

La Candela	A sea walking demon, which shows itself as a light twinkling at night. May be *El Riviel* when he is walking on the sea.
Gente llevado (Los Muertos) (zombis)	Men who die but are either taken from their coffin, or who find a way to leave it on their own. Men who die in *"mal estado"* (sinners, without anyone to perform alabado for the spirit) may also wander in terribly disfigured form after their death. Such people are controlled by *El Diablo*. Many seek reburial. They come and go from El Infierno entering and leaving by the cemetery.
El Diablo (the Devil)	Ruler of *El Infierno* (Hell). Sometimes takes the form of a serpent to bite and kill men in the forest, to convert them into zombis; sometimes takes a corpse from casket for the same purpose.
Los Duendes	Little male spirits with very large sombreros. Known about in San Lorenzo, but of no real importance. Are not fearsome, nor do they pester women or young girls as they do in inland Colombia. A latent incubus.
La Sirena del mar (sea siren)	A siren living under the present wharf in San Lorenzo who whines out her song from time to time. The singing is heard all over town, and went on long before the wharf was constructed.
El Buque Fantasma (Phantom ship)	A ship which sometimes tries to get into port at San Lorenzo. Once a pirate ship that took a great grandfather of one important family years and years ago. Run by a black (dead) captain who speaks all languages. Very dangerous if encountered outside of the Bahía de Pailón at night.

There are many variations on the descriptions of such visiones, and indeed, a given speaker is supposed to elaborate from first hand experience. Some themes remain constant, though. First, a general notion of a witch-ghoul (called *bruja*) exists. The bruja usually takes the form of La Mula, La Tunda, La Viuda. Fear *(espantada, asustada, entundada)* is the crucial weapon of the bruja (manifested through the spell, *hechicera*), and one can combat it by strength, courage, counter spells, amulets, proper diagnosis and adequate preparation (e.g., knowing how to stay fed in the forest or on the sea, knowing how to rest and avoid over-exertion in the blazing sun). One can also trick these witches, if one is sufficiently clever. Secondly, diviners, called *brujos*, can help one foresee unfortunate encounters, and plan more effectively for future undertakings. *Brujos* have many sources from which to draw their powers: genetic (as is the case of the offspring of La Mula and a normal man), through knowledge gained from books or from foreign contacts, or by special entrance to other worlds by the use of Pildé (a *banisteriopsis* species comparable to L.S.D. in effect). Brujos may also help diagnose and combat hechiceras. They do not usually *cast* spells, though, which is why I do not call them "sorcerers."

Third, there are some inevitably superior male adversaries to over-come—they are represented by El Riviel, El Hombre Sin Cabeza, El Diablo and the "living dead." Physical courage is of no worth here; the only defense against such spirits is through clever handling of the situation, forewarning, and planning.

As each individual relates his cuento, he stresses not only complexity of life, but the means by which he, as a particular individual, was able to overcome each obstacle by strength, wit, and planning. *La décima*, too, stresses individual skills. The narration is much shorter than the cuento (which may take a half hour to an hour), and is supposed to be memorized from a written source. Since all men present may know the particular décima being recited the person giving the recitation must be accurate, or his abilities will be questioned. Not all men try the décima, most preferring to stick with the cuento.

Finally, *adivinanzas* (riddles) provide a means for individual asser-tion. Here one man gives the riddle, and looks to another to answer. To be able to give the correct answer is to re-assert one's self posses-sion; but if one fails he may fall back on décimas, or cuentos, or stories of personal encounters with visiones, or stories of inside knowledge of politics.

"Truth" has no place in the cantina context. This is a setting for male, individual self expression. Men pass information of emotional tone, and potential complexity, but do not pass accurate information about economic, political, or social events. The context it seems asserts *the primacy of the male individual in the competitive dyad: man against man, man against spirit, man against any system*. To search out the ritual bases for cooperative dyads we must turn to other secular and sacred contexts. In this chapter we pursue such bases of organization in the secular saloon and currulao contexts.

The Saloon Context

The saloon context depends upon music, without which none of the behavior I am about to describe takes place. In the town niche the saloons normally have a gramophone, and at first the speaker is turned outward so that the vibrant rhythms and raucous Afro-Latin cacophony blare forth. When there is live music the band usually consists of three guitars, one or two large single headed drums called *tambora,* and a set of bongos called *bongos.* One man plays the maracas, and another the *raspa*—which is a notched stick, or gourd, or corregated thermos bottle, played with a stick scraped across the notches. All musicians are men, and all sing as well as play. In the urbanized large town niche the marimba may be used in the band, but is played in a style totally different from that described later on in this chapter.

Men with some money enter, either in pairs, or in groups of five to eight. In the latter case the men sit together, one person buys, and all drink; then another buys, and another, the expense going from one to another and all drinking the same amount. Unless an outsider, or "blanco," joins, or takes the lead in buying, the men pour for themselves, drink, shake out remaining drops, and spit on the floor. If a blanco or outsider is present, all will pour for him first, and drink as he drinks, saying *"salud,"* health, cheers. Often outsiders (especially *gringos*) think they are supposed to drink as soon as the glass is filled, the result being a hilarious succession of drinking and filling and drinking and re-filling—with drunken states developing in short order! The outsider is not really under such an obligation; he may sit for some time without drinking, and when an insider-black companion wishes to drink he will signal the outsider-blanco to "drink." But the sensitive outsider soon learns that to sniff the drink, or sip the foam will suffice.

Men working together (such as a dock gang, or group from the lumber mills or malarial workers) engage in this form of one table, intra-group drinking behavior, all contributing about the same amount of money. Such men will also take a shot of aguardiente, or a glass of beer if there is enough money to buy it, and carry it to another man at another table, handing the drink to the man and looking away. The other man accepts, drinks, shakes the glass out and spits on the floor. He hands the glass back to the original man and says nothing. Sometimes, for an outsider who is not liked (a blanco from the sierra, or gringo) the recipient might not shake out the glass, but take off his bandana, or handkerchief, and wipe out the glass before handing it back. This is known as a subservient but hostile gesture reluctantly signalling a possible asymmetrical relationship. A more common gesture to one of disproportionate status is to say *"gracias,"* thank you, and by so doing discharge the implied return favor.

As black men move from one table to another they carry themselves erect, with back slightly bent, elbows slightly bent, arms swinging moderately, palms to the rear, in the pre-dance body style. They walk in time to the music. A blanco who wishes to be treated as "local" or "coastal" should also carry himself in such a manner when proffering a drink, in which case he will normally get the expected black behavior pattern in return, even if he is a stranger to the community, and regardless of his racial appearance. Also, a black man carrying himself in another manner will not get the expected response when he proffers a drink to another.

Men without money usually stand outside the saloon. They are also taken drinks, either by those buying, or by someone who has received a drink from someone who is buying. For example, Jorge, drinking with two brothers, gives Hernán a drink, and Hernán goes outside and hands it to someone who he will later ask to go on a money making work project—*minga*—with him, or to someone else whose house he may want to stay in when traveling on the Nadadero Chico River.

Men who have just made a sum of money by the labor of others keep giving drinks to the workmen, and the pattern of not returning thanks just described continues, as does the pattern of recipient becoming donor by giving to someone else, either within the saloon, or outside of it.

At this time (when the music has been playing for only about an hour) there usually will be only a few prostitutes in town saloons, or perhaps no women at all. Such a prostitute, at the early period of saloon interaction, will chat with the men; a man may invite her to dance with himself, or with *another* man. In the former case the man simply wants to dance, for it is too early to form a sexual liaison. Neither local man nor local or visiting prostitute would think of making a financial arrangement early in the evening. In the latter case, the man takes the woman by the hand, walks with her to another man, and proffers her hand. The recipient takes it, looks away from the man, and dances. When he finishes he walks back to the donor with the woman, hands her back, and walks away. The donor may walk the woman to her seat, or dance, or walk her to another man. Such loaning of dance partners is equivalent to the giving of a drink. The donor signals his interest in a cooperative relation with another man; the woman as dance partner is a token in this dyadic transaction.

As the music continues to blare away other women begin to arrive, singly, or in small groups of two or three. They move slowly and sensuously toward the saloon, carefully picking their way so as not to muddy their shoes (if they have any) or dresses. They stand erect, slightly arched waist, and talk little. On a bright Saturday night after a rain in town one sees women moving toward the saloon on boards hastily placed over the mud and water around the building; the impression when seen from above (the roof) is that of swaying spokes of a wheel, all converging on the source of hot coastal, national, music.

One or two women fry fish for sale outside the saloon, and the others cluster, waiting to be asked to dance. Rapidly now the men move outside and ask women to dance, entering with them. Single men who are courting women will bring their girl in immediately. If such a man has money the couple will sit together, dancing nearly every number for the first hour or two. Then, if they stay, he will proffer her to another man, and begin dancing with a friend's girl. Others move around from woman to woman, both by inviting women to dance with them, and by accepting the loan of a woman someone else has invited to dance.

Men almost never, to my knowledge, bring their wives with them at this phase of saloon behavior. The wives ordinarily stay at home if their husbands are drinking in a particular saloon, but may go to the saloon if their husband is away, or known to be spending the night with another woman. Men who have invited women into the saloon to dance may, while dancing, initiate overtures for sexual activity later that evening, but men who have been given a woman to dance with are expected *not* to suggest sexual intercourse. If I take my sister, or comadre, to Hernán and he dances with her, I transact a brief agreement with him, the most important consideration being that he *not* go home with her following the evening in the saloon.

Men who *first* approach a woman and ask her to dance signal their sexual intentions. This is easily done: a man simply leaves the saloon, walks rapidly in time to the music, swings his arms with palms facing straight back, and with a large grin approaches an arriving woman. This signals his intentions not only to the woman, but to all others in viewing distance. On the first dance he may suggest that they go somewhere together later—to his home, her home, or even to his brother's home. She need say nothing at this time if she consents. Later, he will simply take her by the arm and off they go. If she does not consent she must forcefully say *"no."* It is not uncommon for a sexual union initiated in a saloon context to continue, even eventuating in marriage. A man may initiate such a union while married to another woman, holding then two positions in two households at the same time. Women, however, are only free to engage in such a change of male partners when their man has left their household. In this sense, the saloon provides a context for weakening affinity (marriage or consensual union) in a particular household, and strengthening affinity in another.

Two important social adjustments are enacted in the saloon context: 1. the solidifying of social relationships (dyads and chains of dyads, called networks) through the ritual giving and taking of alcohol and the loaning of dancing parners; and 2. actual household rearrangement as men and women enact new affinal relationships. In the first case ritual giving and taking goes on week after week, the male dyads and networks so formed are activated in various community work settings, and provide a broad basis for potential co-operation among men. In the second case a man may leave his wife during any saloon context. In this sense, the saloon provides a setting for potential permanent fission, or trial separation, or merely a "one night stand" (which may carry on for two or three days). In the latter case people related to the woman do not forget such "stands" when pregnancy occurs. By such sexual behavior, however brief, a man may incur an obligation to a woman and her kinsmen, or at least be reminded by the woman's relatives of his responsibility when they are in need of economic assistance.

The patterns I have just described are particularly apparent when a boom is on—when there are opportunities in the money economy for *short run group labor,* or when it is expedient for a man to move to take advantage of a new opportunity. The social relationships signalled in this context, when carried out now and then in everyday life, are "long range." One knows upon whom he may call for help year after year. But actual activation of groups of men within the same network reckoning from a central individual (jefe de la minga, political party leader) are for brief periods—a few days intensive work, or a few day intensive politicking.

But let us return to the saloon context. As women arrive in proportion to the men the loud-speakers from the gramophone are turned inward, though not diminished in volume. Now the dancing picks up in intensity. When primarily lower class black people are present the dancing becomes quite stylized, and all begin to revolve around the room in a counterclockwise direction. At first men and women keep their elbows in close to their bodies, elbows very slightly bent, hands slightly rolled, rolled fingers facing the partner. The steps are essentially standard for the particular kind of rhythm. As the people begin to dance in near unison with the dominant beat, they circle one another, counterclockwise, all the while moving around the entire room. One can hear the beat of the feet, together with the rhythm itself, as far away as one hundred yards. This unity of dance style is what many community residents wait for, and now some well settled couples, and more young courting couples, begin to arrive. They enter directly into the circle of dancers and continue for several hours (or until curfew time—anywhere from midnight to 3:00 A.M. in the towns). Over this period elbows slowly become more bent, hands come up, fists become more clenched, and more arm movement takes place.

At times, during the *cumbia* or *gaita* (slow sensuous Afro-Caribbean beats with their origin on the north coast of Colombia), black men dance with handkerchief in their right hand, and lighted candles in the left hand. The women hold their skirt out to the side with one hand, and also use a handkerchief—usually colored—to move in time with the man's hand movements. This sort of dancing becomes highly stylized, and normally takes place only when a group of Colombians who have danced together before are present. It is more common in the wet littoral for excitement to grow as the circling goes on and on and the rhythms switch from one type to another. Some men begin to raise their hands over their heads, fists clenched, thumbs pointing straight back, both arms moving backward and forward in time to the dominant beat. Women twirl more, with fists clenched, and some young men actually engage in mild acrobatics—falling to the floor, swinging around a house support, cutting diagonally across the circle to cut in on the dancing on the other side, and then weaving through rapidly to return to their own partners.

The patterns I have been describing contrast with inland behavior; they are part of the dance pattern of Afro-Hispanic culture, just as the specialized signalling of dyadic links is a part of the cultural code. When a few blancos or mestizos are present they soon learn either to participate in the black manner, or to sit the dance out. One must be skilled in the proper circling movements, or he will be forever underfoot, and actually trip the dancers. But when larger numbers of blancos or mestizos are present the circling funciton is curtailed, and the more individualistic styles characteristic of the national dance patterns prevail.

Asymmetrical deference across color lines in the towns leads many black men to proffer a dancing partner to outsiders. Since there are many prostitutes working the saloons the prostitute may be the first proffered. Outsiders invariably take this to be an offer of the woman herself, which indeed it may be *in the early hours*. But as other women arrive, and men make their own sexual liaisons, and *then* proffer the girl they have chosen as a dancing partner, serious mis-understandings arise as outsiders also take this gesture as an offer of the woman. Finally, most serious intercultural communication flaws arise late in the evening, when men offer their wives or sisters as dancing partners, and the outsider thinks the woman has been "given" to him! Because the cultural code of black frontiersmen insists on silent profferral of the token of exchange (the woman), the outsider often thinks the black man uncommunicative. Because the outsider may make allusion to later sexual relationship with the woman while dancing, the black woman and man think the outsider in search of only women, and thereby disrespectful of all family and kinship structure in the Pacific littoral. In areas where black people have seen a good deal of outsiders they are careful to offer *only* prostitutes to newcomers, thereby reinforcing the outsider notions of "free" or "loose" black women.

The saloon context then may be a secular means of expressing some aspects of black culture—through stylized dancing as a group, and through ritualized exchange of tokens of alcohol and women. The context also heightens mis-communication between outsiders and black frontiersmen, particularly in terms of norms and expectations of sexual behavior.

There is no saloon context in the rural scattered dwelling niche, but the settlement niche has such a context *when a boom period is on.* The saloon context, as described here, is most apparent in the town niche, though in a bust period (when there is virtually no money) it transforms to the cantina context. In the large town-urbanized niche saloon contexts as herein described occur in the outlying barrios— those that resemble the settlement niche—and the dance halls in the central areas of such towns resemble in all respects those of other national towns of comparable size.

The Currulao Context

Every settlement of 200 or more people has one marimba house, *casa de la marimba,* and every town has two or more marimbas placed in the older barrios of the community, as well as in the newly forming ones. In the rural scattered dwelling niche there is normally a casa de la marimba available within four to six hours' canoe travel. The house is a completed frontiersman home as described in Chapter IV. The builder of the house or his sons make the instruments and hang or set them in the sala: one *marimba,* a xylophone with 20-28 hardwood keys and graded bamboo resonators; two *bombos,* double headed "base drums" made from hollowed logs; and two *cununos,* single headed "conga drums" made from hollowed logs. Sometimes, the drums are classed respectively as *macho*, male-large, and *hembra*, female-small. The owner's wife, or mother, makes one or two *guasás*, a bamboo tube filled with corn and seeds into which hard wood nails

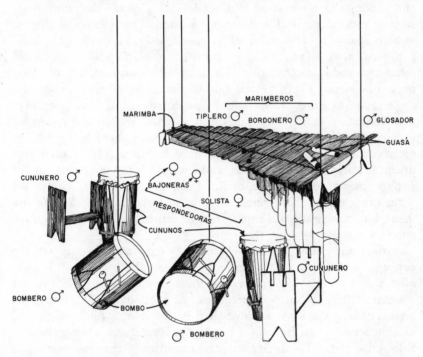

Figure V-2, *Instruments for the* currulao, *with the musicians and their positions indicated.* [♂ – *male*, ♀ – *female*].

are driven. Sometimes a man carves geometric designs on the guasá. A small shelf is also made and two or three glasses for aguardiente, or a couple of calabash dishes for guarapo, are kept there. Benches are placed along one or two walls, and there are stools for the drummers.

The actual event of marimba dancing is frequently called *el currulao*, though many simply say *"baile marimba,"* marimba dance. In the settlement and scattered dwelling niches there is usually a currulao on Saturday night, although, during a boom period, the saloon context tends to preempt the currulao. In towns there is frequently a currulao on Saturday night, and on state and religious holidays.

The context is established in the early afternoon as two men begin to practice the marimba. One man, the *bordonero*, begins to pick out one of the distinct melodies (I know of about thirty), using the lower half to two-thirds of the keyboard. He is joined by the *tiplero,* who harmonizes with him on the upper one-third to one-half of the board. After an hour or more one *bombero* (playing the bombo) joins in moderately softly, beating on the head of the drum with cloth beater, and making sharp rim shots with a stick. This sparks the marimberos to more redundancy in the choruses, and signals the particular rhythm to accompany the various songs. I have heard nine distinct rhythms: *bambuco, agua larga, caderona, fuga, caramba, torbellino, patacoré, amanecer,* and *andariele,* all of which may be used with any of thirty or so melodies. (There are also other names in different places for these same rhythms). There will be no currulao unless the bombero and bordonero can hit on songs and rhythms within the sphere of their mutual competence. By late afternoon, after three or more hours of rehearsal, one or two *cununeros* have begun to play the cununo drum, beating with their hands, and tuning it by hammering on the wedges inserted on the sides of the drum to tighten the rawhide (or wire) head strings. The cununeros fill in with rhythmic accompaniment, but the bombero is supreme in establishing the beat. A woman enters, too, softly shaking the guasá.

Various men now begin to "drop in" and many people try the cununos, and one or two others substitute on the bombo, all leaving after they have played. To some of these men the jefe de la casa, or his mate, offers a shot of aguardiente, or a calabash of guarapo, the gestures being the same as those used in the saloon. Such offering of alcohol serves as an invitation to play an instrument during the currulao that night. The reciprocal understanding is that the participating musicians will have alcohol to drink.

Things begin to quiet down as darkness suddenly closes in. Women begin to put on their best clothes, and men sit around in houses or cantinas (if there are any) and begin to interact as I described for the cantina context. In the towns men and women may go to a movie, and others go to the saloon. Those interacting in the cantina context will probably later attend either the currulao, or the saloon, *but not both.* The cantina context is important, for it is here that a *glosador* should emerge. The glosador is the lead singer, a man who knows songs, knows words and phrases that others are not familiar with. If he is particularly adept he is called *culimocho.* He also knows how to interact well with the women singers, who as yet have not been to the casa de la marimba, but who know of the preparation by the sound of drums. A glosador is usually good at cuentos and décimas, too. He is frequently found in a particular cantina setting and is invited by either the jefe de la casa, or by his brother, or one of his sons.

The mate, *mujer,* of the jefe de la casa goes directly to the home of known *cantadoras,* singers, and invites them to serve as *respondedoras* in the currulao. The respondedoras "respond" to the verses and shouts, *gritos,* of the glosador. There are two respondedora roles: the *solista,* who directly answers the glosador, and one or two *bajoneras,* who harmonize with the solista. Having invited the respondedoras, and appropriately offered some token—usually a verbal compliment, or a promise to give some conchas, or something else, "tomorrow"—the mujer of the casa de la marimba has yet another job in the towns. She must now get permission from the teniente político, or comisario nacional de policía, or from the jefe of the policía rural to hold the "dance."

The routine is almost always the same: she arrives at the "jefe's" home after dark. He tells her to return during office hours, that saloons make their request during the day. She explains to him that this is not a saloon dance, it is a *baile de respeto,* a ritual dance, or a dance involving respect relationships. If he is from the local area he says "give me ten sucres." If he is an outsider he laughs and argues, until the woman offers ten sucres. Unless under pressure from a new *outside* saloon owner (who may think that he must compete with the casa de la marimba, as he does with other saloons) the official accepts the money and issues a certificate to allow the currulao to take place.

Somewhere around eight or nine o'clock at night the marimberos begin to play, and after a few melodies have been moved through in satisfactory shape the bombero joins in. Now he beats more strongly, and soon one or two cununeros join him. Then a second bombero joins and the beat intensifies with a slow-moving, very complex African rhythm, which in no way whatsoever resembles the Afro-Caribbean beats so popular today both in the Caribbean and South America, and in Africa itself. The sound of the full rhythm ensemble (with whatever women may be present in the house shaking guasás) signals the beginning of the currulao. People move to the casa de la marimba, not in couples, but singly. Husband and wife do not usually attend a currulao together. When they do, they do not acknowledge one another's presence. Men sit on the benches, staring straight ahead, and wait for the women to take the lead. The next moves are left to women, as the rhythm throbs away. As women begin to arrive they ignore the men, greet one another, move around the room, some going through a few dance steps with one another.

The respondedoras approach the marimberos, move within the circle of drums (see Figure V-2), shake the guasás which they have brought with them, and sing a chorus of a favorite tune, such as *Adiós Berejú,* "goodbye Berejú," or *La Pangora*, "the little crab." The bombero strengthens the beat, the marimberos look down at the marimba and increase the redundancy of their rhythm as more women move around in dance form. The music stops, with some gestures, smiles, and noise by the respondedoras—aaaaaeeeeeiiiiii—*"baile el currulao!"*

Now the jefe de la casa and/or his mate takes a drink to the band. He pours first for the bordonero, then tiplero, then bomberos. Then he moves to the respondedoras, urging more than one drink onto each of them. Then he serves the cununeros. The glosador should, by now, be in the room, quietly talking to some of the men, and taking a couple of drinks of aguardiente or guarapo. One of the respondedoras, or the woman of the house, pours some aguardiente over the keys of the marimba—to female gritos of pleasure—aaaaeeeeeiiiii, *esta tomando la marimba,* "the marimba is drinking." This latter gesture is necessary for final tuning. The hard ebony-like chontaduro palm keys exude oil when beaten, and "drying them" by letting the marimba "drink" alcohol facilitates accurate beating with the crude rubber-headed mallets.

Now the marimba ensemble rapidly regroups, the marimba plays, drums enter, women shake their guasás and begin to sing a chorus:

Allá viene uno	(Here comes one
Allá vienen do'	Here come two
El Uno es El Diablo	The first is The Devil,
El Otro, Ocoró	The other, Ocoró

or

Los que están bailando	(Those who are dancing
Bailen con cuidado	Let them dance with care
A debajo de casa	Under the house
Está el Diablo parado	The Devil is standing)

The glosador finishes his conversation and moves to the marimba next to the bordonero; he listens to the melody, looks at the women, and enters with a grito:

oooooooooaaaaaaaaaiiiiiii	
iiiiiiiiiii	
Cantadoras vengan	Come, singers
Contando de mis trabajos	I tell of my labors
Hasta que le haga llorar	Until I made him cry
Oye la marimba	Hear the marimba
Como quiere hablar	As it wants to speak
Como es que la toca	How is it that she says
la sabe tocar	What she knows how to play

Figure V-3, El Currulao.

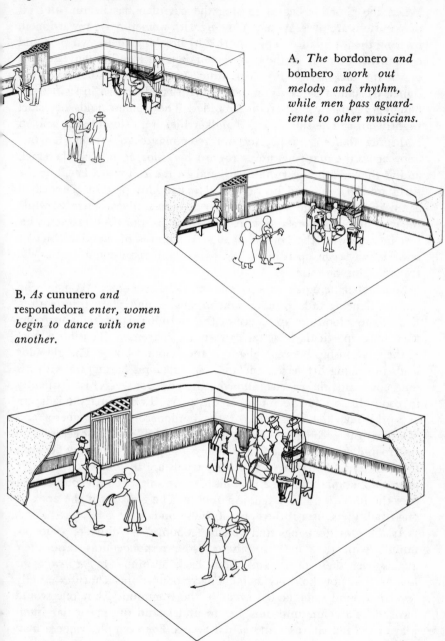

A, *The* bordonero *and* bombero *work out melody and rhythm, while men pass aguardiente to other musicians.*

B, *As* cununero *and* respondedora *enter, women begin to dance with one another.*

C, ¡Baile el currulao! *Full band plays while men and women move in "advance-retreat patterns."*

When the glosador begins to sing the currulao has begun, and all preparations are over. Women dancing with women move toward men, inviting them to dance. They do this by breaking their own pair and each inviting a man, or the two women dancing together move toward one man, and both dance with him. A man who wishes to dance signals by standing quietly, and erect, with handkerchief in right hand hanging gently over his right shoulder. The woman holds her skirt slightly out to one side, swings handkerchief from side to side, and in a distinct dance step bearing no resemblance to saloon dancing, approaches the man; he moves toward her, moving his handkerchief, and as they nearly meet she turns, and he moves toward her, but she turns toward him, and he rapidly retreats. This pattern is repeated again and again. The woman steadily advances, pivots, retreats, while the man becomes more and more excited, leaps into the air, stamps his feet in time with the bombo, shouts, and waves his handkerchief or hat. He may even open his arms as if to grab the woman, but as she turns to him, he retreats.

Men not dancing sit quietly and watch the dancers. Women who are not dancing talk to other women, gossip, and share information. Unlike the saloon the ambience of the marimba dance remains somewhat tense, particularly as far as men are concerned. Tension is part of the relationship between glosador and respondedoras. The glosador leads in singing his verses, and the respondedoras harmonize with his long notes. But the chorus following the glosador's verse is frequently in contradiction to the intent of the verse. Two primary triads are at work. The first is formed by the bordonero, lead–bombero, and glosador, the second by solista, lead-cununero, and bajoneras. The tiplero and other drummers take their cues from the interplay between the two triads. And, the two primary triads are in *continuous antagonism* to one another, the antagonism expressing sex role competition over the initiation of an action sequence. The glosador is the apex of one triad, the solista is the apex of the second.

As the glosador sings and yodels "goodbye"—"Adioooo, Adiooo-uuuu" (with the "uu" in falsetto)—the respondedoras raise their guasás over their heads and shout back at him, "*yo ya tengo mi hombre*," "I now hold my man." The respondedoras' choruses usually revolve around some actual event in the community, but one would have to be a community member to understand the particular interplay of stylized choruses and actual events. For example, when a man has just left his wife the respondedoras sing:

Adiós, adiós por un hombre   (Goodbye, goodbye by a man,
Ay hombre, espérame, hombre   Ay man, wait for me, man)

While the respondedoras sing such choruses the glosador yodels and improvises verses about going on a trip, leaving a woman, injuring women through his great penis, becoming the Devil. The women sing back that their own men are being held, they are not losing their men, allude to the venereal disease in other women, and how the marimba chases the Devil away.

The music and pitch of voices continue to crescendo; as this happens the respondedoras and glosador sing their phrases simultaneously, until finally all words dissolve into an intricate harmonic structure of yodels, falsettoes, and glissandoes up and down the scale.

The respondedoras inevitably "win" in their struggle for dominance with the glosador. Before the end of the song they are loudly singing the choruses, and may even take over some verses. As they do this the glosador may walk away from the marimba to have a drink, or to dance. The music continues until the women stop singing. However, if they wait too long he may return and trick them by beginning yet another song, giving the women no rest and exhausting the particular respondedoras. There are many other actual patterns, which symbolize the same male-female struggle for initiation of a consequential set of actions.

I have been describing the most common currulao—the *bambuco*. Other fairly common styles include the *caderona* (big hipped woman, who symbolizes the sex image capable of luring men away from their homes in the saloon context). Here the women keep singing:

Remeniate caderona	Shake it baby,
Caderona, vení meniate	Baby, come shake (bump and grind)
Ay, Vení meniate, vení meniate	Ay, come shake

Couples do a waltz-like step, loosely embraced, during the caderona. While the man sings of his particular sexual episodes, bragging of his ability to "dry up" women, the women keep singing "shake it, shake it" as a torment to the man. The man also sings of the inherent responsibility for progeny in sexual intercourse, particularly with young girls who have been certified as virgins by the midwives. He does this by alluding to the marimba as the girl:

Esta marimba que suena	This noisy marimba
Tiene una tabla quebrada	Has a broken keyboard
El mozito que la toca	The youth that plays her
Tiene su hembra preñada	Has a pregnant mate

Also, in the *torbellino*, "restless person," dancers may dance in a loose embrace, while the women sing of a lost child, and their search for

SECULAR RITUAL.

The male musicians begin to play African rhythms.

The female singers enter and sing. Then they are joined by a male singer.

The currulao, *or marimba dance, is an important aspect of Afro-Hispanic culture.*

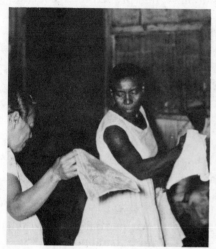 

Women begin to dance with one another as the rhythm develops, and as the female singers begin their choruses.

As the male lead singer enters, women ask men to dance with them, and couples move in advance-retreat patterns.

him, and the glosador yodels. Although the loose embrace is common in these two types of currulao dances, all participants *deny* that they dance in this manner. Dancers will tell any outsider that they *never touch* in the currulao; that there is "too much respect" for touching; that touching is for the saloon. When pressed for reconciliation of this seeming inconsistency people tell me once again that the dance is the *baile de respeto,* and insist that people are not *really* dancing embraced—this is just a symbol for the caderona, and the torbellino. By listening to his teachers and discussing his own observations with them, the anthropologist comes to realize that, indeed, the people are *not* touching in the same sense that they are in other rituals and in everyday life. They *symbolically portray* an embrace in the caderona and torbellino, but do not signal any dyadic contact between actors by this particular portrayal.

In the *agua larga* a man sings a tale of travel and sexual adventure, while the respondedoras shake guasás, but do not sing. Ordinarily, a strange glosador will sing an agua larga, "big water," indicating fantastic travels to all parts of the world and other worlds (a sung *cuento*). But the agua larga, as well as all the other marimba songs and rhythms, may be done *"bambuqueado"*—with a bambuco rhythm—wherein the patterns previously described take over.

The currulao normally lasts until dawn, but it may go on for two or three days. Seldom does a currulao end until the dancers and musicians are in a state of exhaustion, too tired to continue. By this time the singers have all completely lost their voices. All participants return to their own homes, to their own spouses. Unlike the saloon context, no rearrangement of sexual partners takes place. When pushed to explain *why* no one initiates sexual advances or tries to leave the dance to sleep with a new partner, I am invariably, and forcefully, told (again) that this dance is a *baile de respeto.*

I suggest that among other things the currulao enacts complementary male and female role prerogatives which take place in daily life as men acquire a second spouse before terminating marriage with a first. This process is called "serial polygyny." I see serial polygyny as an effective social adjustment within a purchase society. The adjustment allows for fluid household arrangements which accommodate the fluctuations of money sources in the environment. Although household structure itself remains constant after a currulao (the currulao as stability-maintaining mechanism), the *right of men to move,* and the *right of women to try to hold their men,* and the inevitable role complementarity, but interpersonal conflict, between the male rights of self-assertiveness and the female rights of household dominance and maneuver to hold a particular man, is expressed and portrayed. While the ritual portrayal goes on, however, participants are prohibited from engaging in the actual activities that would bring about a change of household dyads. Severe criticism is instantly leveled against anyone who attempts to engage in behavior characteristic of the saloon context, and when outsiders familiar with the saloon context attend the currulao such sanctions are readily apparent. Women march up to a man flirting with a woman and announce so that many can hear that this is not a saloon, this is a respect dance.

In the secular currulao ritual context male and female sex roles are equal and antagonistic—both strive to dominate action sequences, and the strife is portrayed in gesture, song texts, dance styles, and the structured tension between glosador and respondedoras. A competitive, egalitarian, male-female dyad is enacted. We shall say much more about the various sorts of dyadic ties which form the social basis for Afro-Hispanic culture in this frontier zone in Chapter VII. Let us merely introduce here the idea of *attenuated affinity*.

When a man known to be the mate of one woman goes to live with another and is regarded as having taken the second as a mate, we could say that he has broken his bond with the first. But, in the Pacific Lowlands, he remains responsible to the first mate for certain obligations and may even use the previous affinal bond to assert a relationship to another black frontiersman. Women, though they may be "left" by a particular man, are not "abandoned" in the social sense. A man who has moved on and set up another household (even in the same community) still cooperates, not only with his former wife in caring for children, but also with her relatives, and with his immediate kinsmen by involving them in his network of reciprocities. Furthermore, it is the woman's prerogative to keep the original household, and her right to recruit another man, after her husband has clearly moved on. Most importantly, though, attenuated affinity is a criterion of membership in Afro-Hispanic kinship groups. The currulao gives ritual enactment and support to this criterion. In the wet littoral the lattice of persons connected by links of attenuated affinity, together with affinity and consanguinity, ties together most people within a given niche, and between niches.

SYMBOLIC OPPOSITION

When people are attending a currulao they tell me that they never, under any circumstances, go to a saloon. And all people in a saloon tell me quite forcefully that they would never, under any circumstances, attend a currulao. People attending a currulao say that the saloon music is very bad, that the dancers there do not know how to dance, and that there is no "respect." Saloon goers insist that the music in the currulao is very crude, the rhythms cannot be danced to, and there is too much "respect" (associated with the old generations). But the same people do attend both currulao and saloons—young and old—and in the respective contexts make the appropriate remarks about the other context. I regard the two contexts, then, as being in symbolic opposition. The currulao provides a symbolic setting in which the male prerogative to change spouses complements the female prerogative to maintain her spouse and their household. The saloon, by contrast, provides the instrumental context where men can enact actual spouse acquisition and signal separation with a prior spouse. It also establishes an expressive context in which reciprocity and cooperation between men can be signalled, through the exchange of acceptable tokens.

The symbolic opposition manifest in the contrast between saloon and currulao contexts contributes to the overall stability of adapting aggregates of black frontiersmen. Female roles expressed in the currulao build a strong intra-household, intra-community base from which men maneuver as individuals, and as action-sets, to exploit extant natural and cash resources. Male assertiveness, expressed in the currulao, and in saloon and cantina, symbolizes male prerogatives aimed at mobility. Such prerogatives provide economic stability in daily life through various mobility strategies. Female sexual solidarity, and female household maintenance, provide the domestic basis for the maintenance of local kin groupings. We will discuss this social system in Chapter VII, after the sacred domains have been set forth.

In the settlement and dispersed dwelling niches there is *either* a saloon *or* marimba context in a given week. The latter prevails when there is no boom, and the former when there is a boom. Sometimes the marimba house is used as a saloon setting during the early part of a boom period, but when this is done certain changes are made: the bombo is not used, the cununo is called tambora, maracas are substituted for guasás, and the marimba (if it is used at all) is played in the Mexican-Guatemalan style, not in the Afro-Hispanic style discussed above.

In the town niche men and women choose one or the other, week by week, but do not move from one to another in the same night. I have known women in towns to attend the currulao, while men go to the saloon, but I have never known a woman to go to a saloon while her man went to a currulao. The currulao, then, can symbolize activities actually taking place in another context, in the town niche. Clearly, though, in the towns, the instrumental and expressive contexts for household fission and fusion are regarded as being in symbolic opposition: the choice made in favor of one context generates a stylized negative sentiment toward the opposite alternative.

As race lines stiffen in the town niche (discussed in Chapter VIII) there is a tendency for the growth of marimba houses to match the expansion of saloon contexts. I think there are two reasons for this: 1. Black men are increasingly cut out of opportunities in the money economy by stiffening race lines; and 2. with an influx of outsiders there is less opportunity in the saloon context for the ritual behavior described above. These two reasons may help us understand a particular adaptation taking place in the large town niche.

In Buenaventura, Colombia, and Esmeraldas, Ecuador, both the saloon and currulao contexts exist in the outlying black barrios, just as I have described them in this chapter. But in some areas near the docks, market, and in otherwise ethnically mixed areas there is a combining of the two contexts within one edifice—such buildings are called *"bar currulao"* in Buenaventura, and referred to as *both "el salón"* and *"la casa de la marimba"* in Esmeraldas. In these settings I still find the contexts to be distinct, but the contexts can go from one to another in the same evening. The personnel changes completely during such a switch, and for the most part the instruments change, too. But musical instruments for both currulao and saloon, and juke box, are kept in the house. And, the marimba may be used in both contexts (though not with the same accompanying drums and shakers —these are separated, as indicated above for the settlement niche undergoing a boom period).

More study is needed of this symbolic opposition in Buenaventura and Esmeraldas. One final point about method should be mentioned in this regard. For the outsider to hear a currulao in the urbanized milieu, it is necessary for him to behave as though he were attending a currulao in the rural area. He must quietly provide the woman of the casa de la marimba with aguardiente, and ask her to make the arrangements; he must find musicians willing to go through the slow build-up from rehearsal through participation. Otherwise, if he simply pays for a currulao but does not behave properly, he will get saloon music played on traditional instruments! Many black frontiersmen have learned that folklorists will pay for their music, and they readily accept folklorists' money. But they will not play in the typical manner. Sometimes they will add some "bambuqueado" to the cumbia, but one will not get a true bambuco, or caderona, or agua larga unless he already knows the behavior set of Afro-Hispanic culture in the currulao context.

THE SECULAR, RITUAL CORE OF AFRO-HISPANIC CULTURE

Music itself is peripheral in the cantina context. Here men assert the primacy of the individual, and ritually relate ways of overcoming human, organizational, and supernatural adversaries. Although the men participating in the cantina context frequently work together, and help one another out when in need, cooperation is not symbolized in this particular setting. It is within male-female mixed settings, dominated by musical expression, that we find the greatest evidence for the reinforcement and maintenance of flexible personal networks in the wet littoral. In the saloon context personal networks are reinforced by ritualized exchange of drinks and dancing partners, and a context for actual weakening of marital ties is provided. In the currulao attenuated affinity is ritualized and considerable attention given to it by various means of symbol play. This is important because the criterion of attenuated affinity is one of those used by black frontiersmen in sorting themselves into minimal survival groupings—called "kindreds." I shall summarize this material a bit later on, after we have more fully explored the reciprocal role expressions of men and women by an examination of sacred contexts.

The particular ritual of the currulao is not found outside Afro-Hispanic culture, though Cayapa and Coaiquer Indians also play the marimba in the Afro-Hispanic style. Nor is the means signalling dyad formation by exchanges of aguardiente and dancing partners found outside Afro-Hispanic culture, as far as I know.

During the currulao and saloon context a great deal of attention is given to the nature of music itself—none of the interaction described takes place without music, and poor, or uncoordinated performance of music will cause the entire context to be dissolved (this frequently happens in the currulao, and also occurs in the saloon context where there is live music). Music itself may be regarded as a *cultural focus*. The Afro-Americanist Melville J. Herskovits (1945:164-65) defined the cultural focus as: ". . . that area of activity or belief where the greatest awareness of form exists, the most discussion of values is heard, the widest difference in structure is to be discerned."

In the currulao we have evidence for perhaps the most African music in the New World being played in a secular ritual setting—not associated with any sort of "cult." In secular contexts dominated by musical expression we find means by which black frontiersmen solidify a viable social organizational adjustment to their environment. At the same time, in the cantina context, they maintain a viable individual adjustment to their social adaptation by asserting the inherent strength, ability and manipulative capacity of the individual in competition with other individuals, with demon adversaries, and with complex social, political and supernatural systems.

The next chapter takes us into sacred contexts, where saints and spirits enter into the stylized interaction of this Afro-Hispanic culture.

NOTES

1 Chapters V, VI, and VII discuss normalized cultural patterns which characterize the wet littoral from the San Juan river south to the Esmeraldas river. I explicitly *exclude* the Chocó of Colombia. The two areas are very similar, but many Chocó patterns diverge from those presented herein, and there are Chocó patterns not found in the segment of the wet littoral that I am discussing.

CHAPTER SIX

Sacred Rituals and Social Structure

A more rapid drum beat than that used in the currulao is often heard in the Pacific littoral; and the voices of many women singing in call-response pattern together with the rattle of maracas tells the community resident that *arrullos,* "spirituals," are being sung. They are sung to support the ascent to heaven of the soul of a dead child, or to symbolize that ascent; they are also sung to summon or symbolize the descent from heaven of a saint. Sometimes the ability of saints to descend and ascend at will is symbolized by arrullos at Christmas, Easter, or early May. In many towns and settlements there is even a parade, called *Belén,* that takes the arrullo out of house, and through the entire community.

A casual visitor to a community would not know that another musical event, the *alabado* (dialectically *alabao*)—"hymn of praise"— was taking place unless he happened to pass the very door of the house in which a corpse was laid out, or to pass the same door a week to nine days later, when a second wake to the soul of the deceased was being held. The visitor would hear the mournful strains of a Spanish dirge being sung, without any rhythmic accompaniment.

Two musical settings which occur after the death of a person signal contrasting sacred contexts. The contrast depends on the state of the deceased person's soul. The state of a soul, in turn, relates to the degree of independence the person achieved during his or her life-time. For a dependent person—a child—a *chigualo* wake is held, and *arrullos* are sung. For an independent adult person, an *alabado* wake is held, followed a week or so after burial by the *novenario. Novenas,* or *rosarios,* or *alabados* (different terms for the same songs) are sung during the novenario. At the end of the last song (*última novena*—the last rite) a final rite, called *la tumba,* "the tomb," may be performed.

Music dominates chigualo and alabado contexts, but in all ways the musical style contrasts in the two contexts.

THE LIVING WALK, THE DEAD WANDER

A structural relationship exists between the degree of responsibility achieved by the living, and the souls of the dead. A male child must achieve a degree of sexual independence before he is considered ready for marriage. And when his sexual independence leads to the pregnancy of his lover, it obligates him, to some extent, to her relatives. Having achieved this independence with consequential responsibility, the soul of the independent man is thought to wander after his death, in this world, and in other worlds. A woman who bears a child is regarded as achieving a new independence and a new set of responsibility-dependency relationships with kinsmen.

Let us pursue the symbolic relationships suggested by Afro-Hispanic concepts of the living and the dead. It is common to hear it said that a male must *andar y conocer* (literally "to walk [travel] and to know" [learn]) before he becomes a man. The phrase expresses the positive value placed on traveling and learning to cope with the environment and the various niches. There is a deeper meaning, too, for *andar* means "to strut" in the black idiom. Walking in the manner prescribed for saloon giving, or for making sexual overtures to a woman, or for breaking the circling pattern described for the saloon dancing as an act of individual assertion is known as "walking." If one asks a black frontiersman what he means when he says "concocer" in the above phrase he will invariably laugh, raise both hands above his head with elbows bent, fists clenched, thumbs pointing back and move his arms and upper torso back and forth—the gesture symbolizing sexual intercourse. To *andar y conocer* also means to learn the ritual style for symbolizing cooperation, and attracting a woman, and to learn the proper styles for sexual intercourse. The appropriate styles of behavior in the saloon context, it will be remembered, relate to the ritual means of signalling male-male dyadic relationships, which ramify into networks of association. The combination of *andar y conocer* is important, for it expresses the need for a man to know his way around in the social lattice of male support, as well as to know what he is about in his sexual relationships with his lover or wife. In brief, an adult must know the appropriate styles of social intercourse and sexual intercourse, and relate them to appropriate contexts.

For men, the phrase *andar y conocer* has still another meaning, for independence also refers to individual skill in handling the fear creatures discussed in the last chapter. Although men do not interact with ghosts and spirits in the cantina context—they merely pass information about them—it is thought that all individuals encounter such a creature at one time or another during their maturing years. Intelligence, strength, and appropriate tricking procedures must be immediately brought to bear, or a maturing man will be overcome by supernatural forces. Men encounter such creatures outside of the household domain—in the streets of town or settlement, on estuaries, rivers, or the sea. Since mobility for men is tied up with their independence and the particular male prerogative to "move on" when necessary, a truly independent man must be able to move within and between the niches with relative impunity, for the fear creatures are also there, ever-ready to seize an advantage over the weak male adversary.

It is said that the *alma*, "soul," of a *man* who has died *tiene que vagar*—must wander. People seem less clear about whether the souls of dead women *must* wander, but when pressed for an example about a specific woman they invariably say that she, when young, would be found by her mother *andando con cualquiera,* "walking with anyone." This phrase applied to a specific woman means that she was having sexual affairs as a young girl. When we press further and ask if *anyone ever* avoids such sexual affairs the answer is yes—*las virgenes,* "the virgins"—and the speaker immediately lets us know that they live in *la gloria,* "heaven," which is part of *el cielo,* "the sky." So it seems that all souls of deceased adults do indeed wander, and the living participants in Afro-Hispanic culture seek to direct the soul's first trip away from the specific settlement in which the deceased lived. This is done in the *novenario.*

The souls of pre-pubescent girls, and pubescent girls who everyone agrees have never had sexual intercourse with a man, and the souls of boys up to an indeterminate age when they become somewhat independent, go directly to *la gloria* when they die—to live as *angelitos,* "little angels," with God, Jesus, the Saints and the Virgins. They alone do not wander. Their ascent is symbolized in the *chigualo.*

Saints are also mobile, and women are able to summon them from la gloria, and make requests of them. They do this by having special saints' days, at which time they sing *arrullos,* "spirituals," until the spirit of the saint enters the house where the spirituals are being performed. These same spirituals are sung during the chigualo—the wake for a dead child—and it would seem that the relationship between living and heaven-spirit is the same in both cases. The soul of the dead child ascends as an angel into la gloria to the accom-

paniment of arrullos, just as the saints descend from la gloria to help
the women to the accompaniment of arrullos. Sometimes this third
sacred musical context directed to saints is simply called "arrullo,"
and sometimes it is referred to as *"velorio."* Although "velorio" means
"wake" in standard Spanish, it refers to spirit or saint propitiation
in Afro-Hispanic culture.

SACRED MUSICAL CONTEXTS

Three sacred contexts, each dominated by music, will now be discussed: the *alabado-novenario,* the *chigualo,* and the *arrullo* to saints.
In order to better consider the relationship between the sacred
musical contexts and social structure, on the one hand, and the sacred
musical contexts and general sacred beliefs, on the other hand, I shall
first indicate the structure of the universe, as I understand it from
my residence in the wet littoral.

The Universe

The accompanying diagram gives a rough sketch of the universe.
I am inducing structure from a fairly vague set of concepts which
most black frontiersmen hold, but which nevertheless seem to portray
their consensus. The earth, *la tierra,* is of course bordered by the sea,
el mar. Beyond the sea are other worlds, *otros mundos,* which some
brujos visit by taking banisteriopsis, an L.S.D.-like hallucinogenic
drug locally called *Pildé. Brujas,* witches, come and go from the otros
mundos, as do spirits such as La Tunda, El Riviel, La Candela who
seem to use the sea as their entry point. The Barco Fantasma and
Sirena del Mar (phantom ship and sea siren) also come and go between
the sea and other worlds. Social hierarchies are far more elaborate in
the other worlds, too, for here live kings and queens, and dukes,
counts, commoners, and slaves. Trickery in the other worlds is far
more developed than in the wet littoral.

On the other side of the earth there is the sky—*El Cielo*—which
consists of two parts: Heaven, *Gloria,* and Purgatory, *Purgatorio.*
Underneath the sky (but not necessarily underneath the earth) is
Hell, *Infierno.*

Everyone is clear about who definitely lives in Gloria: God, Jesus,
virgins, saints, and the souls of dead children. Perhaps there are the
souls of some very good priests or nuns there too—must they be good
enough to be saints? No one is sure. Souls of adults leave the house in
which they die somewhere between Purgatory and Hell. Were it not
for the último alabado, or *la tumba* (discussed below), the soul might

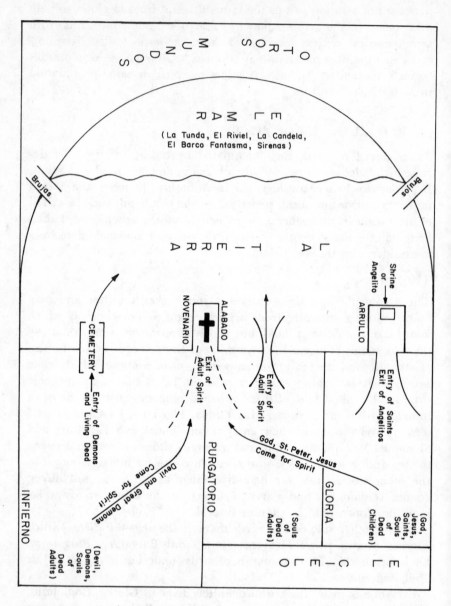

Figure VI-1, *The Afro-Hispanic universe.*

not leave the earth. People say such a soul *"queda vagando"*—keeps wandering. God, Saint Peter, and Jesus come for the spirit of the deceased, and so does the Devil, *El Diablo,* great demons, and souls of dead men and women who died in sin. The latter group of Devil, demons, and evil souls come from Hell, where they live. People never know the disposition of the soul once it leaves this world. Some day, perhaps, a soul will reach Heaven from Purgatory, but it is not thought likely.

Humans-Spirits-Saints[1]

There are portions of the earth where the connections between humans and sky, or humans and Hell, are particularly close.

The Cemetery. The cemetery provides an entry into Hell, and an exit from Hell into this world. All relatives, friends, and neighbors normally accompany the adult corpse to the cemetery. The quality of the cemetery is cold, and if one is ill, or upset, he must have sufficient aguardiente in his system to maintain his inner heat while there. The grave does not provide the route to Hell for the soul, for the soul remains in the house after death, and only the corpse goes to the cemetery. The corpse itself could be stolen by the Devil, as we noted in the previous chapter. There are many stories about the opening of the casket to dump the corpse into the grave—only to find it empty. If someone is suspected of dying in sin, or if he is a stranger to the community, he may be interred within his casket, so as to allow him no chance to escape and become a zombi, *gente llevado.*

At the burial of a child, the parents stay home. They are too emotionally close to the child to feel elated at the fortune of the child to dwell forever in Heaven, and so they do not normally risk the cold of the graveyard with their grief. Godparents of the child, though, together with grandparents, enact ritual joy, and go to the graveyard with the coffin, *cajita,* of the child still singing arrullos, and bury the physical remains of the angelito.

Alabado-Novenario, and La Tumba. The house in which an adult dies is precariously balanced between the earth, Purgatory, and Hell. After the death of an adult, people from the community gather who regard themselves as related to one another through the deceased. Men make a casket, while women cover the corpse with a sheet and lay it out on a table, with candles around the table. Flowers are laid on his chest, and sometimes by his head. That night the alabados are sung. These are dirges, lead by known *cantadoras* in the community who are called *rezanderas,* "prayer singers." They are often the same *cantadoras* who are favored for currulaos. Doors and windows are left open, and people drink coffee and aguardiente to combat the *hielo de difunto* (cold radiating from the corpse). The soul of the dead person leaves his corpse in the form of a spirit, but remains close to the house. As the corpse is taken to the church (if there is one) in the morning for final rites, the spirit remains around the house, and stays there for a week to nine days after burial of the corpse. During this nine day period other people related to the deceased usually come from other communities to visit. People talk quietly, and all doors and windows are left open for the deceased's soul to remain around. Should the doors and windows be closed the soul could wander, and not find his way back. Or, worse, he could become angry. And an angry spirit is something no one wants to have around the house.

Sometime from a week to nine days after death a second wake— the novenario—is held. Sometimes the term "novenario" refers to the entire time from death through second wake. Dirges are sung (sometimes only nine: *los nueve rosarios*—the nine rosaries), and at some time during the night the soul as spirit departs for the sky. The last dirge sung is always the same:

Adioooooo, primo hermano	Goodbye first cousin
Primo hermano, Adios	Goodbye first cousin
Vo' [te] vas y me dejas	You go and leave me
Solito con Dios	Alone with God

Now the soul should be gone. If it has not departed it must be forced out. If a man dies in sin, as in a fight with another man—in which case he would have died "too hot," *con mucho calor*—then it is probable that he will not leave gracefully. A ceremony, called *la tumba,* is then performed.

Men build steps about four feet high, and place four poles over the steps, about six feet high. Women lay a sheet over this. Then a black paper cross is laid over the steps, the bottom of the cross facing the door. Candles are placed on the four corners of the steps. All other light is extinguished and the soul enters the covering. Everything inside the cover is called *la tumba.*

The people form two lines leading from the front of la tumba to the door of the house. Sometimes men are on one side, women on the other, sometimes not. The space between the two lines is called *el callejón,* the alley. All windows are closed. The organizer of the ceremony walks to the front of the tumba; he blows out the candles, leaving the room in darkness, and then rips off the black cross forcing

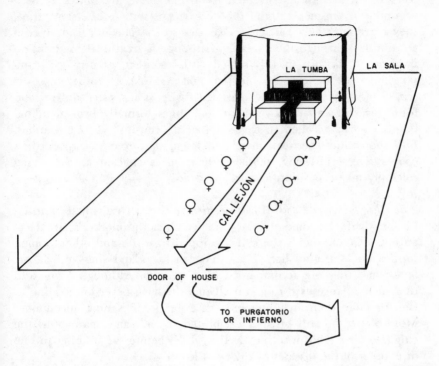

Figure VI-2, La tumba.

the soul, as spirit, to leave the tomb and enter the callejón. Now everyone sings together:

| Te vas y me dejas, Solito con Dios | You go and leave me, alone with **God** |
| *Adios,* primo hermano | *Goodbye,* first cousin. |

The soul leaves the callejón with a swoosh and goes out the door and into Purgatory or Hell. Some people cry at the swoosh of the departing spirit; others shout, "Don't cry, have courage, he went out well!" (*no llore, no llore, tengan valor, él sale bién*).

Sometimes the tumba may be performed immediately after the novenario. This occurs when it appears that, in spite of a proper novenario, the soul of the dead has returned from Purgatory. For this reason I indicate the "break" between Purgatory and the earth near the house of the novenario on Figure VI-1.

During the alabado, novenario and, when necessary, la tumba, men and women from the local community cooperate in all endeavors with incoming hinterland relatives. They express equality in their roles which are jointly oriented toward maintaining solidarity of a grouping of kinsmen around the deceased person. At the same time, they rearrange their particular kin ties so that no one can trace a relationship through the deceased. Although a great deal of attention is given to kinship in this sacred ritual context, affinity and consanguinity are deliberately blurred. For example, a brother of a deceased man may regard the deceased's wife as his sister during and following the alabado-novenario. Sometimes formally broken affinal bonds may be recalled in a re-linking of "cousins" to one another. Full cooperation between male and female sex roles is expressed; a cooperative, egalitarian, male-female dyad is enacted as the living solemnly take a position against the dead.

The Chigualo. When still birth occurs the tiny corpse is first baptized by a midwife, or some elderly woman. Then the mother's ritual co-parent, *comadre,* holds the child wrapped in white and other women form a circle around her. They shake maracas and sing and dance. Sometimes they are accompanied by a cununo. Although I am told that such a dance used to go on all night, I have never known one to last for more than an hour, and the event itself is now uncommon. More often, the still birth is celebrated in the same manner as the chigualo for a child who has lived a while, before succumbing to one or another of the diseases of the wet littoral.

The chigualo context takes place following the death of a child. It is not so solemn as the alabado-novenario, heaven is open to the setting, and women are the interaction initiators. Most chigualos occur in the first two years of life, for infant mortality is very high during this time. Usually, the child has been baptized by a priest, or by a midwife, *partera,* or even the godmother. If this has not taken place the child is called *moro*—moor—and is quickly baptized by a midwife or godmother just before, or even after, death. The corpse is washed by godparents and close female relatives, and wrapped in white and laid on a table with crepe paper wreaths, flowers and variegated leaves. Candles surround the table. If night has fallen when the child dies women immediately send for a *bombero* and two *cununeros* for the child must be protected from Tunda. Women also make sure that well known cantadoras will be on hand for the singing of arrullos. If the child dies during the day the drummers arrive by dark. The bombero brings a bombo, and the cununeros also bring their drums, if none exist in the house. The actual ritual is signalled by a man beating a rapid rhythm on the bombo. When the bombero begins people come within minutes to see who has died; some remain, some leave. Two rhythms distinctive of the chigualo—*bunde* and *jota*—are played, as are two rhythms also heard in the currulao—*bambuqueado*, and *fuga*—but it must be stressed that the rapidity of the bombo's beat clearly signals the context of arrullo (whether for child or saint).

Men become linked in *compadrazgo*, ritual co-parentship, relationships if they are invited by the child's mother to help with preparations, burial, or expenses involved in the chigualo. Kinship terms often later replace the *comadre-compadre* terms used in the chigualo. When this occurs the mother of a dead child becomes the crucial locus for the reckoning of kinship ties within a set of kinsmen tied together through the specific household in which the arrullo was held.

The child is placed at one end of the room, and candles surround the corpse on the table. The mother, father, and mother's close siblings sit near the corpse, while other women assemble on either side of the room. These women make up a chorus, sing arrullos, and clap their hands for rhythm. The male drummers group themselves against the opposite wall, and still other men and women sit at the far end of the room, near the main door of the sala. The scene is set for the arrival of the cantadoras. The chorus has been singing since dark, and the ambience is moderately solemn, but amicable. Drummers "obey" women, and "follow" their leads; men (including the deceased child's father and/or mother's husband) serve aguardiente and coffee as women tell them to do so.

The chorus has been singing songs symbolizing the entry of the *angelito* (dead child, soul of dead child as a spirit) into heaven, and the bombo has been frightening the body or soul snatching Tunda apparition away, so that life within the house now opened to the sky is safe for all children, living and dead. The cantadoras enter around eleven or twelve at night. They take up their position, begin to shake maracas, and sing choruses more complex in rhythm and counterpoint than those sung by the general female chorus. Some of the cantadoras summon personal saints, or saints for all women, such as San Antonio, and petition things for themselves as the chorus steadfastly sings the child's entry to heaven. After about ten or fifteen minutes the chorus sings again without the aid of the cantadoras, while close relatives, or compadres, serve aguardiente to the cantadoras and to the drummers, as well as to those classed as kinsmen, and to guests of superior rank.

Soon after the arrival of the cantadoras the ambience of the chigualo loosens. Adults come and go, and many take turns on the drums. Young men and women even engage in mild sex play, and children climb over everyone, and everything, poking at the dead child, and listening to the songs telling of the ascent of its soul into heaven.

Within the house there is no danger for the still dependent children, for the only avenue open to el cielo is to gloria—saintly spirits enter through gloria at women's request. The only danger at this time—the Tunda apparition—is kept at bay by the male bombero. Only if dependent children wander from the house without an accompanying adult are they in jeopardy, for Tunda could appear before them, leaving them *entundada*—frightened by the apparition—to be henceforth unable to cope with life. So the children either leave with an adult, or stay and sleep in the house of the chigualo, within comforting range of the male played, ghost-frightening, bombo and with doors of heaven opened to them by the women.

It should be noted here that Tunda also attacks children without adult escorts who make themselves vulnerable by insulting, or being rude to, someone in the mother-role. Mothers also threaten children with the "entundada" phenomenon, and are regarded by strong male children as being capable of invoking Tunda to punish them, should the young growing child use his increasing strength, or wit, to challenge female authority. When a boy is ready to challenge his mother, he must also be ready to thwart Tunda. This again demonstrates the structural relationship between male independence, and the ability of individuals to cope with supernatural forces, as well as with exigencies of social and sexual relationships in daily life.

The chigualo continues unabated until dawn, when it abruptly ends. The cantadoras go home; those who have been served, and have accepted, aguardiente throughout the night hurriedly put the child in a little coffin, *cajita,* close the lid to the cries of the mother, and with the drummers still beating away head for the cemetery, singing arrullos and waving the coffin. This latter behavior does not go on much in towns, because of the instant interruption by priests or nuns, but the behavior is typical when priests are not around. If the cemetery must be reached by water two or three canoes are held together by the now rowdy participants, and the drumming and singing continue until the corpse is interred.

A cooperative sex role relationship where women initiate interaction, dominate men, and solidify a network of kinsmen radiating from the matricentric cell (mother-dead child) is portrayed in the chigualo. Women have direct access to the doors of heaven and use such access to their advantage, while at the same time assuring ascent into el cielo to children who die before reaching a degree of independence.

Some adolescents die before they are fully independent. They are too independent for their souls to become an angelito spirit, but since no one is yet dependent on them, their wandering spirit can do no harm. In such cases they are merely buried, without chigualo, and without alabado-novenario. The tumba may be performed for such an intermediate status, however, if the person died while "hot"—as when committing violence, or if he were murdered.

Arrullo to a Saint. The set up for a saint's propitiation is about the same as for the chigualo. Instead of the table with corpse, though, a shrine is built. Drummers and singers arrange themselves more or less as described above. There are usually at least two bombos during the arrullo to a saint, and there may be even more. The sound of more then one bombo most clearly differentiates the music of this event from that of the chigualo.

It is women in a particular settlement, or barrio of an urban area, who undertake to organize an arrullo for a saint. Women must keep the dates for the saints clear, they must arrange for the arrullo, which means renting the drums and paying the drummers, if they cannot find a way to get men to play for aguardiente and guarapo. They must build this shrine, decorate it, and, if necessary, hide their preparations from local priests who may feel the arrullos to saints represent pagan rites to be stamped out. Women and only women reap the general benefits of saintly aid which may occur after an arrullo, and men must petition through women for luck in fishing. This they may do only once a year, though women may summon the saints at any time.

Because there is always aguardiente and guarapo served by women (to the drummers, and to one another) in an arrullo to a saint, men also attend. And the women frequently have difficulty maintaining the sacred ambience as some men may try to turn the arrullo into a saloon context, described in the previous chapter. When men begin exchanging shots of aguardiente, or trying to dance, the women may even abandon the house in which the arrullo is held, and retire without drums to shake maracas, sing, and invite a particular saint to enter the house.

By far, the most significant saint in the Pacific Lowlands is *San Antonio,* Saint Anthony. The majority of songs sung in all arrullos (even in the chigualo) are directed to him. Although his own special day is June 13, all special days, in one way or another, may turn into invitations of women to San Antonio to enter the house, and to help them in their pursuit of, and endeavor to hold onto, a man. In San Lorenzo, for example, men say that San Antonio is the *alcahuete de las mujeres,* a pimp. San Antonio's picture is always one of the many placed on the shrine, and girls petition him for greater sexual prowess to attract a husband, just as older women petition him for the power to hold their particular man. A picture of San Antonio may also be placed with that of another man (whom a woman wishes to attract) but this sort of picture manipulation is done in private, not at an arrullo. Price (1955:181) reports that, in Tumaco, San Antonio is

> Said to be the "lawyer" for the dead and for fishermen, and to be effective in the recovery of lost articles, he is the only saint who does not need permission from God in order to work miracles. He is considered to be the most intelligent and *milagroso* — miracle-working — of the saints. His color, beige, may be worn as a vow if a request has been answered.

My experience indicates that Price's statements would hold from Buenaventura south to Esmeraldas. San Antonio is also a broker between the living and the dead, between the living and the spirits, between saints and spirits and between spirits. He serves women in all matters, and fishermen in their exploitation of the marine environment.

Regardless of the particular day in which an arrullo is held, the songs to San Antonio tend to be of the longest duration, and represent some of the most complicated rhythms, such as the *bunde*. Frequently, during a song to San Antonio (there are more than 40 of them), the cantadoras engage in complicated counterpart symbolizing competition between women: one petitions one thing from San Antonio, while another petitions something else. One may be asking where in the house San Antonio is, while a second sings that "he is under my bed" while a third woman responds "he is having sexual intercourse with me." After such a back and forth theme—counter-theme textual and musical play, the women give shouts, and hug one another. By so doing they seem to symbolize a oneness of general endeavor (attracting and petitioning San Antonio) together with an individualness of specific purpose (the different petitions, and notions about what San Antonio is doing).

No particular tension exists in the arrullo—except that provoked by men refusing to acknowledge the importance of saints to the women's stratagems and needs. But the saints are not bothered by men's irreverence, for they are propitiated and petitioned by women, who are the sole legitimate action-initiators in this sacred context.

Although intensive questioning in any community can elicit over fifty known saints, special arrullos actually given vary from town to town, with certain exceptions. Arrullos actually given in 1967-68 in San Lorenzo included the following: Virgen de Ceibol, Cristo de las Aguas, Virgen de La Laja, Virgen María (Virgen Pura, Virgen Rosaria),

Virgen de Carmen (Virgen Dolorosa), Santa Bárbara, San Antonio, San Vicente, Virgen de Atocha, San José, Virgen de Fátima, Fiesta de Mayo. Of these, consensus over dates and significance occurs throughout the Pacific littoral only with the following: June 13, San Antonio; July 16 or 17, Virgen de Carmen; August 15, Virgen de Atocha; September 15, Virgen de La Laja; January 23, Virgen de Belén; May 3, Fiesta de Cruz. In addition, there is usually an arrullo to Baby Jesus on Christmas Eve, where the ascent to el cielo of Jesus as a dead child, lying in a manger, is symbolized and a ritual chigualo performed.

Saints are regarded as vain, and they like ceremony. They often find the intra-household ritual context too restrictive, and prefer to include the entire community in a public arrullo. Especially at Easter and Christmas, but at other times too, a "street parade" called *"Belén"* is arranged, if not blocked by the clergy. Such Beléns may feature as many as twenty bombos, and as many as one hundred or more singers with maracas in such towns as Barbacoas, Guapi, and Buenaventura, Colombia. Women arrange the Belén, and they work closely with men on formal Belén logistics, which include rehearsals and a formal plotting out of the route that the Belén should take. During the rehearsals the women bring the saints into the household, and arrullo contexts are held.

Although the women set a route for the day time procession in terms of main streets, or dominant trails leading past the fronts of houses, they begin to vary the route as the procession gets under way. The women soon begin to lead the Belén to and fro across the *back* yards of houses, weaving in and out to the delight of the saints (who enjoy this) and the frustration of the men (who are not sure where they will be led next), as the women follow their day-to-day back yard visiting routes, with the saints.

In the arrullo context women dominate everything, summoning saints into the home from heaven, and leading them during the Belén through their community visiting routes. They give the saints the variety and ceremony which they enjoy, enacting both female sexual solidarity and individuality in trapping and holding men. The men in this ceremony are paid for their drumming, and dispensed with if they do not follow the female lead.

Only when fishermen wish to petition San Antonio, after he is summoned by women on his own special day, can a man take an active role in the arrullo. This is done when the women stop singing, and tell a particular man to recite a sacred *décima*, called *la loa*. Such a man will be well-known in the community as an expert décima reciter in the cantina context. The loa is supposed to be memorized from a written text. Everyone is silent while it is recited. The texts which I have heard and collected are quite simple; they include parts of rosaries, phrases of praise to San Antonio, God, Jesus, and terminate in a request for good fishing for the ensuing year. Immediately after the loa recitation women shake tin cans with a few "*reales,*" pennies, inside and go from man to man saying "*San Antonio, San Antonio, otro año, otro año*" (Saint Anthony, Saint Anthony, another year, another year) and all the men are supposed to contribute money to pay for this ceremony. The arrullo then returns to patterns described above. Regardless of the specific day, the specific significance, or specific saint, a core phenomenon seems to take place in every arrullo. Women dominate the context, and express both their female sexual solidarity and their independence in trapping and holding men.

RITUAL STRUCTURE AND SOCIAL STRUCTURE

It is clear by now that an understanding of Afro-Hispanic culture, and its particular adaptation to the political economy in the wet Pacific littoral, involves us with a variety of role relationships, and considerable variation in the patterning of kin obligations. Among other things we must understand the patterning of *sex roles,* the idea of *genealogical reckoning,* and the *criteria for inclusion in a kinship network.* The three secular and three sacred ritual contexts help us sort out some of the structural components. Let us begin with sex roles.

The six ritual contexts which I have portrayed range on a continuum from male to female initiation of interaction. These differences in role activation seem to reflect a continuum from male self assertiveness to female dominance. In the cantina context males assert their individual power over women, their mobility, and their ability to trick spirits and the dead. In the saloon context men express male network solidarity by the exchange of women as tokens, and also express and enact actual change of spouses. During the currulao, also a secular context, men express their prerogatives of mobility, and allude to their relationship to the Devil, while the women collectively express their prerogative to hold particular men, and seek in turn to resist male innovation in song and dance. In the sacred alabado-novenario context men and women express equality in sex role relationships as a human group against the unwanted dead. In the chigualo context women control interaction patterns and become central to intra-household reckoning of responsible kinsmen and contributors while opening the household to spirits of heaven. In the arrullo to saints women assume a dominant intra-household and intra-community position, bringing the saints from heaven to the community, and manipulating them to female bidding. There is, then, quite a variety of sex role portrayals according to context, and we shall have to understand this variety in terms of domains of activity within Afro-Hispanic culture.

Next, let us turn to criteria for reckoning kinsmen. We have not yet characterized the kinship system, but we do have enough information drawn from our ritual contexts to find out what some of the *ground rules* are. The alabado and novenario rituals so clearly portray one rule that it is instructive to begin with it. In this sacred ritual it becomes quite clear that not only is the deceased himself gone, but his position in a kinship system is also gone. The deceased's kin-status cannot be used again in plotting a relationship from one kin reference point to another. The chains of connections which result from either parent-child links—called consanguineal links—or from affinal links, constitute what anthropologists call *genealogical space*. During the alabado-novenario kinsmen must dismiss one linkage in their genealogical space, and transact another if the relationships between them are to continue. We say that the cultural code of Afro-Hispanic culture stresses the criterion of *decedence*, since death itself effects linkages in genealogical space.

Consider the following diagram. The triangles represent men, the circles represent women, a single line is a consanguineal link and a

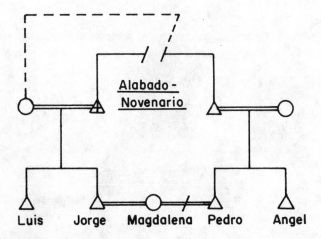

Figure VI-3, *Attenuated consanguinity symbolized by the* alabado. *Dotted line indicates possible fictive consanguineal tie.*

Construction of a shrine to San Antonio precedes an arrullo for him. During the arrullo *this special Saint descends from heaven into the house.*

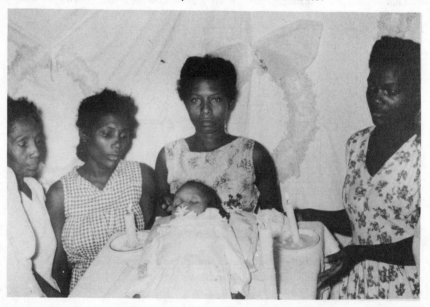

Child corpse arranged for the chigualo. During this ceremony the soul of the deceased ascends from the house into heaven to the accompaniment of arrullos, "spirituals."

Three sacred rituals provide symbolic support for Afro-Hispanic social structure.

Adult corpse arranged for the alabado. *His head is bandaged because the man died from a blow received in a fight.*

End of the chigualo. *Inebriated participants take the tiny corpse to the cemetery.*

On the way to an adult burial in San Lorenzo. Youth in front carries rum to warm participants experiencing the cemetery's cold.

double line represents an affinal link. The slash through the affinal link refers to attenuated affinity, as we discussed in the last chapter during the analysis of the currulao. The cross with a triangle inside indicates death. Luis and Angel are cousins. Furthermore, they refer to one another as *primo hermano,* first cousin, not only because of the actual consanguineal tie, but also because they live near one another, and engage in activities bringing economic gain (or, at least, subsistence). In this diagram the criterion of decedence, symbolized by the alabado for the soul during the novenario, indicates a break in the most convenient dyadic linkage—between the two brothers who are respectively the parents of Luis and Jorge, and Pedro and Angel. If Luis and Angel, in this example, wish to continue cooperating, they will symbolize this during the alabado, during the seven to nine days prior to the novenario, and during the novenario. They will use the kinship term "primo hermano" constantly, help one another in small things, attend to preparations of the corpse, and spend a good deal of time around the house of the deceased. They will also discuss, openly, so that others can hear, the nature of their kin ties. They might, in this particular example, talk about the closeness of their mothers—Angel's father might even refer to Luis' mother as his sister, thereby maintaining the consanguineal basis for the Luis-Angel cousin dyad. For this reason I drew the dotted line on the above diagram indicating the possibility of a fictive consanguineal tie. But as one after another of Luis' and Angel's parents die, attention is increasingly given to dyadic ties in their own generation. In Figure VI-3 the crucial tie becomes that of the attenuated affinal arrangement between Magdalena and Pedro. We saw in the last chapter that this dyadic linkage is given symbolic enactment and support in the secular currulao ritual.

A stranger to a community might not understand why, at a particular time, a glosador or the solistas in the currulao introduced some subtle jokes about Pedro and Magdalena, especially if he knew that they had separated long ago. But the symbolic supports in Afro-Hispanic culture to the maintenance of dyadic chains (when actors wish to maintain them) are strong. It is highly likely that such an actual affinal tie would be alluded to in a currulao if, indeed, actors such as Luis and Angel were busily rearranging points in their genealogical space so as to maintain a satisfactory set of mutual obligations within a web of kinship. Note, though, that this web cannot ensnare one for more than a generation or so, for the criterion of decedence allows one or the other actor to deny a critical linkage, should he care to do it. One must work, symbolically, to maintain kinship ties through several generations in Afro-Hispanic culture. Most people do not maintain a recognizable set through more than a couple of generations, but some do. In the next chapter we shall see how kin decisions are made in terms of processes of mobility.

The chigualo, too, provides a context for maintaining kinship ties. Let us elaborate on the diagram just examined a bit, to see how this is done. A number of years ago Magdalena and Pedro lived together in Pedro's house, with Pedro's brother, Angel, and Pedro and Angel's parents. Their only child, Nelson, died in his second year, and Angel and Jorge's brother, Luis, and his brother-in-law, Lenín (not illustrated in Figure VI-4) saw to the arrullo and burial as co-parents, *padrinos,* of the child. Pedro left a year later to go north to Tumaco and work unloading ships, and Magdalena went back to her mother's home in San Lorenzo. Her sister had just left, and her mother needed an extra pair of hands. Word came back to Angel that Pedro had another wife, Anita (not illustrated in Figure VI-4) in Tumaco and, since Magdalena had been sleeping with Jorge and was now pregnant, she decided to make a fuss and told Angel and all others around her that Pedro had "moved on," as he had a rig to do. Then Magdalena moved in with Jorge, who had constructed a new home, and began to build a life around Jorge's main shop. Later, Pedro returned, bringing Anita with him, and began to dabble in politics. I return to this case and its day-to-day practical implications in the next chapter.

The following diagram will allow us to consider the consequences

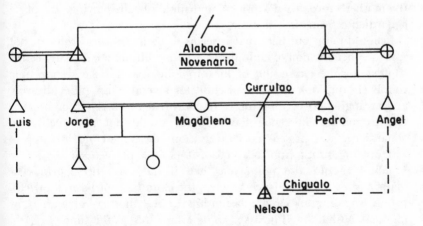

Figure VI-4, *Genealogical space may be traversed by ritual kinship* (compadrazgo) *which is symbolized in the* chigualo. *Dotted line indicates* compadrazgo *tie.*

of the chigualo ritual in enacting another criterion for kinship reckoning through genealogical space.

Right after little Nelson's death, Luis and his brother-in-law and their sisters and female cousins saw to the preparations for the chigualo, and undertook the actual burial. Luis and Angel were asked to be *compadres* to Pedro sometime during the first year of Nelson's life. Had Nelson lived, and had the compadre dyad between Pedro-Angel and Pedro-Luis remained, then Nelson would have called Angel and Luis *"padrino"* and they would have referred to him as their *ahijado,* "god-child." By referring to him in this way, a dyadic tie between each of the three men, Luis-Pedro-Angel, is symbolized. Denial of responsibility, on the other hand, indicates an unwillingness to be tied together in a dyadic agreement, or "contract."

Willingness to cooperate, by work, and by providing money for aguardiente, crepe paper, a white sheet, a white dress for the corpse, and to pay the cantadoras symbolizes an important agreement between compadres, and between parents and compadres, following the death of a child. Participation in drumming is also an important way by which men signal membership in kin networks radiating from the mother of the dead child, her husband, and/or the father of the child. During the chigualo women closely related to the mother of the child serve aguardiente to men regarded as being "in" the localized kindred of the mother, or her husband and/or father of the child. Sometimes a man symbolizes his intent to cooperate with the kin grouping by asking for a shot of aguardiente, and then participating in the drumming. But more frequently, the drummers are genealogically close to the mother's recognized kinsmen, and simply begin playing, accepting aguardiente from time to time.

I should point out here that it seems to be the *musical context,* not just the phenomenon of child death, that establishes a culturally coded context for the expression of kinship solidarity. I have seen people simply sit and look at the dead child for several hours (after dressing and arranging it) because the cantadoras had not arrived, or because the drummers could not play well (or would not play well). No aguardiente was passed, no conversations developed, no attempt to sort out important from residual visitors took place *until the music ·began.* I should also point out that, if there are no padrinos or madrinas for the child (such as when the child has not been baptized), people standing in close relationship to the mother, or father, or mother's husband will be asked to be compadres, at the time of death, and the behavior I have been describing goes on. For this reason I regard the compadrazgo bonds as an idiomatic adjunct to kinship criteria.

Returning to Figure VI-4, we now see still another option for symbolizing kinship for Luis and Angel. They may consider themselves related to one another through the dyad signalled when they cooperated as ritual kinsmen, compadres, to Pedro, at the death and chigualo for angelito Nelson. Having established this bond, they continue to call one another *cousin*, but, if their parents are dead (as in this illustration), they refer either to the bond through the Magdalena-Pedro dyad, and/or to that established at the death of Magdalena's child. Of course, the Pedro-Magdalena dyad is itself signalled in the community through the birth as well as death of Nelson. In Figure VI-4 we see how three rituals—alabado-novenario, currulao, and chigualo —provide ritual contexts for symbolizing different ways to traverse genealogical space for participants in Afro-Hispanic culture.

Once the anthropologist has a basic understanding of the environment and political economy, and has worked out some of the cultural ground rules to which cultural participants refer in daily interaction, he is ready to describe the social organization. During the last two chapters we have tried to understand aspects of the specific adaptation of Afro-Hispanic culture in western Colombia and Ecuador by focusing on rituals, and relationships between ritual contexts. The unique dimensions of this Afro-Hispanic culture are most apparent where the cultural focus on music dominates a particular setting. By contrasting and comparing behavior in the particular settings a sense of the structural components of Afro-Hispanic cultural adaptation emerge. As we move to social organization we begin to see an adaptive system in more general dimensions. We begin to understand the social system as an on-going adjustment to economic marginality. But we must not forget that the uniqueness and the general are complementary aspects of the same process of cultural adaptation.

NOTES

1 For a detailed comparative discussion of "saints" and "spirits" in the Pacific Lowlands, and on the North Colombian Coast, see Thomas J. Price, Jr. (1955), *Saints and Spirits: Differential Acculturation in Colombian Negro Communities* (unpublished Ph.D. thesis, Ann Arbor: University MicroFilms). Nina S. Friedemann (1966-1969) makes a very valuable contribution to ritual and symbolism in a contemporary black mining town near Barbacoas in "Contextos religiosos en una área negra de Barbacoas (Nariño, Colombia)." *Revista Colombiana de Folclor* 4(10).

CHAPTER SEVEN

Adaptive Strategies

The political economy of the wet littoral responds to booms and busts, brought about by sporadicity of requirements for certain products sought by world markets. This chapter presents the social organization of black frontiersmen as an adaptive response to sporadic surplus. It draws on structural components introduced in the past two chapters, and also introduces more data drawn from other contexts of interaction.

The fundamental survival plan for black frontiersmen involves the *maintenance of an exploitable set of dyads*. A dyad is an interpersonal relationship between two actors, where each actor is indebted to the other. Obligations to repay the debt, however small the original debt may be, are manipulated by the respective actors to achieve some goal. The goal may be simple, as when Hernán asks Jorge to help him strip mangrove bark and bring the bark to a buyer. Or, it may be complex, as when Hernán asks Jorge to ask his wife (Magdalena) about her former husband's attitude toward a particular form of taxation. In the latter case the former husband, Pedro, has some political influence because of his position as the brother of the teniente político, Angel. In the latter case several dyads—Hernán-Jorge, Jorge-Magdalena, Magdalena-Pedro, Pedro-Angel—are involved, and the dyadic criteria vary. Hernán-Jorge have no relationship to one another, except that which they maintain by exchange of information and services; Jorge-Magdalena are a husband-wife dyad; Magdalena-Pedro were once a husband-wife dyad, and maintain a special relationship due to intersecting ties with their respective families, as we saw in the last chapter; and Pedro-Angel are brothers.

When a chain of dyads such as this is manipulated by an actor toward some goal we say that he is using his network. The analysis of dyad chains is called "network analysis."[1] In order to carry out such an analysis we must know what is in the dyadic relationship that allows partners to continue interacting, to feel responsibility toward one another, or to have the power over one another to force compliance. Such a knowledge lets us deal with factors which impinge on interaction. We call the resultant analysis a "transactional" one.[2] In the wet littoral, black frontiersmen tend to successfully use criteria of consanguinity and affinity (their kinship system) to transact dyads. As an auxiliary system, they use the Latin American idea of "co-parents," *compadrazgo-padrinazgo*. I think, though, that the compadrazgo-padrinazgo system may best be thought of as an idiomatic adjunct to kinship in this Afro-Hispanic culture, for reasons discussed in the last chapter. Let us first consider the nature of reciprocity and the transaction of dyads, and then look at some dominant dyadic ties in family, household, and kinship systems. The analysis takes us into the household domain, extra household or "street" domain, community and supra-community domains within the various niches.

DYADS

When friends, relatives, or co-parents meet one another in the street, or on a river, they typically pass by before speaking, and then call back a greeting, or rapidly exchange information or emotional tone without turning back to look at one another. When two people of the same socioeconomic position barter for goods, or buy goods, they do not look at one another, and they do not introduce pleasantries or animosities into the conversation until the actual transaction is over. Even in some credit relationships a black townsman may walk directly into a shop and ask for a pound of rice. On receiving the rice he can state flatly *"no tengo plata,"* "I'm broke," and walk out. Provided that he pays within a day or so, this sort of credit relationship is regarded as equivalent to direct payment. Should he not pay, however, he loses all possibility of credit in the future—the shopkeeper will simply say *"no puedo,"* "I can't," and take back the rice the next time the buyer tries to buy on credit. Following Sahlins (1965:147) I call all of these examples, including the short-term credit relationship, "direct exchange" which results in *balanced reciprocity*. Such direct exchanges go on all the time. They may be immediate (as in the exchange of greeting or goods), or delayed (as in the case of short-term credit), but the style is always the same: abrupt interchange of words in the exchange context, no eye contact, no extraneous pleasantries or animosities or symbols of deference or degradation on either side. No dyadic contract is transacted by such balanced reciprocities.

Deference is brought into the direct exchange relationship by black people when clearly higher social, economic, or political standing exists. For men this may include hat tipping, or a smile (but with eyes averted), or even a shuffling of feet and mumbling. Women manifest deference by tilting the head to the left, averting eyes, and talking softly. But such deference is *uncommon* in Afro-Hispanic culture, even *vis-à-vis* relatively powerful, prestigeful figures such as a local physician, or head of a governmental malarial campaign. Black frontiersmen all know these deference signals, but are very reluctant to use them unless they get something in return. Short-term credit (or delayed direct exchange) is common with professionals, or officials. Black people needing medical attention typically walk into a physician's home (or his dispensary), avert eyes, shuffle feet, and mumble their ailment. After treatment (a shot of penicillin, if any is available) they walk out *without saying "thank you."* Normally, the fee for such treatment is paid within a month. It takes professionals from the interior some time to become used to this behavior. One physician told me that it took him years to learn that the black man or woman walking out of his office without even saying "thank you" was actually telling him that he would pay as soon as possible. He also told me that the few times that he insulted the person who did not immediately pay, he never received payment. Black people also tell me that they will not repay anyone who abuses them, not because their dignity is wounded, but because they have submitted to some degradation instead of offering money. Deference will be *given* by a black person toward a visibly more powerful townsman, particularly when the more powerful person is still a stranger to the community, but *degradation will not be accepted.* He who degrades a black person is fair game for non-payment.

If we are to find the transactional basis for the dyadic contract we must leave balanced reciprocity, and look to forms of interpersonal behavior with a built-in mechanism for continued goal oriented interaction. There are two mechanisms for this: 1. giving a person something with an implied contingency, 2. allowing someone to take something and then later holding him accountable. I see the two (giving and taking) as facets of the same process.

Sometimes, when two people meet (not necessarily friends, relatives, or co-parents) one of the two greets the other *before* they pass, and with slight preamble directly asks for something: "loan me ten sucres," "help me raise some roof poles," "give me some fish." If the person asked is not a recognized close relative he has two options: he may say "I can't," or he may *immediately* do what he is asked to do. If he wants to give that which is requested but cannot, he then asks a close relative to respond. For example, Hernán meets Jorge and says "good morning, Jorge, how are you, where are you going, loan me your machete." Jorge does not have a machete so he goes to his sister's house and takes her husband's machete and carries it to Hernán's house. He leaves the machete in the cocina and goes on about his business. Such exchanges are not without tension. A machete is expensive, and a basic tool of survival. When Jorge's brother-in-law, Lenín, finds his machete gone he will be angry and hold Jorge accountable. But Hernán is now in Jorge's debt, and Jorge will call on Hernán when he needs help in some undertaking. Provided that Hernán acts in the culturally prescribed way and remains in the town, thereby maintaining a readiness to help Jorge, or someone Jorge designates (his brother-in-law, for example), we can say that a dyad has been formed. Hernán would normally return the machete, of course, and this could balance the exchange. But, in such a case, Hernán would more likely return something *more*.

By returning to Jorge's house with some peccary meat and the machete, Hernán "gives a present" to Jorge. To get peccary meat one must buy shot and powder, go into the forest, and take the risks of a hunter (or get some cash and buy the meat). Since peccary meat is favored, the gift is significant in its difficulty to repay. Jorge is now in Hernán's debt. And, he is in his brother-in-law's debt, too, because he "took" his machete without asking. So Jorge sells some of the meat and buys a half bottle of aguardiente (white rum) and goes to Lenín's house. He walks in without greeting, puts the machete down in a corner, sits down at the table (if there is one) in the sala, opens the bottle, finds a glass (which, perhaps, his sister gives him), pours out two ounces and hands the glass to Lenín without saying anything. Lenín accepts the aguardiente, drinks it, shudders, spits on the floor, puts the glass down on the table. Jorge fills it again, and the process is repeated. After three or four times Lenín indicates that Jorge should drink, or Jorge simply takes a drink. Now they begin to talk about something, and *exchange information, not pleasantries*.

Typically, they begin by talking about prices, the drift of the conversation moving toward the impossibility of either of them buying everything they need. It is clear that a dyadic contract—an informal relationship based on continuous reciprocities—exists, and that the two will continue to use one another, and one another's property, as it becomes necessary to do so. Hernán, Jorge and Lenín are bound by series of dyadic ties. Before we can understand more about the lattice of interpersonal dyads in the wet littoral, and the means by which they form into cohesive groupings of people, we must understand more of the cultural content brought into the dyadic relationship. We must examine some of the fundamentals of consanguineal and affinal dyads, in the contexts of family, household, and kindred formation and maintenance.

FAMILY AND HOUSEHOLD

The inescapable biological phenomena of procreation, birth, growth and maturation, adult maintenance, and eventual deterioration to death establish the universal bases for certain primary dyads. Two of these—mother-child and mother-husband—provide, through culturally patterned role relationships, basic intra-familial, intra-household dyads from which various dyadic chains radiate. Radiating dyads provide the capital support for the fundamental units. The first of these dyads is consanguineal, related through blood, and the second affinal, wed to the (mother) locus of the consanguineal relationship. Why don't I just say that father and mother are married (affinally related) and children are related consanguineally to them? Simply because such a statement negates the important surrogate roles often played, and also ignores the *recruitment process* of a spouse in household formation and development. Further, it does not adequately describe the nature of the universal matricentric cell (mother-child dyad) which is adequately supported by father recruitment, and by ramifying family and kinship dyads in the wet littoral.

Mother-Child Dyad

First pregnancy signals a new dyadic relationship for every woman in the household. Such pregnancy often occurs before the mother is actually living with the child's father. In such cases the mother looks for economic support to her father and brothers, or to her mother's husband. In order to support her child she *must* find a minimal set of men and women capable of supporting her new role relationship— mother-child. If she cannot find such a minimal set then a surrogate mother will take the child. Such a surrogate mother may be her mother, grandmother (maternal or paternal), sister, brother's wife, or mother-in-law (more precisely child's father's mother). Provision for possible surrogate motherhood, and for economic responsibility for at least the first two years of life, are made through the ritual co-parent system.

Prior to the birth of the child the mother will ask two men and two women to be her *compadres* and *comadres*. They will share responsibility for child rearing for a time; and should the child die they will see to the expenses and ritual involved in its chigualo. With four co-parents, normally selected from the available near-kin, the mother is provided with her primary supportive set, and bound more closely than before to certain kinsmen. These ritual co-parents, or reinforced kinsmen, have a *padrinazgo* relationship to the child. The child is called *ahijado* (-*a*), and (when he is old enough to know this, and talk) calls the godfather *"padrino"* and the godmother *"madrina."* Comadres share the mother-son incest taboo, and compadres accept the brother-sister respect relation prohibiting sexual relationships.

Ritual kinship almost always extends beyond the household of the mother. Every household has a male or female "head" who is known as *jefe de la casa*. This status is one of economic responsibility to household residents not one of authority over residents. To maximize her future residential options, it would seem, the new mother (or sometimes her lover) asks people closely related to her, living nearby, to be her co-parents. As the mother-child dyad matures and strengthens, some residential shift takes place. Such a shift signals tightening of some affinal or consanguineal dyad as a particular man, or a couple of brothers, begin to assume more direct responsibility for the mother-child continuing relationship. The mother may move to her brother's house, or to her lover's house. In the latter case she is regarded as "married." If she remains in the house she has been living in she is expected to take over more and more adult tasks. If a man moves in with her, then she is also regarded as "married."

Mother or mother surrogate nurses a baby for six months to a year and a half, usually terminating around the end of the first year. The child is carried virtually everywhere during this time, except that the mother tries to avoid going into the open sun on river or sea for more than a few minutes, for fear of the intense heat which transmits *"pasmo,"* which refers to any debilitating illness. She also keeps the child from the intense cold radiating from dead adults (*hielo de difuntos*), and from the cold, cold cemetery. She protects it, too, from the body snatching ghost, *Tunda*, who hangs about the towns and settlements, and from cold moon rays and night water lights.

By the time the child is two years old he accompanies the mother wherever she goes, or she simply leaves him in the household with a couple of boards loosely nailed across the bottom of a doorway. It is up to the child to stay in the house, or to climb over the flimsy barrier and chase after the mother. If the child aggressively follows the mother, she takes him wherever she goes, but the prerogative becomes his by age two or three. A child left at home in this manner may seek another household for comfort rather than follow the mother. When a little child enters another household comfort and shelter are automatically given. By this time (age two) mother's protection is verbal—she warns the children, but does not physically restrain them. In some cases children beyond two may make their own selection of a new surrogate parent, or take up residence in a congenial household of people closely related to, and normally physically close to, the mother's household.

Children between a year and a half and three normally accompany the mother to ritual events, the mother holding them gently, and tapping complex rhythms on their bottoms and backs as the drums, rattles, and marimba are played. By the time children are three we see them repeating such rhythms on tin cans, batea or canoe bases, or on the drums themselves. Rhythm in this sense seems built into the mother-child dyad; but more formal instruction in the melodic structure of the marimba demands the attention of a man in either padrino or father role.

Mother's discipline is short and severe. One verbal order is normally given to children when they are misbehaving or annoying the mother, or someone who the mother does not wish to be annoyed. Then the mother takes a willowy branch and swings at the child, who dances, ducks, runs and tries to escape. One sees two-year-olds hastily crawling over the boards placed to restrain them with the whip lashing their bare bottoms. They scream in defiance and pain, mouths open and tears streaming. The mother does not normally pursue children beyond the household, unless she is extremely angry. In the latter case, she, too, may yell as she beats the child, and when he runs he may find the mother's mother or sister waiting with whip at his point of escape! But as the child gets older and escape becomes easier he "behaves" in order to stay within the matricentric cell, for his escape from a whipping may preclude rapid return into the home. Those inadequate to injure the mother (toddlers and children up to five or six years old) fight back, even grabbing the whip and swinging back at the mother (and thereby incurring even greater punishment). They also place themselves in jeopardy with Tunda, as we saw in the last chapter. Those who are becoming strong—say an eleven or twelve year old boy—are *not* expected to fight back, their only option is flight. Should they fight back the wrath of manly punishment will fall upon them. When men must take over such discipline they do so with a thorough drubbing, usually followed by expulsion from the household for a time.

The woman without growing children is probably more lonesome than one without a resident husband. And in fact, except for exceptional economic roles, women without some resident children are extremely rare. A woman depends on children of both sexes up to ten or twelve years old for women's work—cleaning the bush around the house, harvesting root crops, corn, cane; diving for conchas; carrying laundry; weaving baskets. In other words the mother-mother surrogate and children make up a minimal household work cell, supported by adult men bound to the mother-child dyad in a variety of manners. In turn, the children depend on their mother-mother surrogate for basic transmission of certain types of cultural information such as the proper manner to perform rituals, days of saints, uses of saints, and the repertoire of songs sung at the death of children and adults. They also depend on her for their economic well-being, particularly in her ability to plan an adequate work schedule for the basic sustenance of this mother-child unit. Such planning, of course, includes the recruitment process of the male role in family affairs, to which we turn shortly.

The mother-child cell is basically intra-household, but not totally so. When the cooperative unit living within one house becomes too large, the matri-centric cell may extend between households, maintaining many of the basic functions of cooperation and socialization, even though children and mother (or mother surrogate) are eating and sleeping apart. For this reason I refer to the mother-child dyad as the fundamental *family unit*. The fundamental *household unit,* however, must be seen from the standpoint of the mother-husband dyad.

Mother-Husband Dyad

Mother may recruit a husband for her family in a number of ways. If a young girl's mother wishes to establish a basis for early marriage she gets a midwife (or in the town niche a physician if there is one) to certify that the girl is a virgin. Later, when the girl's mother knows that the girl is having sexual relations with a boy she will demand marriage from the boy's parents. Marriage in this case normally involves the girl's moving into the boy's household, and also usually involves the formation of compadrazgo ties with someone other than the parents from the household the girl came from, when the girl has her child.

It is more common for the girl to become pregnant, have her first child, and to call on the father for assistance. If the assistance is adequate, and if the couple continue their sexual affair, the boy will usually move into the girl's mother's house before the second child is born. In this case compadrazgo ties are normally established with someone in his natal household. But if the mother becomes pregnant by another man she may remain "single" in her household through two, or three, or more children, going through a series of affairs with different men.

The mother-husband (or lover) tie is *affinal;* it forms a sexual-social bond between the couple, *and between members of the immediate families of the couple. The bond created between the families of the couple, reinforced through compadrazgo ties to individuals in their respective households, endures even after the couple cease their sexual relations.* Consider, again, the case of Magdalena and Pedro which I introduced in the last chapter. The ties created by the Magdalena-Pedro affinal dyad forged an enduring relationship between Luis and Angel, the relationship being reinforced after the death of the child. Before the death of their parents, Luis and Angel were *cousins.* But now they are *concuñado* or "distant in-laws" and *compadre,* co-parents, to one another provided they recognize the bond forged through Magdalena's and Pedro's past affinity, physically manifest through their dead child. This "in-law" relationship stands, when reinforced, if the relationship can be traced through any affinal bond, or series of bonds, whether or not the affinal bonds are "active;" that is, whether or not the couple forming the affinal bonds are still sharing their affinal relationships. The relationships I have just described look like this:

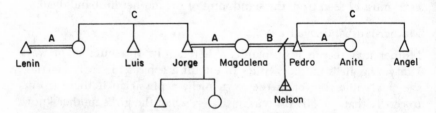

Figure VII-1, *Dyads linked in three ways: affinity (A), attenuated affinity (B), and consanguinity (C)* [△–*male,* ○–*female*].

The same people are involved as in the diagrams in Chapter VI (Figures VI-3, VI-4), except that Lenín and Anita have been added.

When Hernán activated this network segment by approaching Jorge (see page 146), he reinforced dyad classes A, B, and C. All three classes are culturally recognized linkages in kinship networks in the wet littoral, and we shall say more about them presently. I should remind the reader here that the relationship between Jorge and Angel is *also* consanguineal, as their parents were brothers; when their parents were alive they regarded one another as cousins.

Thus far we have only mentioned the form of marriage, *casada,* in which partners enter the affinal dyad by economic cooperation, continued sexual reciprocities, and change in residence by one of the spouses. This form of the affinal dyad is the most common, though partners may also register their marriage, *matrimonio,* with civil authorities (making them *"bién casada"*), or even go through Catholic ceremonies of marriage. The latter is quite rare, and ordinarily tied to processes of upward mobility.

Whatever the degree of actual marriage contract, men expect to go through a series of affinal dyads in their lifetimes, and women attempt to hold a particular husband for as long as they can. Sometimes men have more than one wife, and occasionally such polygyny takes place within a household, even in towns. Women are not allowed by their spouse to share their sexual relationships with another man. Since the man with two wives is often in the process of change from one to another (witness the above case of Pedro, Magdalena, and Anita) I characterize the affinal pattern of the wet littoral as *serial polygyny.* (For a more detailed analysis see Whitten 1965: Chapter VI).

We noted in Chapter VI that maturing men had to learn to *andar y conocer* and that at one level this phrase referred to the learning of appropriate styles of sexual intercourse. Male initiated styles of coitus signal the degree of responsibility which a man is willing to take in providing for his sexual partner. Since men and women talk about these styles, the contrast between the spouse style of sexual relation, and the non-spouse, or "casual" style, reveals the ideal intent of a man in terms of continuing sexual relationships.

Sexual behavior is warm and tender between spouses, and according to all those who talked to me about this subject, rougher sexual behavior on the part of the man may signal eventual break in the marital bond. Intercourse between a couple is described as *"suave"*— smooth (groovy). A man is expected to copulate with his wife when relatively sober, to be tender, to avoid, for example, squeezing her breasts to pain, or violently thrashing around on top of her during coitus. He should care for her position during intercourse and if she must move because of discomfort brought about from the bamboo floor, or rough hewn bed or matting, he must let her do so. She, in turn, should undertake to bathe his genitals in perfume, *agua florida,* or, at least, clean water, from time to time, building slowly toward arousal, and endeavoring to prolong the period before orgasm.

When men go drinking they do not usually take their wives, with the exceptions described in Chapter V. They dance with other women, and should they wish sexual intercourse after becoming inebriated they go with a prostitute, or with someone else's wife. By going out with another woman they avoid rough, abusive intercourse with their own wife, and thereby maintain respect for their wife. But a signal of pending polygyny, or new wife acquisition, can be made in such brief affairs. If the man and woman show the tenderness toward one another normally reserved for the husband-wife relationship, such a signal is transmitted. Sometimes, after a drinking bout, men take a woman on a *peli,* or gang bang, and may injure the woman in such activity.

Women show respect to their husbands by refraining from intercourse with them when menstruating. A woman is not expected to tell a man that she is menstruating if the affair is casual, or if the man is intoxicated. A man who is tricked into intercourse with a menstruating woman is the butt of masculine jokes. It is his fault if he gets a blood infection referred to as *bota mucha,* "big bag," (probably limphogranuloma in its venereal form) because he did not take time to recognize the *manchón roja,* "red stain."

A man has authority over his wife's sexual activities and he backs it up by physical force. Should he find that she has been unfaithful to him he may severely beat her. There are cases, during such a beating, where a man snatched a machete and swung at his wife, either wounding her badly, or killing her. Only where death or permanent disability results from such a beating will the woman's brothers or other family members seek revenge. I have no reliable data on actual killing of a man following the killing by a man of his wife. The only situations I know about resulted in arrest of the killer, or escape to another distant town, or country. Arrest or escape were followed by vows that should the man return to the area of his wife's relatives he would be killed. I know of no return after such an incident.

The mother-husband tie often involves traveling together, usually with at least one other man, preferably the husband's brother. In such cases the husband and wife are quick to make the brother padrino of their child, demonstrating paternity of the child by the husband, not the brother.

In an enduring affinal relationship there comes a point where the husband-father undertakes the construction of a house for his nuclear family. In such cases he becomes, automatically, *jefe de la casa,* "household head." The house may be built in the pioneering sense in a rural zone (rural scattered dwelling niche) or in a town or large town where he has no relatives. When a man does this I call him a *first generation settler*. As his household expands and marriages occur a network radiating from himself begins to form into a viable economic unit, called *"parentesco,"* "kindred." Or, a man may choose to remain in the immediate vicinity of his parents' or even grandparents' kindred, as in the settlement niche. He builds adjacent to his relatives, or in an area economically propitious to continuous interaction. In such a case the locus of his kinship system will likely be a generation or two back—to the original settlers. Relatives connected by consanguineal, affinal, and attenuated affinal bonds are all included in his ego-centered kin network, but he reckons his kindred from a focal settler.

House and household are not synonymous concepts, and they can only be separated by understanding the usage of the Spanish term *casa* in social context. When referring to a physical structure—the house—people in the littoral say "casa." But, when referring to a grouping under one roof with a responsible head, the term casa refers to the grouping itself, in relationship to the *jefe de la casa*. In this latter, social sense, there may be more than one house*hold* within the house, and the household may include people who are not always in residence. Also, in this sense, a person may have a position in more than one household, as for example when a man has two or more wives living in different households. He may be jefe of one household, but dependent upon (and obligated to) the wife's father, who is jefe of his other household.

A man is always jefe de la casa when present in the house. But when a man leaves his woman she becomes "jefe" and remains in that role until she finds another husband, who then assumes the headship position. Succession of household possession is normally from man to spouse, to mother's son remaining in the house, to his wife if he abandons her, and so on. It is quite rare to find a male head of a household without spouse, more common to find a woman head without spouse, but most common of all is the head of a household, with his spouse.

The mother-child dyad is dependent to some extent on a suprahousehold set of men for food and social comfort. The mother-husband dyad may provide the minimal linkages for this set, provided that the husband can maintain sufficient ties external to the household to allow him to bring food and information necessary for decision making into the family. The head of a given household finds others within his casa dependent upon him, and so he too must maintain a series of interpersonal ties with exploitable companions. The maximal inter-locking set of individuals culturally recognized in the wet littoral is made up of those people reckoning their relationship from certain focal kinsmen. We call this interlocking set the *kindred*.

THE KINDRED

The kindred is the maximum kinship grouping, and in the wet littoral it is usually referred to by the term *"mi parentesco"* (my kindred, my relatives), although in parts of Colombia, particularly the Chocó, *"familia"* takes on this meaning. The prefix *"mi"* is essential, for the *kindred is a set of relatives reckoned from a common kinsman, for some purpose.* Anthropologists refer to such a kinsman as an *ego*. From the standpoint of any ego there is a set of *alters* related to him by some culturally coded dyad. The code is suggested by the set of kin terms used by ego to refer to alters. In the Pacific littoral the set is comparable to that to which we are accustomed, since it is com-posed of Spanish equivalents for brother, sister, mother, father, son, daughter, cousin, uncle, aunt, etc. However, in the code some criteria for tagging (using a term in the code to name an alter) are different than we are used to in our system. Particularly, the criteria of affinity, proximity, decedence, and genealogical space must be considered in more detail. We analyzed some of these criteria in the last chapter, as structural components. We now turn to the kinship code itself. Here are the terms used in the wet littoral to address and refer to relatives.

Figure VII-2, Consanguineal kinship terms of address, ego male or female. For reference add prefix "mi."

Primary Term	Variants	Relationship to Ego
Papá	papí, papita (intimate) padre, señor (formal)	Father
Mamá	mamí, mamita (intimate) madre, señora (formal)	Mother
Hermano (Colombia & Ecuador) Ñaño (Ecuador)	ñañito, hermanito (intimate)	Brother
Hermana (Colombia & Ecuador) Ñaña (Ecuador)	ñañita, hermanita (intimate)	Sister
Abuelo	abuelito (intimate) papá grande (Ecuador)	Grandfather

Figure VII-2 (continued), Consanguineal kinship terms of address, ego male or female. For reference add prefix "mi."

Abuela	abuelita (intimate) agualita (intimate-Ecuador), mamá grande (Ecuador)	*Grandmother*
Hijo	mihijo (intimate)	*Son*
Hija	mihija (intimate)	*Daughter*
Nieto		*Grandson,* Nephew's son, Niece's son
Nieta		*Grandaughter,* Nephew's daughter, Niece's daughter
Primo (Prima)		*Cousin,* including children of parents' siblings, *may* include spouses of parents' siblings, parents' siblings near ego's age, children of cousins. Children of anyone classed as Tío (a).
Primo hermano (Prima hermana)		*First Cousin,* when ego wishes to make this distinction.
Tío		*Uncle,* parents' brothers, spouses of parents' sisters, grandparents' brothers, spouses of grandparents' sisters.
Tía		*Aunt,* parents' sisters, spouses of parents' brothers, grandparents' sisters, spouses of grandparents' brothers.
Sobrino		*Nephew,* may be son of primo hermano, prima hermana.
Sobrina		*Niece,* may be daughter of primo hermano, prima hermana.

Figure VII-3, Affinal kinship terms of address and reference, ego male or female.

Primary Term	Variants	Relationship to Ego
Mi hija (pronounced and used as one term, "Mija")	mujer (reference only) hembra (reference only) esposa (formal, reference only)	*Wife, co-habiting woman.*
Hombre	esposo, marido (formal, reference and address)	*Husband, co-habiting man,* man with whom woman is having sexual relations

Figure VII-3 (continued), Affinal kinship terms of address and reference, ego male or female.

Cuñado		*Brother-in-Law*
Cuñada		*Sister-in-Law*
Concuñado		*Husband of Sister-in-Law, man connected to ego by series of affinal, or attenuated affinal ties.*
Concuñada		*Wife of Brother-in-Law*
Suegro		*Wife's Father, husband's father.*
Suegra		*Wife's Mother, husband's mother.*
Hija		*Son's Wife*
Hijo		*Daughter's Husband*
Sobrino		*Spouse's Nephew*
Sobrina		*Spouse's Niece*
Padrasto		*Stepfather (mother's husband)*
Madrasta		*Stepmother (father's wife)*
Hermano paterno	hermano, ñaño (Ecuador address and commonly for reference)	*Father's Son*
Hermana paterna	hermana, ñaña (Ecuador address and commonly for reference)	*Father's Daughter*
Hermano materno	hermano, ñaño (Ecuador address and commonly for reference)	*Mother's Son*
Hermana materna	hermana, ñaña (Ecuador address and commonly for reference)	*Mother's Daughter*

In Figure VII-2 I separated ego's collaterals (his cousins, aunts, uncles, nephews and nieces), from his lineal relatives (mother, father, brother, sister, grandfather, grandmother, son, daughter, grandson and grandaughter). We must understand how an ego in this system uses the criteria of affinity, proximity, decedence, and genealogical space to group himself with some collaterals, and exclude others. We have already defined affinity, and introduced the concept of attenuated affinity. "Proximity" refers to how "close" a kinsman is to ego: either socially, as defined by the intensity of the dyadic tie, or physically, as defined by residential proximity. "Decedence," as we have seen, refers to how people use a dead relative as a kin link. We introduced the concept "genealogical space" in the last chapter, and we now require a technical definition. Ward Goodenough (1970:74) provides this one:

> . . . genealogical space is composed of a chain of connections between two persons as ego and alter. These connections consist either of one or more parent-child links, in what can be called a consanguineal chain, or of one or more marital ties, or of both together.

In the wet littoral black frontiersmen regard affinal and attenuated affinal ties as linkages equal to those formed consanguineally; they regard physical proximity as more important than consanguinity or affinity, and social proximity as equally important to consanguinity. And, once again, remember, *they will not trace a linkage through a dead relative.* Genealogical space, then, may be traversed by consanguinity, affinity, or attenuated affinity, but such linkages must recognize the criterion of decedence. In other words if you are related to your mother's brother's son (your cousin), your consanguineal linkage is the mother-mother's brother dyad. If your mother's brother dies and you wish to maintain a link in your genealogical space to affirm a kindred tie, *you then must find another linkage.* Such a linkage may be found in affinity, attenuated affinity, or in the compadrazgo-padrinazgo system. Let us now turn to the notion of "uncle," "aunt," "cousin" and "first cousin" (collateral relatives in ego's kindred) and see how the cultural code works.

The maximum genealogical space *for ego* defined by ties of consanguinity, affinity, and reinforced by compadrazgo-padrinazgo extends for only two generations upward, and two generations downward. The focus for reckoning is always a living ego, not a past ancestor. There is *no descent* system involved. Ego's tíos and tías (uncles and aunts as defined in Figure VII-2) are his father's and mother's contemporaries in both relative age, and in work habits relative to ego. If their ages or work habits approach ego's then he normally tags them as "primo." All those men and women two generations removed from ego whom he recognizes as kinsmen he calls tío and tía. A child has many uncles—contemporaries of his mother and father. But an adult has few uncles and many cousins—children of those people in his parental and grandparental generation whom he groups as his close kindred relatives. Cousin marriages in the dispersed and settlement niches assure affinity bonds to cousins, and compadrazgo-padrinazgo ties in the town niche also assure ego that he will have linkages necessary to maintain his kin set through two ascending and two descending generations.

Cousins who are genealogically close (first cousins), and who share intensive dyadic responsibility, or are in ego's household or close to the household (which I loosely call a compound) will be called primo hermano. On the death of any close collateral relative the standard term to call the deceased (unless he is lineally related) is "primo hermano." "My cousin is dead," may be glossed, "I have lost a close link in genealogical space." Affinity is also used to include a spouse of a cousin as cousin, provided that physical proximity (living in the household, or compound) is also included.

Part of ego's kindred is grouped around him in what I call the compound. This sometimes forms an early settlement, or the core of a new town *barrio*, "neighborhood." Other members of ego's kindred are dispersed, living with their spouse's relatives. Within the household and within the compound ego calls both his "hermano paterno" and "hermano materno," by the term "hermano." Ego usually uses the term "primo" for half-brothers and half-sisters living in the same town or settlement, if their primary residential responsibilty lies outside his household or compound. The actual term designating "half brother"-"half sister" is reserved for children about whom ego knows, but has never met, or for his half siblings residing in other communities, who he may wish to visit when traveling.

Most egos do not have a symmetrical set of relatives radiating out from them in all directions. The residential compound normally has certain founders—a siblingship or set of primos hermanos with spouses and perhaps one or two in-laws—*from whom other relatives reckon their relationship to one another.* In other words, all men and women do not reckon outward from themselves—most use another ego locus (their father, or a first cousin) to figure their place in a system of genealogical space. Such reckoning is necessary, for example, when a man is planning to move. How can he attach himself to a settled grouping? What is his relationship to those who are relatively more settled then he? The cultural code including the above stated criteria for membership is invoked to answer such questions. The code provides a set of rules which black frontiersmen strategically manipulate in order to transact a satisfactory position in social and geographical space.

The localized segment of the kindred of relatively successful settlers provides a symbolic net of potentially cooperating kinsmen, and the dispersed set of kin variously attached to other settled groupings provides tangible points of reference for the ubiquitous spatial mobility in the wet littoral. Lineal relatives and those classed as primo hermano are regarded as making up the core of the kindred, and reciprocity is expected from all at all times, according to the capacity of an ego to give, or the ability of an alter to take. Primos are *in* ego's kindred, and other kindreds as well, so their relationship to ego must be reinforced and demonstrated by processes of reciprocity sketched earlier in this chapter. Cuñados and concuñados are linkages *to* other kindreds. These linkages are forged or transacted exclusively by manipulating ties of affinity and attenuated affinity. For ego, manipulation of his set of primos and cuñados-concuñados is of utmost importance in the maintenance of his own ego-centric network of friends, relatives, and associates.

NETWORKS

A basic adaptive mechanism in social organization is the dyad. All black frontiersmen bring into their dyadic contracts sets of pre-coded cultural capital—their kindred system. Beyond the kindred system there lie culturally coded means of signalling dyad formation, and I described some of these early in this chapter. Let us return to the chains of dyads which make up networks, and see what network analysis can tell us about the social organization of people in the wet littoral. Let us consider a network segment in San Lorenzo.

The Network Broker

Earlier I mentioned Hernán's establishment of a dyadic link with Jorge by the borrowing of a machete, and the return of the machete and peccary meat. Hernán likes the deep forest and is willing to spend much time outside of town and settlement hunting. He also has three small farms, maintained by three different women and their children. When he is in town he depends on his brothers and their spouses, offering them, in return, meat and some fresh vegetables, as well as information about the forest and its resources. Remember, demand for resources from the external economy vary from time to time.

Jorge is a very different sort of chap. His father and two of his uncles have little shops in town, having moved to San Lorenzo from La Boca as the railroad terminus became established. Jorge helps in the shop, and maintains a coconut grove about a one hour canoe trip from the town. Such maintenance is important to his family because a grove of near-mature trees, properly planted and spaced, should *average* about one coconut per 12-15 trees per day figured over a year. Groves are typically 100-200 trees, and therefore can be figured as providing at least 7-10 maturing nuts per day or somewhere over 3,500 nuts per year. One nut sells for 1-2 sucres at the dock at San Lorenzo, so the potential cash value is obviously great. Besides the actual labor involved in maintaining the grove (ditch digging and maintenance, planting other crops, etc.), Jorge must keep tabs on the coconuts themselves. People tend to take coconuts when in need of cash. Jorge and his father expect this, and *use their knowledge of such "theft" as a means of demanding reciprocity from "thieves" from time to time.*

Jorge could lie in wait for "thieves" in the coconut grove, but this would be terribly inefficient use of his time. Instead, he hangs around town a good deal, engages in gossip, and attempts to find out through rumor, hint, and innuendo who might be fishing or hunting in the territory of his grove, who might be suspect if coconuts are disappearing. Of course, information gained about all sorts of things through such behavior is considerable, and this brings us back to the sort of role he plays in the town.

Jorge learns a great deal about the social and economic bases of kindreds of important egos, and about the habits and preferences of people such as Hernán. And he endeavors to translate this knowledge into advantage for himself and for his kindred. *Jorge is a specialist in social capital.* He knows much about who owes who what, or who might owe who what, and seeks to use such knowledge by tapping into the exchange system of kindreds, and other networks. I call him a *network broker.* In Chapter IV (page 88) I noted that in the town niche:

> People must adjust their activities not only to the egalitarian and ranked behavior of fellow men and women, but also to the activity and organizational patterns of people with differential administrative, political, and economic power.

This is what Jorge is really good at—he not only knows what his fellow black men and women are doing through their networks of exchange, but he also knows what at least some of those in classes higher than he (administrators, etc.) need, want, and *what they will pay for.*

Action-Sets

To play the broker role in the town niche, information must be translated into action. Jorge must make some things happen, or at least *appear to do so in the eyes of those more powerful than he.* Let us take the example of timber delivery to towns with sawmills, as this occurs in San Lorenzo and elsewhere. Timber buyers will usually buy at any time from a jefe de la minga. It is the responsibility of the jefe to deliver the logs to the buyer at the sawmill, and the sawmill owner names the price. The sawmill owner then sells the cut lumber to buyers in the highlands (shipping by rail) or elsewhere on the coast. All lumber buyers and shippers are blanco.

Lumber buyers normally buy all logs brought to them, at a low rate, to insure that the minga group will continue to operate out of the sawmill town, and not turn elsewhere when in need of cash. But sometimes the buyers know that they can sell many boards if they can secure the timber in time. They could go directly to the minga jefe, and succintly state their need. But this would cost them more, for the jefe would indicate his other responsibilities, the cost of a minga, and would ask for increased pay in advance for the requested lumber. Characteristically, the sawmill buyer turns to someone like Jorge, who knows the needs of "his people."

If Hernán (who is a jefe de la minga) is in debt to Jorge then he may be requested by Jorge to undertake a minga to deliver logs to the sawmill of don Henri, an immigrant Frenchman. Usually, Jorge will propose this as a mutual business venture, and advance the money for food and drink for the minga party, provided that Hernán activates his social capital (usually a couple of brothers and cousins, together with a concuñado and maybe a friend or two) to go into the forest, cut, and transport the timber. Jorge, in turn, borrows the money from don Henri to lend to Hernán, and may even ask for a cut of the profit when the logs are sold. He will not normally be granted this last request, but, by refusing, don Henri remains obligated (in Jorge's view) to again "use" Jorge to tap into the labor force of black frontiersmen through their respective ego-centered networks.

Hernán, in turn, asks each of the men who have previously accompanied him to again aid him. He promises them the same work time at a later date, when they are in need. On delivery of the logs to the sawmill Hernán takes most of the money, sharing only with Jorge by returning the original loan, and some of the profit. To show his good will Hernán ordinarily buys aguardiente for the men at a local cantina, or saloon. He does not go with "his men" in a group, though. Rather, they show up at the same place, having heard from someone that he is drinking there. They come with friends, relatives, and compadres, and sit where they please. Hernán pours a shot of aguardiente (or beer if a boom is on) and carries it to the worker, averting his head. The worker accepts without thanks, drinks, spits, shakes out the glass and returns it. This process continues, and some recipients from Hernán take the glass but pass it on to another person, not a participant in the minga. The glass goes back through the route which it came, tracing symbolically lines of potential future exchange.

Hernán, in this context, represents a node in intersecting networks built on dyads, with different social and economic bases for the respective dyads. A cantina context is often established, by at least some of the men in such a setting, and as more alcohol flows a saloon context is normally established.

As time passes those who worked for Hernán ask him for favors— loans of food or material goods—and he repays until he is without money and without goods. An odd bumpkin character this—he earned so much in a short time, but within a couple of months he is again without anything. As he approaches the bare minimum level his prestige goes up because of generosity, and his susceptibility to the operation of network brokers such as Jorge increases. When there is cash to be made for short run labor Hernán can mobilize those now again in his debt. And when there is no cash to be had—no demand for a forest product—Hernán will borrow from those with whom he prefers to work. In a system of economic fluctuation exchanges of prestige for goods allow for distribution of bare necessities among those with no control over the market.

Those who actually do things together—such as cut and deliver timber—make up an *action-set*. But the activators of this particular set lie outside the set itself, and work in different ways. For example, Jorge normally stays away from ritualized drinking following Hernán's minga. Should he show up having made a profit on their labor he would be expected to initiate series of prestations of aguardiente or beer, and thereby also enter into the continuing series of future obligations to the men and their respective kindred sets. Jorge works opportunistically as a broker, carefully selecting creditors outside of his kindred, while intensifying his debts and credits within his kindred. He can always list his debts to his kindred and to his patrons (those above him for whom he "does favors"), when approached by non-exploitable companions in need. He must transact dyadic contracts with people such as Hernán if his broker function is to work, but must avoid Hernán's particular series of debts.

Don Henri has been in town for some time and understands fairly well the nature of action-set manipulation. He usually shows up in the drinking context, talks loudly and makes many jokes. He buys a bottle of aguardiente and sets it down on the minga head's table, and then quickly departs before he can be thanked. He publicly supplies the minga head with symbolic capital to be dispersed through an evening of drinking, thereby intensifying bonds within the action-set, which he will again eventually activate through brokers such as Jorge.

Stem Kindreds

I mentioned earlier that Jorge's parents have established themselves with small shops in town. As petit bourgeoisie these men and their wives and children have established the basis for upward mobility for coming generations. By finding some way of maintaining a relatively dependable source of income—which is usually a combination of a shop in town, together with two or three small farms on which they raise subsistence crops and cash crops such as coconuts, pineapples, bananas, sugar cane or rice—such people become the focus of attention of all their kinsmen. A relatively permanent action-set emerges. Imagine a family composed of husband, wife, and three children living in a community where the husband and wife both have a number of brothers and sisters, cousins, uncles, aunts, and all the relatives through such people by affinal bonds. Suppose that the family has taken all its cash, and set up a small store with a dozen cans of tuna fish, twenty coconuts, some ropes of rolled tobacco, a few boxes of macaroni, bundles of dried fish, a few bateas, fire fans, canoe paddles, dynamite, some laundry soap and a jar of candy and a bunch of *cachimbos* (clay pipes). And suppose various members of their kindred ask for these goods when they are in need. Obviously, in no time, the store would be depleted, and although the family would be able to ask for things back, it would be difficult to ever re-stock in time to sell anything! Such is often the case in the settlement niche. And this very thing does happen again and again in the town niche as well.

In order to get an enterprise running a family with kinsmen must be ruthless in severing intra-kindred dyads. They *must* say no to all kinsmen who cannot reciprocate with something which they can use. Characteristically, such kinsmen who can help are those who live in other communities. The family aspiring to such a settled way of life usually keeps dyadic ties with dispersed relatives open—particularly those living in settlement and dispersed dwelling niches. And within the community only those contributing to the enterprise by supplying either political information, or actual goods (e.g., making bateas and paddles in return for purchased macaroni or tuna fish) are included. As the number and value of material goods, and size of the shop itself, expand in the enterprise, the jefe de la casa assumes larger importance. Social bonds of contributing affines and consanguines tighten around him, and the capital investment increases. As the children grow and assume responsibility in the enterprise, the family name (taken from the father) comes to reflect the enterprise's continuity. This occurs not because of the cultural code with its rules for kin membership, but because of the successful strategy played by certain action-set activators through time, in response to demands and constraints in the political economy.

People in the kindred, reckoning from the *children* of the settler-founders, become a definite *group* of people defined in relationship to their consolidated socioeconomic interests. Jorge's last name is Rodríguez. People in San Lorenzo know that the Rodríguez set owns two shops, and once had a saloon for a couple of years. They know also that one or the other of Jorge's in-laws is forever being recommended for teniente político, tax collector, or secretary to the teniente político. They associate the Rodríguez set with both economic and political activity. The Rodríguez kindred becomes a structural part of the political economy. Kindreds that are identifiable through time by a particular name, and which function in the political economy as wholes, rather than as temporary ramifications from particular ego nodes, are called *stem kindreds* (as distinct from *personal kindreds*). In another book (Whitten 1965) I argue at some length that the politics of San Lorenzo revolve around the mutual striving of particular stem kindreds toward domination of town politics, and, consequently, economic life.

Strategies of Adaptive Mobility: Peasant-Proletariat-Entrepreneur

To simplify description it is possible to construct a strategy model of successful mobility in the wet littoral. The model is described in technical form in an article (Whitten 1969) in which I also try to show that peasant, proletarian, and entrepreneurial activities are not mutually exclusive, but that *one grows out of another as a consequence of socioeconomic mobility in the town niche.* In Chapter I, I introduced the concepts of peasant and proletarian activity and the concepts have been with us in subsequent chapters. I wrote that a proletarian activity involved an investment of time and energy in cash gain, supplemented by some direct harvests, while a peasant activity referred to pursuits bringing a direct harvest, supplemented by some cash gain. In the process of mobility the two activities complement one another, and contribute to the general adaptability of Afro-Hispanic culture.

The first generation of socioeconomic mobility can be summed up as follows (Whitten 1969:238):

1. Balance activities bringing direct economic gain at the local level with those maintaining social capital of a dispersed personal kindred (normal peasant strategy and first generation proletarian strategy).

These are the general strategies that Jorge's parents had to use to survive in the town niche. But Jorge's activities are predicated on the relative success of his parents; had they failed in the establishment of an enterprise, then his activities would resemble theirs. But they did succeed in the rough and tumble politics of the town niche, and so his task, and that of his siblings, must be summed up differently (Whitten 1969:238):

2. Dispense with dispersed social capital and invest in local social capital of close kinsmen and affines directly contributing to the acquisition of political and social power. This is normally done through polygyny,[4] direct political activity and the accumulation of symbols of local social prestige (late first generation and early second generation proletarian strategy).

Jorge has a woman living at La Tolita de Pailón who keeps a small farm for him there, from which he supplies his shop. He also has a woman up the railroad in a small town, where she runs a small shop together with her brother (who, by the way, is also a jefe de la minga). In San Lorenzo he lives with his wife, Daisy, and three small children. He has two brothers, both of whom work in their respective shops. All spend extra money on clothes for their wives, and encourage their wives to dress well for any community event. If Jorge's children move the enterprise to the next step, the Rodríguez set will take over an important role in community politics. I summarized this strategy generating the new role as follows (Whitten 1969:238):

3. Consolidate economic, social, and political capital and serve as a necessary middle-range organization for economic, social, and political power. This is done by acquiring high prestige and using consanguinity, affinity, and money to manipulate local politics (late second generation, third generation and early fourth generation entrepreneurial strategy).

Few stem kindreds are able to do this. But in every community up to around 1000 population, at any time, there is one kindred so placed. Everyone knows the family name of the third generation stem kindred, and (through at least 1965) it is an open secret that local appointed officials in the community are normally cuñados or concuñados to this kindred. The kindred is grouped in the center of the community. Brokerage nodes in the third generation stem kindred maintain contracts with virtually every person of importance in the administrative, economic, and political system. Regardless of physical type, members are regarded as "zambo," "mulato," or even "blanco." The competitors for power are the second generation rising stem kindreds, who have their own brokerage nodes. Remember, access to sources of economic gain remain in the hands of people residing outside the littoral, or with those of higher class who have come into the littoral from outside. Brokerage dominance by a stem kindred represents the maximum indirect access for black townsmen and frontiersmen.

Many members of the second generation stem kindreds and the dominant third generation stem kindred are related to one another. But in this context (competition for power between the kindreds, often represented by [somewhat overlapping] membership in opposing political parties) individuals are regarded as being in one enterprise, or the other, but not both for ordinary purposes. But for exceptional purposes, such as an all-out community effort to build a people's park (which occurred in San Lorenzo in 1963, see Whitten 1965:183-186), the linkages between members of the otherwise competing stem kindreds will be emphasized, and an *extended, effective* organization of community power structure emerges.

Even for the dominant third generation stem kindred, though, the economic resources of the wet littoral available to black people are inadequate for sustained mobility, or sustained dominance. Children in the fourth generation are born into a *class* higher than their fellow black townsmen, but other upwardly mobile groups seem to force them out of *power*. Also, they tend to run out of spouses in their own situation, and begin to move out of the community, or to marry into rising kindreds. Anyone in a community can tell you the family name of the formerly important kindred,[5] including stories about the history through two or three generations of the important kindred members. Here is how I have summarized the final strategy of adaptive mobility (Whitten 1969:238-239):

4. Break all contracts within the kindred and marry out; cash in social prestige and economic and political power for their utility to a rising kindred, or to the local elite (fourth generation strategy of individual survival at acquired socio-economic level).

It should be clear by now that the fundamental adaptation of Afro-Hispanic culture in the wet littoral is tied to processes of mobility. I have described three such processes: the process of *spatial mobility* where black frontiersmen move their residence in response to cash and subsistence economies, *horizontal mobility* where people rally around a traditional work group head, support his drive to higher social status, while leveling his economic income, and *vertical mobility* through which individuals and groups move upward within a community by consolidating social capital to exploit economic and political opportunities. I see the process of vertical mobility as a dominant, central one, around which other activities aggregate. Brokerage nodes in the upward mobile groups transact channels of access to the actual social figures through whom opportunities and money from the national and international economy are funneled. Peasant, protetariat, and entrepreneurial behavior are considered as complementary facets in the process of mobility, the dynamic relationship between them making up the basic social adaptation of Afro-Hispanic culture within its environing purchase society.

SUMMARY

In the past three chapters we have moved from a delineation of sex roles and kinship criteria in this Afro-Hispanic cultural system of adaptation to the mobility strategies that provide basic adaptive mechanisms allowing for rich cultural elaboration. We can now draw together a summary statement of the social system.

Specific households are embedded in networks radiating from male broker nodes strategic to socioeconomic striving. Household maintenance tactics tap a localized kindred. Affinity, attenuated affinity, and consanguinity are all manipulated in traversing genealogical space for any ego central to household maintenance. Within the household the matricentral cell—regarded as *universal,* and not specific to Afro-Hispanic culture (Fortes 1949, 1953, 1958, 1969)—is maintained by the mother's recruitment strategies for male support. She uses both affinal and consanguineal dyads for such maintenance, the ramifications of these ties extending well beyond the household.

Recruited men in the role of husband are the authority figures in the household, when they are actually present, but their responsibilities to the household involve them in constant strategies of male-male network maintenance outside of the household which tap a dispersed kindred. Male mobility—spatial, horizontal, vertical—eventually leads to polygyny, or serial polygyny. Responsibility to "abandoned" wives for aid in child rearing accrues to the husband-father's matricentral consanguines and affines.

Male self assertiveness provides continuity in this Afro-Hispanic culture through mobility strategies. Female interaction initiative provides stability through household permanence, and through maneuvers between households in a residential community which allows for community permanence. Community and residential permanence, in turn, contribute to male mobility by providing bases for dispersed networks. Supra-household and supra-community networks of reciprocating males themselves are necessary for intra-household and intra-community stability in the boom-bust political economy. The male interaction initiator role and the female interaction initiator role complement one another, and their respective relationships are differentially enacted in different ritual contexts. Each sex role contributes to social structural continuity while allowing considerable organizational variety and adaptability.

Women stabilize the domain of household and community; men stabilize the domain of kinship and network maintenance. Each domain is activated by maneuvers in the other domain. The specific role complementarity in the household domain leads to apparent conflict during actual separation of spouses, but provides continuity of the household by reference to the intra-household female prerogative, and male mobility prerogative. Taken together the various ritual contexts described in Chapters V and VI enact the full range of sex role differentiation necessary to household, kinship, network, community, and inter-community maintenance.

Kinship criteria such as decedence, proximity, and attenuated affinity assure the maintenance of a flexible web of cooperating men and women which can be rapidly expanded during boom periods, and yet contract into minimal kindred and compound units during times of total economic depression. The coalescence of stem kindreds through three generations of upward mobility in towns provides a social clearing house for brokerage transactions involving participants in Afro-Hispanic culture and the agents of national and world demand for marketable products from the wet littoral.

Afro-Hispanic culture contains, at one and the same time, a system unto itself—a particular cultural adaptation to a special environment and political economy, with particular history—and a system which is now part of a world neocolonial system in which hundreds of ethnic cultures generally adapt to external demands for raw materials by industrial economies. The ethnic cultures so adapting are themselves parts of national political economies. We turn now to the implications of Afro-Hispanic ethnicity within national settings.

NOTES

1 A review of network analysis which includes the perspectives used here may be found in Whitten and Wolfe (1973). Many anthropologists are now working on refined concepts and ideas, and putting their notions to the ultimate test of data analysis. See, for example, Mitchell, ed. (1969).

2 In the last 10 years many anthropologists have been trying to come to grips with the dynamics of social interaction. For example, Fredrik Barth (1966:3-4) gave us this definition:

> In any social relationship we are involved in a flow and counterflow of prestations, of appropriate and valued goods and services. Our own and our counterpart's ideas of appropriateness and value affect our relationship . . . *one may call transactions those sequences of interaction which are systematically governed by reciprocity.*

In my view, no sequence of interaction can exist without reciprocity, provided that we properly understand that any exchange of goods or messages is, by definition, reciprocal. Although not specifically recognized as such, transactional analysis in most of social anthropology bears remarkable resemblance to the largely sociological perspectives presented by the authors in Grinker, ed. (1967). This transactional perspective

> . . . concerns the interface between the subsystems and whole systems and between whole systems themselves. Each one of these sub-theories . . . is dynamic, since they are all concerned with behaviors or actions rather than with the essence or the naming of parts in a metaphorical sense. (Grinker 1967: x)

Theories, or sub-theories, variously labeled "exchange theory," "strategy theory," "game theory," and so forth have recently been reviewed together in an effort to come to grips with interaction strategy and adaptive strategy within a unified framework of anthropological thought and analysis (see Whitten and Whitten 1972).

3 For an excellent discussion of the concept of network specialists see A. Mayer (1966) and J. Boissevain (1968).

4 Within a town polygyny is most pronounced in terms of the frequency of plural wives per kinsman in this generation. In the dispersed settlement niche polygyny is also sometimes very common. This occurs in the special cases of today's mazamorreros, or placer miners, who continue the mining activities discussed in Chapter III. These mazamorreros typically have two or three, or more, wives working with them. Far up some of the rivers such as the Santiago, in Ecuador, and the Telembí, in Colombia, such groups are at work today. The man shovels gravel and supplies meat, while the women pan the gravel, work the garden, and cook.

5 We noted in Chapter VI that the deceased ancestors are dismissed as kinship linkages. Those calling one another "cousin" within an upwardly mobile kindred focus on linkages within their own generation as their parents die, and fictive or real alternative dyadic links through ascending generations become increasingly difficult to maintain. Although they will not trace relationship to one another through any link to a dead person, they nevertheless symbolize affiliation through prior generations through veneration of important dead parents. A votive stone is placed in the graveyard, and cooperating men and women will visit the deceased's grave, and clean it, for many years after death.

CHAPTER EIGHT

Blackness In Northern South America: Ethnic Dimensions

During most of this book I have considered Afro-Hispanic cultural adaptation as supra-national in a frontier cultural ecology. This particular frontier is now being incorporated into the nations of Ecuador, Colombia, and Panama, and the national structures have a profound effect on cultural adaptation. Blackness is a socio-biological construct tied increasingly to nationalization. National impact in the wet littoral spreads outward from urbanizing centers. In this chapter I analyze the effects of early urban*ism* on people classed as "black" in one sector of the wet littoral—northwest Ecuador—and state the implications of urbanism for black disenfranchisement. Where possible, I will note commonalities with the Colombian experience.

NATIONAL CONCEPTS OF MISCEGENATION

In both Colombia and Ecuador the predominant viewpoint is that three primary races—European, native American Indian, and African —*mingled,* and miscegenated, in the wet littoral. Yet the majority of people in this zone, or from this zone, are still tagged as a phenotypic stereotype of one of these primary races—the African. The criteria used in such ethnic tagging alerts us to values involved in the concept of race, and race mixture ("miscegenation") in these two countries. Let us first see what the criteria are for the primary races, and then turn to the mixtures.

A person of European appearance, if a national, is normally tagged *blanco,* "white." Regardless of class standing and regardless of regional culture a person who *looks like* a European (southern or northern) will be regarded as "white" by most people at all national levels.

To be Indian in Ecuador or Colombia one must be known to be a native speaker of an indigenous New World language, or dress in a costume stereotyped as "Indian." A person so identified is tagged by the pejorative term *Indio,* "Indian," or more polite *Indigena.* Everybody uses this form except the Indians, who have a variety of non-Spanish terms for themselves meaning "human" or "us." Many Indian groups who use Spanish refer to themselves in Spanish as *gente,* "people," in distinction to all others.

To be *negro,* "black," by national definitions, a person must *look like* a Colombian or Ecuadorian image of a West African. This image varies from place to place, but such an image is applied to people with the following characteristics: black skin, wooly hair, and a relatively flat wide nose. The concept "negro" (lower case "n" means that the Spanish term is being employed) is particularly apt to be applied to a residential aggregate of people—household, settlement, town, barrio —when the aggregate shares a common dialect of Spanish and is known to have a particular regional history. Extremely pejorative terms such as *Africano,* "African," or *Congo,* "Congo," may be secretly applied to individuals identified as belonging to a "negro" aggregate, and the more common, pejorative term, "negro" or the more euphemistic *negrito* are publicly used for individuals, as well. Terms such as *negro puro,* "pure black," and *negro azul,* "blue black" and especially *negro feo,* "ugly black" are also used to assert the concept of a West African primary race.

To completely understand the concept of blackness, and how it effects life in the wet littoral, we must first understand the *ideology of racial mixture.* Remember, I said that the basic Ecuadorian and Colombian concept, shared throughout both nations, is that three primary races *mingled* in this area. The initial mingling resulted in the development of three concepts which suggest both phenotype (what one looks like) and descent (the supposed ancestry of a person). Simply, the offspring of *negro* and *blanco* produced a population of *mulatos;* the offspring of *negro* and *indio* produced a population of *zambos;* and the offspring of *indio* and *blanco* produced a population of *mestizos.* The offspring of various mixtures of mulatos, zambos, and mestizos were categorized during the colonial era into many sets of people. For example, the offspring of mulato and blanco were differentially classed as *quinterón,* "five parts white," *cuarterón,* "four parts white" and *tercerón,* "three parts white," and offspring of mestizo and mulato were classed as *zambo de mulato,* and subsequently through more sub-divisions according to the degree of blanco in both mestizo and mulato. In a couple of generations such categories as *zambo de quinterón* ("zambo with five parts white") emerged and underwent further subdivision (see Pavy 1967, Mörner 1967).

What is crucial to remember in such classification systems is that both *appearance* and *ancestry* were used in determining the degree of mixture. Since appearance depends on many factors, cultural as well as "physical" criteria were applied and considerable ambiguity resulted in the placement of most individuals regarded as "mixed" into the expanding numbers of categories. By the time the twentieth century rolls around we have a very large set of terms suggesting mixture, all of them set out in contrast to "blanco" as superior, and "negro" and "indio" as inferior.

The majority of people in the nations of Ecuador and Colombia regard themselves as being of mixed racial ancestry. Yet, in spite of this, the *concept of color* is often used to state class, status, or power positions among those regarding themselves and others as racially mixed. In such ranking this rule holds: the higher the status of a person relative to another, the lighter he is regarded as being. "Blanco" is the most desirable term used to refer to someone at the top of some hierarchy, but actual *appearance* nonetheless plays an important part. One can be classed "blanco" because he is some local big shot, but he can be brought down a peg or two by referring to his racial appearance. "Negro" is not a general term for those on the bottom of a hierarchy. It is used to refer to the negative attributes attached to West African features. Audrey Miles (1968:17) succinctly describes the pattern from the standpoint of a young, black, North American Peace Corps Volunteer working in the highlands of Colombia:

> As a newly-arrived Peace Corps Volunteer I was very uncertain about how I should react to being called *costeña, negra,* and *negra fea* (ugly) on the streets . . . gradually I've come to realize that the more *moreno* (dark) one is, the uglier he is in the eyes of the average Colombian. Everyone in Colombia wants to be *blanco* (white), so *negros* are *feos*. *Negra fea* means, "if we can't be white we must constantly remind you and ourselves that you are darker than we are."

The majority of people in the wet littoral show pronounced Black African features; they live a subsistence existence at the bottom of national class hierarchies, and they share a common supra-national culture.

Afro-Hispanic ethnicity varies according to the means by which people manipulate the concepts "blanco," "negro," and the concepts which denote "mixture." Such manipulation is directly tied to the political economy and particularly manifest in the contrast between niches. In 1968 I returned to San Lorenzo to find that many effects of urbanism had altered the social demography of that town. Until this visit I had only contrasts between different towns and settlements to work with, but the changes taking place in San Lorenzo also allowed me to see the effects of niche transformation. Because of this temporal perspective I shall present material on San Lorenzo, building on the illustration introduced in the past three chapters. I first elaborate on the various identity referents used by people residing in Northwest Ecuador to refer to themselves, and to tag others. Although specific terms vary somewhat from town to town, and from one nation to another, the set of constructs suggesting stereotypic thinking can be found throughout the Pacific Lowlands. Since San Lorenzo has been directly connected to the Ecuadorian highlands by a railroad linkage since 1957 it is particularly instructive to examine the coastal and highland perspectives separately.[1]

The Coastal Ecuadorian Perspective

Costeño, from the coast, is the primary identity referent for everyone living on the coast or on the rivers west of the Cordillera Occidental of Ecuador and Colombia. The contrast is with *serrano,* from the Sierra, in Ecuador. All people who share Afro-Hispanic culture prefer the term *moreno.* The term literally means "brunette," but in the wet littoral, as in much of the rest of northern South America, it is a polite term which lumps people otherwise classed as "negro," "zambo," and "mulato." A participant in Afro-Hispanic culture is first a "costeño," and secondly a "moreno." Very dark people tend to regard almost everyone except the very light as "morenos," but the lighter skinned people themselves may use other categories when it is economically or politically advantageous for them to do so. The term "moreno" may be elaborated upon in discussing the actual phenotype of a person. Examples include *moreno obscuro,* "dark moreno," *moreno colorado,* "red moreno"—meaning rust colored skin—*bastante moreno,* "dark moreno." The most important aspect of the use of "moreno" is that it includes all participants in Afro-Hispanic culture who cannot be regarded simply as costeño because of some degree of African descent. In short, it corresponds to current usage of the concept "black" in United States Afro-American ethnic categorization. Until the term "black" began to be used in its present sense, the term "Negro" would have been the best translation of the usage of "moreno."

While the term "moreno" ethnically groups participants in Afro-Hispanic culture, the terms "negro," "zambo," and "mulato" make ethnic and class separations based on concepts of primary versus mixed racial heritage. The term "negro" is a pejorative term for a black person, zambo, or mulato when used by someone classed as non-negro.

Black people refer to one another as "negro," but do so in a manner comparable to that apparent when black people in the United States refer to acceptable members of their own ethnic category by the term "nigger." Sometimes people identifying as "costeño moreno" in Ecuador apply the term "negro" with its pejorative meaning to highland black people or to Colombian blacks, when a fight is imminent. But by so employing the term they use it in the *highland sense,* discussed below. In San Lorenzo, as elsewhere, the term "negro" can be an insult, or a sign of affection, depending on who uses the term, and how it is used. Sometimes participants in Afro-Hispanic culture wish to refer to the actual degree of skin color for descriptive purposes. To refer, politely, to blackness, *bién negrito* is used. To be rude, one might call another's color "negro azul." Shades of darkness are often applied by men to women in a discussion of beauty.

"Mulato" refers to a very light skinned person in this area, whose ancestry is known to include someone classed as "negro." "Zambo" is a local intellectual term in Esmeraldas province used to deny African origins of blackness, and to assert the fundamental Indian-African mixture of the 16th century to have established a non-black dark race. The concept has nationalistic overtones, for it is also often asserted that the predominant numbers of African-appearing people in Esmeraldas come from Colombia.

The terms *cholo* and *montubio* also signal contrasting categories in Afro-Hispanic culture. "Cholo" in this area refers to a dark person with long straight hair. Only when long straight hair is manifest can one be classed as cholo, from this coastal perspective. Color does not ordinarily enter into the designation "cholo." An inner feature— strength, or personal power force—is also crucial in using the category. One may be dark and have straight hair, but he must have some radiation of inner strength or he will not be regarded as "cholo" from the coastal perspective. Noanamá and Emperá (Chocó) Indians from Colombia are labeled *Indios Cholos* and the connotation of inner strength is applied to them by black frontiersmen.

There are three overlapping meanings of the term "montubio" in northwest Ecuador. The first refers to a monolingual Spanish-speaking phenotypic Indian native to the coast. The second refers to any person who is uncivilized, inherently dirty, slovenly, and dangerous, and who does not respect the personal rights and personal property of others. Regardless of physical appearance, a person who commits murder, or a person who has a rural style of life and is distinctly antisocial, is "montubio." From the standpoint of townsmen all dwellers in the rural scattered dwelling niche are "montubio." Third, all middle and lower class light skinned coastal Ecuadorians and Colombians who are non-participants in Afro-Hispanic culture may be called "montubio." In this latter sense "montubio" as used by black Ecuadorian frontiersmen is the reciprocal analog of "negro" used by a light skinned costeño.

Black frontiersmen refer to all Indians in native dress as either *indio* or *indígena*. In the rural scattered dwelling niche the Indian is addressed with respect, and shown deference; in the settlement niche he is regarded more or less as an equal, although many factors impinge on indio-negro interaction in this setting. In the town and urbanized town niches he is regarded as inferior by blacks but, again, in the barrios surrounding urbanized niches which resemble rural settlements the ambiguities apparent in the settlements are present.

Serrano is used to refer to anyone from the Sierra, regardless of physical appearance, and sometimes Indians and non-Indians from the highlands are lumped as serrano. *Gringo* is used for all outsiders, including other Latin Americans.

The Highland Ecuadorian Perspective

Serrano, from the highlands, is the primary referent for everyone coming to the coast from the Sierra. This term is used as a respectful contrast to "costeño," which means any mestizo, mulato, or blanco from the coast. Serranos do not usually use the term "zambo." They accept the idea of a special zambo race of Esmeraldas, when told about it, but tend to lump individuals as either "mulato" or "negro" according to their concept of mixture. The term "blanco" is used to refer to any middle class or upper class highlander, or to any highlander to whom respect is given, and "montubio" is used to tag *all* poor, light skinned costeños, particularly if they come from a coastal province south of Esmeraldas. Serranos may call a light costeño "blanco" when he, or his friends, are listening, but they almost always refer to such a person as montubio when in Serrano company.

The term "indio" is used pejoratively by non-Indian highlanders to refer to all highland Indians, but they use it without pejorative intent to refer to lowland Indians. "Indígena" has been the polite term for highland Indians, but it seems to be taking on the pejorative connotations of "Indio." "Cholo" is used both to tag a poor, phenotypic Indian highlander, and as a term of endearment for children, close friends, and spouses. It is also a pejorative term used by blancos to mean a lower-class highland mestizo.

"Negro," to the serrano, refers to any costeño or highlander with black skin, wooly hair, and flat, broad nose. It is also a term of endearment when applied to close friends in the same age-sex-ethnic category. To be used as a term of friendship outside of the same age-sex-ethnic category it must be made diminutive, *negrito*.

The term "mestizo" itself is not often employed by serranos coming to the wet littoral, in spite of the ideology of race mixture. It is usually heard only when comparing skin complexions with foreign whites. In the highlands, though, it is quite frequently employed in contrast to "blancos" who are people of reputed European descent occupying the top of a social hierarchy (national, regional, or local). It is often assumed in Ecuador, as elsewhere, that a speedup in economic development will result in a concomitant speedup of racial mingling. The Ecuadorian historian Alfredo Pareja Diezcanseco (1970: 88) sums up a prevalent intellectual view of his country:

> Ecuador is not a country inhabited by white folk, for as an ethnic minority they only add up to scarcely one tenth of the total population. Neither is it a country of Indians, for in that case its history would be one of regression, or else, of stratification . . . the nation is Mestizo . . . Once the Indians enter civilized life . . . the Mestizo part of the population will be more homogeneous.

As highland mestizos descend the Andes in response to expanding opportunities in the lowland tropics, they enter zones which lack the contrasting, upper-class, blanco category and, it seems, in the absence of that contrast assume membership in the superior category themselves. As a consequence, those who would be cholo, or mestizo, in the Ecuadorian Sierra, become blanco on the coast and eastern forests. "Blanconess" is reinforced by incorporating all the mixed categories, especially "mulato," in contrast to "negro" and "indio" each of which is designated as a pejorative, non-mixed, non-national, category. Such lumping into primary races preserves both the ideology of mixture for the national majority, and promotes discrimination against the Indian and black non-mixed. I shall return to this argument below.

It is readily apparent that the coastal and highland perspectives clash in a number of ways. Specifically, the Serrano uses of "negro," "mulato," "montubio," and "blanco" seriously effect the social environment of black frontiersmen. In particular, Afro-Hispanic culture asserts a primary We-They division as costeño-serrano; and from the darker standpoint a basic coastal We-They division emerges as moreno-montubio. The highland perspective stresses an asymmetrical stereotypic division, blanco (including mestizo)-negro, as fundamental. This is particularly apparent and effective when mestizo-serranos assert the costeño-serrano contrast as only applicable to those who fall into categories suggesting racial mixture (mulato) and when they assume the status of blanco in the zone of Afro-Hispanic culture.

SOCIAL RACE AND RACISM

We have moved from Afro-Hispanic culture into the realm of ethnicity and race relations in a search for the ethnic markers of this one Afro-Hispanic adaptation. By "ethnicity" I refer to what social anthropologists such as Aidan Southall (1961:1-46), J. Clyde Mitchell (1966:52-53) and Michael Banton (1967) call *categorical social relationships*. These relationships are characterized by stereotypic criteria, as distinct from structural relationships which are characterized by group membership, or network relationships which are characterized as chains of association radiating from specific brokerage and patronage nodes as we discussed in the previous chapter (see Mitchell, ed., 1969, Whitten and Wolfe 1973). By race relations I am referring to actual social transactions between people who stand, *vis-à-vis* one another, in contrasting or complementary social categories when the categories themselves are conceived of in terms of physical features or in terms of biological ancestry. Charles Wagley (1959 *in* 1968:155-56) established the basis for this perespective in Latin American ethnography when he wrote "... the way people are classified in *social races* in a multiracial society tells us much about the relations between groups." (emphasis added) One of the clearest statements about a framework for ethnicity in social structure has more recently been set forth by Marvin Harris. In a review of Michael Banton's book, *Race Relations* (1967) he states (Harris 1969:204):

> A theory or race relations must be a sub-case of a theory of social stratification, which in turn must be a sub-case of a theory of sociocultural evolution. It must be able to answer the question of how access to wealth and power is regularized; how groups achieve specific adaptations to each other; and how intergroup relations evolve along general and specific trajectories as determined by general and specific conditions.

We noted above that a symmetrical reciprocal ethnic division—costeño-serrano—which the black costeños favor, is constantly eroded by the highlanders' use of the pejorative and asymmetrical division—"blanco-negro." The asymmetrical division also facilitates the imposition of intermediate ethnic categories such as *mulato* or *mestizo,* and tags them with asymmetrical economic potential. We can now complete our general definition of ethnicity by adding the notion of economic consequence of categorical social relations: *ethnicity refers to patterns of human interaction which form the basis for categorical social relations with observable, or projected, economic consequences.*

When different sets of concepts about social race and ethnicity become intertwined, as they are in the littoral of both Ecuador and Colombia, one set may, under certain conditions, become dominant over the other. Edward M. Bruner (in press) has developed a viewpoint which he refers to as "The Dominant Culture Hypothesis:"

> . . . the concept of a dominant culture may be divided into three separate components of the larger system that are sociologically relevant to ethnic expression in any multiethnic situation. The first component is the population ratio, the social demography, and not just the fact of ethnic heterogeneity, but rather the nature of the particular mix in a given context. The second component concerns the established local culture . . . and the manner in which members of other groups relate to and articulate with it. The third component focuses on the locus of power and its distribution among the various ethnic groups.

Up through 1965 Afro-Hispanic culture dominated life in the town of San Lorenzo. A few incoming highlanders occupied the very top of the economic, political, and social hierarchy, but their need for goods and services forced them to channel various requests through the dominant local stem kindred, or one of the major kindred competitors. Other mestizos falling into the middle or lower class (see Whitten 1965:44-47 for a complete overview) were virtually cut off from the political economy unless they married into a black costeño family, or formed stable dyadic ties in the Afro-Hispanic method. The social structure and decision making processes effecting change at that time emerged only after the structure which I described in the last chapter had been worked out. Then, it was possible to understand how Jorge Rodríguez, and other such network specialists, got themselves into emerging formal organizations, and provided crucial linkages between regional and national political economies. I concluded that study with this statement:

> Change has not been a disrupting element in the social structure of San Lorenzo. By extending traditional lifeways into new contexts, the Negroes and their lighter relatives have retained their own power structure, centered on kindred interaction. Furthermore, they have begun to control aspects of the new economic opportunities, especially in the lumber and shellfish industries. The native townsmen are themselves agents of change so long as they control a large share of power, of the ability to get things done. (Whitten 1965:201)

I knew, at this time, that Ecuadorian colonization of the tropical forest zones was well underway, and that the swelling of national mestizo culture would produce profound effects in the Pacific Lowlands. Data from Esmeraldas, Limones, Tumaco and Buenaventura indicated that people who fit the blanco-mestizo stereotype of "negro" had been excluded from direct participation in crucial decisions effecting their life chances. In each urbanized town the centers of administration and commerce were occupied nearly exclusively by blancos, mestizos, and mulattoes. All political officials except the rural police were blanco, mestizo, or mulatto, and "negros" surrounded the town in identifiable *barrios*, "neighborhoods," each of which bore remarkable resemblance to a rural settlement niche. Between 1965 and 1968 San Lorenzo doubled its population and underwent a niche transformation from "town" to "large urbanized town." Because of my previous familiarity with that community it became possible to work out some of the dramatic processes that contributed to political and social disenfranchisement as a concomitant of economic development. Although the specific events are attributable to only one town, the general process which they represent is applicable to the entire littoral, and beyond.

BLACK DISENFRANCHISEMENT IN AN ECUADORIAN TOWN

In the cold dawn of early June, 1968, I boarded the *autocarril* (a bus on railroad track wheels) in Ibarra, north highland Ecuador, and once again began the 12 hour descent down the Andes to San Lorenzo. We were fortunate on this trip, for though fresh landslides had occurred during the night just west of Lita, another autocarril was on the other side, and a walk of only four miles through knee deep mud was required. I planned to gather more information on symbolism in Afro-Hispanic culture in northwest Ecuador, and toward that end carried with me fresh data from field work in Colombia. My mind went back to information gleaned in 1961 and 1963, and to my short visit in 1965. I wondered whether the Rodríguez kin group was still dominant, or whether it had lost ground in the silent struggle with two rising kin groups which were becoming more and more powerful *vis-à-vis* the Rodríguez set. I thought that perhaps my friends in San Lorenzo might have taken advantage of new opportunities, for I learned in Quito that an airport had been constructed, and that large scale logging operations were underway.

I was not prepared for what I found. Exploitation of the natural environment had greatly expanded, and more money was available

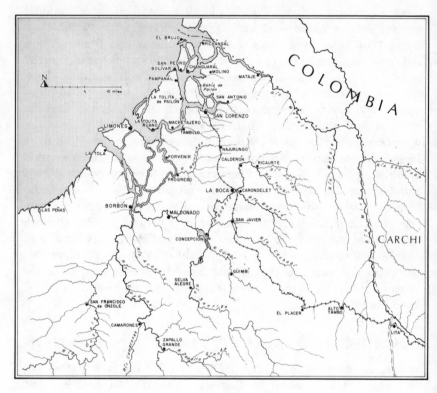

Map III: The Northwest Sector of Esmeraldas, Ecuador

than at any other time since the World War II banana boom. But the social demography had also altered, and national blanco-mestizo culture had become dominant.

San Lorenzo, 1968: New Factors

As the autocarril moved into the outskirts of San Lorenzo in the late rainy afternoon I was surprised to see the numbers of houses stretching out from what had been the extreme limits of the town three years before; and as we rounded a curve and moved toward the center I was again surprised to see the numbers of blanco-mestizos looking out of doorways which had been the portals of prominent black people during my earlier visits. The surprise over the unanticipated spread of outlying black barrios, together with the concentration of blanco-mestizos in the center of town, was only the beginning of my realization that the social demographic dimension of actual white over black in political-economic power was unfolding.

Timber exploitation by large scale company work had sporadically expanded since 1963. The minga system was scarcely operating. Instead, black people were hired by the month to cut trees, dig canals, and float the logs into rafting areas from which they could be shipped to Guayaquil, and on to foreign markets. One sawmill was greatly expanding by using wage labor for acquisition of timber, but it was employing mainly highland blanco-mestizos for the in-town job of cutting the trunks into boards. The timber system had established some hinterland camps where the black men were living while their women remained in the town or settlement niche. Whenever possible, aguardiente and even women were brought to the camps on the weekends, to entertain the men, and to keep them from going to a settlement, or town, where they might decide to remain into the Monday workday.

Great stretches of mangrove trees were totally decimated by stripping the bark, and on the high grounds within the mangrove fringe the stands of soft woods had been cut, and cash farms had been established by outside blanco-mestizos. Resident bosses for the farms had come from the south coast, or from the highlands. They were living on the farm, and hiring black workers from towns and settlements. Houses for the black men are provided there, and the men are paid by the month. Beer and aguardiente, and even women and a record player and records are brought to the farm on payday, to induce the men to stay and enjoy themselves without going to a town or settlement.

While under military dictatorship in 1964-66 the Ecuadorian government virtually abolished the malarial campaign in Esmeraldas province. The campaign previously stressed periodic spraying with DDT, the taking of blood samples in the bush from all people with fevers, and the giving of malarial suppressives to those found to have malaria. During military dictatorship the system was changed to one which demanded that people with malaria travel to a few distribution centers (San Lorenzo was one such) to have blood tests made, and to receive malarial suppressives. Malarial outbreaks occurred in epidemic proportions along hinterland rivers such as the Bogotá, Cachabí and Tulubí, nearly obliterating settlements there, as well as seriously injuring the population of larger all-black towns such as La Boca.

Also during military dictatorship the "conservative party" which had always been dominated by the Catholic church disappeared, and the now "liberal" personnel (the clergy) merged, politically, with the

military and its policy. Church[2] and military stood opposed to other
liberal, socialist, communist, *"Velasquista"* (named after José Maria
Velasco Ibarra, former President of the Republic of Ecuador), or other
independent movements or parties.[3]

Funds from Catholic missionaries and the Ecuadorian government
facilitated the development of a hospital and new trade schools in
carpentry for men, and "home economics" for women. These new
buildings were established in a sector called the "new town." Loans
made from the *Banco de Vivienda* provided capital for the church and
railroad officials to construct houses in the new town, and to rent such
houses to both blanco-mestizos, and to local black people.[4]

The possibility of increased linkage of the north Ecuadorian coast
and the Ecuadorian Sierra together with economic depression in the
rural sectors of the Sierra, stimulated increased in-migration of highland laborers, and petit bourgeois merchants and shopkeepers who
successfully competed with the shops of the black townsmen. They
bought out those of the Rodríguez kindred, and either purchased or
forced out of business the saloon and cantinas owned by rising second
generation kin sets competing with the Rodríguez set for dominance
in 1963-65.

Absentee blanco highlanders have contributed money to facilitate
the building of new saloons and shops. These are run by resident
blanco-mestizos. When people in San Lorenzo have money these new
saloons and shops provide an immediate source of goods and entertainment, and the capital expended flows out of town, and out of moreno
networks. In like manner the establishment of entertainment in the
camps and farms, for which workers pay, serves to direct money earned
by black people in this zone out of the towns and settlement niches.
In 1968 I could figuratively see the processes of ethnic disenfranchisement in a developing political economy. And Jorge, Hernán, and all
of the other black people could see this as well. They were eager to
tell me not only what had happened in the three years since my last
visit, but also expressed to me a new sense of tension and frustration.
This sense of things not going right was not born of poverty, hunger,
and strife, but seemed to be nurtured by an expanding economic
system, in which they could earn more money than before, but they
could still not do anything with it in terms of gaining more power
over events taking place around them. In the short month or so
available to me in the summer of 1968 I worked intensively with a
number of newcomers from the rural hinterland, to understand more
fully the transformation processes in the town niche.

San Lorenzo, 1968: Black Disenfranchisement

The black in-migrants building ever-outward from the previous town
fringes were coming from some of the least accessible hinterland
regions—mostly from north of the railroad near the Ecuadorian-Colom-
bian border. They had been forced out of the settlement and scattered
dwelling niches by rampant malaria outbreaks. People from these
rural areas themselves have more than doubled the community's area
in the past three years, and have contributed considerably to the
density of the population in other fringe barrios. Many new, self-
contained barrios have been developed, and are named after the place
of origin of the settlers. Each of these has an identifiable kindred locus,
with an elected "jefe" of the barrio. The jefe is the central man to a
siblingship which itself forms the core of the cooperating kindred.
The process of localization and time investment in strategies designed
to bring in an economic gain from the town niche seems somewhat
accelerated, while the rural quality imparted to these new black sectors
of San Lorenzo is quite obvious to all. They are freqeuntly not considered as part of the town, by those living near the center.

Budding households and expanding families in the older areas of
town are moving out over the water, beginning to build networks of
houses connected by wet, slippery cat-walks already characteristic of
Buenaventura, and Tumaco, Colombia. As older families forced from
the center of town by lack of economic wherewithall move in with
their children, their own land-based center-of-town houses become
occupied by highland and coastal blanco-mestizos. Such people immediately file for "ownership" certificates with the teniente político
or comisario nacional de policía.

Young black men from the hinterland are encouraged to enroll in
the Catholic carpentry school, and young women are encouraged to
participate in the new home economics school. In these schools men
are instructed by highland blanco-mestizos in methods of home construction and maintenance, while women in the home economics school
are taught home sanitation, maintenance, sewing, and child care, by
white nuns. Both men and women are warned about the dangers inherent in active participation in political process, except through
the church-military coalition. They are also advised of the desirability
of upward socioeconomic mobility but are given no realistic means
to achieve such mobility.

The church-government banking facility overtly favors loaning
money to women, and is clear about denying requests by most men
as a matter of policy. The argument made by the controlling clergy
is that women are "more stable in the community." They do not, pre-

sumably, spend money on drink, or on political bribes. Furthermore, they *remain in the community* on a more or less full time basis, attending to their home and to church approved (and government approved) affairs, whereas men tend to move about, in the forest, and in search of wage labor.

Clergy teach young women how to make budgets and figure credit on a strictly monetary basis. They are also instructed in the nature of banking, loaning, and saving procedures. Men, by contrast, are either taught to build houses with tools which they cannot afford to buy, or are encouraged to work on a wage-labor basis for a timber company, or on a plantation.

Women in this area still have a relatively steady income based on shellfish gathering, and gathering and marketing of the conchas has greatly expanded. But the marketing of the conchas is now almost exclusively in the hands of highland blanco-mestizo merchants. The blanco-mestizo merchants with access to the railroad officials resident in Ibarra have been more successful in gaining concessions, loans, and credit from the railroad than have local people in San Lorenzo (who must deal with local highland administrators within the town). Some local black men have journeyed to Ibarra to ask for credit and concessions to market the conchas, but have met with no success there.

In terms of strategies of mobility, discussed in the previous chapter, first generation male settlers find the most ready cash *away from* the residential locus, in the forest, and on the new small plantations. Women, however, continue to cluster in the new town barrios, aided by the shellfish business and by the church-sponsored banking facility. This leads to a conspicuous absence of men between ages 25 and 40, except those with an investment in upward socioeconomic mobility strategies. A new alternative strategy of investing time and energy in church-sponsored change, including housing projects, and work for the church, has developed. Unfortunately, for continuity with prior ways of doing things, acting in accord with this strategy means severing most local political contacts, and often changing the residential locus from kinship-dominated barrio to the "new town."

The "new town" was designated back in 1957, when the railroad reached the coast. (It is described in Whitten 1965). In 1963 it was a source of considerable amusement, for nothing existed except sidewalks laid out in second growth jungle. By 1964 some development had begun on the basis of economic loans secured by the Catholic church from the ruling military junta. In 1968 I was amazed at the growth and development. The military junta supported the clergy's development plans, and today there are schools, a hospital furnished through discarded equipment of a New York City Catholic hospital, and several housing projects. There is even being planned an advanced high school (*colegio secundario*) which would make San Lorenzo the center of blacksmith training and carpentry specialities in the nation.

To reside in the new town as a family means acquiring credit from the Banco de Vivienda, which in turn means having steady employment *in town*. Such employment is becoming increasingly difficult to get due to the influx of laborers from the Sierra, who lend an aura of in-town white-black competition over the most desirable occupations. Many of the black men or women who have acquired a lot in the new town have a blanco-mestizo spouse. They were either married at the time when male serrano marriage into a black kindred was strategic, or they are successful black men with light coastal wives. In either case their children, the inheritors of this favored location, will be mulato, or non-black, by present means of reckoning ethnic identification.

Black newcomers from hinterland settlements and scattered dwelling niches who locate on the outskirts of town represent an expanding labor force for forest work and plantation work. Special attention is paid to them by those controlling the expanding resources (lumber bosses, farm owners, the Catholic clergy). The Catholic clergy feels that they have "stronger family ties" than the town-dwellers. We could say that the newcomers are at first unaccustomed to the proletarian role, and therefore are more readily exploited by those in search of cheap rural labor. Eventual self-awareness of this proletarianization often occurs *outside of the town niche* instead of within it. It is within the town niche that strategies of adaptive mobility are most effective, as we saw in the previous chapter.

Those proletarian and entrepreneurial black people—people such as Jorge, Pedro, Luis, and Angel—who were already well adjusted to combining town and rural life (and who have long served as cultural brokers) meet resistance from lumbermen, priests, and local officials when they try to engage in the sort of politics to which they are accustomed. Their obvious abilities of maneuver within rural as well as urbanizing contexts are not understood, and consequently feared. They are labeled *"comunistas"* (communists). Jorge's more recent attempts to promise lumber to a sawmill, or to hint that a number of black townsmen would oppose selection of a new blanco teniente político met with heretofore unanticipated reaction by non-black people, now expanded in their numbers and in their control over most economic resources. They felt that such abilities to mobilize men for action indicated outside power, a source of strength generated from external political realms—such as foreign nations.

The organizational format of Afro-Hispanic culture is insufficiently understood by present outsiders. Such outsiders, in an effort to explain the existence of black power structure, tend to project outwards. Such projection, set in today's world of gross dichotomies of political ideology, results in pejorative labeling rather than understanding. Attaching the "communist" tag to black strivers, such as Jorge, makes black maneuver all the more difficult for such people, and increases the potential for confrontation politics.

In terms of my earlier model, briefly sketched in Chapter VII, I found that there were still linked action-sets in the form of stem kindreds which are still crucial to internal politicking in San Lorenzo. But blanco-mestizos now actively compete with the nodes of the black action sets (such as the central people in the Rodríguez kindred) in acquiring the brokerage roles. A consequence of this is a strengthening of the role of any light skinned member of Afro-Hispanic culture, and a tendency to lump "mulatos" with "blancos" and "zambos" with "negros," for some purposes. Such classification gives inordinate weight to phenotypic characteristics, even over cultural and behavioral characteristics.

Money still lightens. That is, a phenotypic "negro" will still be tagged "mulato" or "zambo" if he has wealth and/or political power. But access to wealth for those "negros" without economic or political wherewithall is more restricted than for the non-negro. And, while individuals can be lightened it becomes more difficult for a residential aggregate classed as "negro" to better its social standing. Economically mobile kindreds, if I am correct in this interpretation, must become lighter if mobility is to continue through several generations. The process itself assures some color coding where the darker skinned people cluster at the bottom of an economic hierarchy.

Earlier (Whitten 1965) I indicated that certain, but not all, individuals representative of dominant kindreds within a barrio must manifest respectability symbols acceptable to the Catholic church. Such acquiescence to these symbols assures some involvement with the church's power domain. But such manifestation now includes allowing an indoctrination of young men and women by the priests and nuns through their school. Among other things, this makes polygyny more covert, and increasingly difficult, for the upward-mobile. This is serious for black maneuver, because a phase of upward mobility of an aspirant kindred normally includes a high degree of polygyny as a man establishes several enterprises, using several women to help him in such enterprises, while he himself invests increasing time and energy in local politics.

The rising groups of kinsmen who actively compete with blanco-mestizo brokerage find that the accusation of "communist politics" is readily applied. For example, if Pedro or Angel go to see a new highland lumber buyer, or concha buyer, it is likely that many high-landers competing with the Rodríguez set will first warn the outside buyer of the "leftest" menace in San Lorenzo, and indicate that Pedro and Angel are more interested in politicizing the "negros," than in turning a profit. The notion that "we highlanders have to stick to-gether with church and government" is a powerful incentive to white domination of brokerage, as well as patronage, roles. And, unfortu-nately, tagging black entrepreneurs with the concept "leftist" *izquier-dista,* may carry a stigma ramifying to their kinsmen, and to others with whom they carry out regular mutual cooperation.

Because of such specific communist-accusations based on generalized communist-fear, many local upper-class blanco-mestizos formerly de-pending on such black entrepreneurs, together with many first and second generation rising strivers, have become leary of overt exchanges symbolizing alliance with the accused. In other words, the political label of "leftist" serves to make upward strivers poorer risks as brokers, at the very period in their economic rise when the broker role, to-gether with its political functions, becomes most crucial for continued mobility. If anything is designed to produce tension, I would think that this sort of bind would be bound to produce it.

Also, serrano men who marry women associated with striving black kindreds were seen as "leftist" in 1968, and they found it nearly impossible to play a brokerage role. Because of this the blanco-mestizo with *least personal contact* with Afro-Hispanic culture is in the *most strategic brokerage position,* and the mis-communication across ethnic lines expands.

Finally, during the Summer of 1968, I found that linkages between local middle-class entrepreneurial black and lower-class, upward-mobile, proletarian blacks were being further weakened by the actual introduction of new blanco-mestizo brokers, unidentified with black aggregates, into the local mobility process. Most black strivers found their activities pivoting increasingly around new machinations of highland-bound Ecuadorians, themselves engaged in a very different strategy of adaptation with colonization as one of their prime tenets.

With such data before us we see one clear case of *black disen-franchisement as a concomitant of economic growth and development.* However, black disenfranchisement is not total, for economic class lines include people of mestizo, as well as negro, ethnic categories. The possible necessity of inter-ethnic linkages between complementary proletarian and enterepreneurial black role sets in the town niche (discussed in Chapter VII and in Whitten 1965, 1969) may continue to separate various black frontiersmen into contrasting local class-conscious sectors. Although the vast majority of black people will be (and are now) on the bottom of the hierarchy, there will be enough black and mulatto people in the middle (but not on the top) to allow the casual observer to state that the problem is one of class relations, not race relations. But upward mobility of the few in no way negates the point of general black disenfranchisement.

Carrying on this argument, we could suggest that the growth of national class consciousness could work even more to the detriment of people classed as "negro." The mass of people identifying with the cultural aspects of Afro-Hispanic life find themselves on the bottom of a national class hierarchy which emphasizes a common, mixed, ancestry. For non-black colonists in black frontier territory the rise of class consciousness is favorable to the asymmetric ethnic strategies of the new "blancos."

These new blancos refer to themselves as *"los pobres,"* "the poor." But they have other characterizations for the black frontiersmen. They use such nouns as *sucio, vago, tonto, incivilizado, bruto, infrahumano, feo* ("dirty," "lazy," "stupid," "without national culture," "subhuman," "ugly"—in terms of racial features) to depict black aggregates, but not *specific individuals*. When a blanco wishes to project these attributes onto a specific individual it is sufficient to use the term "negro," *vis-à-vis* that individual. There is a reinforcement of these stereotypes through discussion in which those people "typifying" blacks agree to two or three characteristics, usually discarding one or two of the above attributes. Since the retaining and discarding of attributes through debate is inconsistent, the entire complex attaches itself as a series of connotations to the term "negro." The general drift of such racist-reinforcing discussion follows the line: men are over-sexed and primarily interested in dancing and drinking; women are all interested in lighter men and in having lighter babies. Blanco-mestizos with considerable time on the coast (or coastal blanco-mestizos) dispute the highland or inland-valley stereotype that the black man is over-sexed, and point out the virtual absence of a *"macho"* (maleness) complex amongst black men. They argue that black men would as soon drink and dance as fornicate, and so the black man's woman is easy prey for whites or mestizos who would take her, leaving him with his rum and his dancing to find another sexual partner when the mood moves him.

Blancos who come from the coast often *act like* black people when they are working at similar jobs, but change their demeanor when not at work. Although the pejorative stereotypes noted above are clearly in evidence, actual interpersonal *behavior* in the lowlands in regard to negro-blanco relations usually does not reflect the categories, except in the urbanized town niche. Newcomers from the highlands are soon told by coastal blancos that black people should be addressed as "costeños" or "morenos" and not as "negro" and they normally comply with such preferred usage. Furthermore, most incoming blanco-mestizos clearly *fear* the coastal and riparian morenos, noting their strength, sophisticated use of sea, channel, and river systems, and their abilities to wrest a living from the forest and water resources. Except in the urbanized town the newcomer is almost completely dependent on black frontiersmen for his survival, at least until he learns the rudiments of adjustment to the natural environment. As long as the blanco-mestizos are in the clear minority we could say that race relations are most fluid, and that individual relationships do not reflect the white ideational constructs which derogate the black frontiersmen. But a change in the numerical ratio of mestizo-blancos to black frontiersmen plus the differential access of the former to capital resources renders a crucial transformation in the pattern of race relations, and the case of San Lorenzo shows how very rapid this transformation can be.

After a month of discussing these factors with people in San Lorenzo in 1968 I came to see the following as unfolding. As men make more money in the wage-labor logging and plantation industries, women become more economically and politically important to blanco-mestizo buyers and brokers, and to the church-controlled system of social honor in the residential community. Women still stabilize the household domain, as in town and settlement niches, *but the available male capital resources in the kindred are severely altered.* Because of this alternation the *function* of the mother-child dyad within the context of household and kindred changes in the urbanized niche. Rather than directly serving black frontiersmen in their processes of economic rise, and in spatial mobility, women with primary household responsibility come to represent relatively autonomous loci for family relations. As the church-sponsored "family stability" campaign expands, the actual kinship and family system is made less functional to black husband-mother dyadic relationships in contexts of politics, social honor, and economic gain. The dyads making up the black family become more adjustive responses to increased white dominance than to other vicissitudes of life. Though men may be relatively better off, economically, they are socially and politically less powerful. They are aware of this situation, and vocal about such powerlessness. The adaptive mobility strategies are still played, and barrio organization is what has been previously reported for larger towns such as Buenaventura, and Tumaco, Colombia, and Esmeraldas, Ecuador. The investigator with a model of four generational mobility would understand the various strategies played by black frontiersmen, but to understand the growing sense of frustration and tension he would have to analyze the more general processes of black disenfranchisement taking place as a concomitant of economic development. Some black frontiersmen are already making such an analysis, and are beginning to seek new forms of alliance, thereby continuing to adapt their system of social organization to new contingencies.

But black strategy alteration is not enough; blanco-mestizo patterns of adaptation are cognitive as well as interactional, and a new ecology of race relations seems to be unfolding which necessitates a still deeper view of black and white adjustment to the wet littoral.

THE IMPACT OF ECUADORIAN ETHNICITY ON AFRO-HISPANIC CULTURE

I turn now to a consideration of some *highland* ethnic terms in the broader context of Ecuadorian colonization. Long an "Andean country" in the real sense of the term, Ecuador's blanco (upper class) mestizo-cholo (lower to middle class non-Quechua speaking), and Indio (mostly lower class Quechua speaking) sectors were primarily crowded into the valleys and on the slopes of the Andes mountains. On the central and south coast of the country were large concentrations of blanco-mestizos in all classes, together with some Afro-Ecuadorians, as well. The north coast of the country was predominantly "black" as we have seen, and the eastern forest, or *Oriente,* has been sparsely settled since the 17th century by various aboriginal Indian groups.

But much of the wealth sought after by nations lies in the tropical forests on both sides of the Andes, and foreign exploitation is now underway. A concomitant result of such exploitation (of oil in the Oriente, and timber on the coast) is a process of internal colonization from highlands to lowlands. The colonization programs are ostensibly oriented toward new subsistence pursuits—new homesteads—but in reality, more often than not, they carry an important petit bourgeois and entrepreneurial spirit, where the money economy is sufficiently advanced to allow for such an orientation.

In an article about colonization in Ecuador based on field work nearly ten years ago, Casagrande, Thompson, and Young (1964:202) wrote:

> The theoretical interest in studying colonization lies both in the processes whereby an already established sociocultural system is extended, replicated or reintegrated, and in colonization as a *creative process,* since colonists frequently must accommodate themselves to a new ecological situation, and to novel socio-political and economic arrangements.

In my earlier work I also took this approach to San Lorenzo, focusing mainly on the internal structure of black frontiersmen, and thinking of colonists as having to adapt to the new, local scene. But with the speeding up of colonization processes we must take another view of the creative aspects of internal colonization from the high Andes to the tropical lowlands. This view stresses the *transposition of blanco ethnic values* with a new affect brought about through social demographic shifts. With such shifts local lowland peoples classed as "negro" and "indio" are directly confronted with an effective ethnic block in the political economy. The contrast between blanco and its two primary opposites—"negro," and "indio"—is especially significant when economic opportunities begin to expand.

The new coastal blancos are not in any way incapable of perceiving the relationship between ethnic advantage and economic advantage, but they explain it differently than I do. They feel that the problem with black frontiersmen is that they are not capable of participating in the revised social order. We could say that their own racism blinds them to a more rational interpretation. But we must remember that, in spite of the pejorative ethnic portrayal of blackness sketched above, Ecuadorians and Colombians are, at the same time, tolerant of racial *variety* to a far greater degree than North Americans, provided that West African racial features are not directly associated with observable non-national cultural patterns.

What it seems to come down to is this: the new blancos make *frequency interpretations* based on their limited knowledge of black behavior and on preconceived stereotypes of bio-cultural "mixture." I take this concept from the applied anthropologist Charles J. Erasmus (1961:23). Here is how he defines it:

> . . . frequency interpretation is viewed as predictive interpretation based on the observation of repeated events, the dominant cognitive aspect of human action. Experience or observation is the raw material from which frequency interpretations are inductively derived.

The most immediately apparent traits in Afro-Hispanic culture pertain to patterns of mutual respect (such as eye avoidance, loud talk, passing by before giving a greeting, and the offering of a woman as dance partner), and superficial manifestations of the underlying structural relationship between musical settings and adjustive dyadic transactions. In regard to the music, all that is really "visible" is the rhythm which, in all but saloon contexts, is new to the blancos. And even in the saloon context, the particular behavior set of expectations is also new, but subject to uninformed frequency interpretations such as that black men give their women away and go on about their dancing. We know that the latter interpretation is not accurate; but we can also see how blancos could make such an interpretation.

Also, blanco frequency interpretations are made primarily in the town niche, while most of the actual labor of black people takes place outside of town. Town for the black man is a place to rest, or to politic, not to "act busy" or show deference to newly arriving bosses who know nothing of the wet littoral (but a good deal about what may be planned for the littoral). Accordingly, blancos see Afro-Hispanic culture as composed of lazy men, and strong, willing women. They see black men enacting their willingness to give women away, and to travel virtually at will, when what is really being symbolized is potential dyadic relationships which will be economically valuable in allowing men to provide for their wives' homes.

In the context of the currulao virtually all newcomer blancos first interpret the drums to mean that an African ceremony is being performed. Then, when they learn that there is no sacred or mystical significance to the ceremony, they assume that it is just a noisy saloon context. By attending the currulao (often, in order to symbolize friendship) in the mood in which they attend the saloon; and by buying aguardiente for themselves, by asking women to dance, and by trying to sing popular national songs as the music begins, the potential for an actual currulao unfolding with its symbolic portrayal is seriously damaged. The currulao becomes, in some modernizing contexts, a phony tourist attraction. In such settings the currulao contexts move to the outer barrios, where the larger concentration of black people increasingly amass, and where blancos do not bother going at night.

The interpretation of such removal of Afro-Hispanic ritual behavior away from the center of town or from near the center, is that it is disappearing, that the black frontiersman is becoming "like everyone else" but a little behind in the process of acculturation. By regarding Afro-Hispanic culture as somehow retarded any blanco can easily conclude that the lower class position of the majority of black people is *their own fault*. Such a cognitive warp expands the basis for racism among non-blacks, and makes the categorical relationship defined by the criterion of whiteness (including mestizo, mulatto, and other mixed categories) ever-more powerful as an environing pressure.

We have now seen how the adaptive strategies of Afro-Hispanic culture are being effected by colonization processes bringing increased numbers of blanco-mestizos into the town niche, together with expanding economic opportunities for brokerage roles. We have also seen how the pejorative categories, already a part of blanco-mestizo national culture, can expand and become reinforced in this same setting.

We have noted several times that the favored "costeño-serrano" symmetrical categorical division is subsumed by the asymmetric categorical division "blanco-negro" when the social demography alters. In order to maintain symmetry in the face of such a transformation I found black townsmen in San Lorenzo using the pejorative ethnic terms themselves to refer to black serranos. Back in 1963 when a black costeño would indicate his dislike for a black highlander—usually from the Chota Valley, north of Ibarra—he would simply slur the term "serrano" in referring to this person. But in 1968 I found many black friends telling me about the "inferior racial quality" of highland blacks, stressing the very qualities that new blancos from the Sierra used for all blacks, highland and lowland. Also, economically successful mulattoes and zambos hold forth at great length about the story of a slaver shipwreck off the coast of Esmeraldas where Africans, led by a *ladino* (hispanicized African) seized their freedom, mated with Indians, and came to propagate a race of zambos with such political power that they ascended to rule over the entire province in a couple of generations. In such a story it is stressed to the newcomer that Esmeraldas people are "zambo," that the introduction of "negro" elements is recent, and from Colombia.

In such story telling all of the pejorative connotations will be applied to the stereotype of Colombian "negro" by black Ecuadorians, never specifying, however, specific individuals, or even, in this sort of context, groups of individuals. The only exception to this pattern that I know about is a situation where an obstreperous crew of Colombian blacks, transient in port in San Lorenzo, threatened physical violence. They called certain San Lorenzeños "negro," and in turn, as individuals, were called "negro" by San Lorenzeños just as a fight became imminent. In Colombia, particularly in Tumaco and Buenaventura, I have noted many instances where black men apply pejorative ethnic terms to their own barrio, but never to themselves, or to specific individuals in their barrio.

ECONOMIC DEVELOPMENT AND RACISM IN THE WET LITTORAL

Development of the political economy necessitates an expanding infrastructure, which in turn establishes the necessary conditions for urbanization. As the infrastructure expands nationalization takes place as part of a general process often called "modernization." In South American countries nationalization is in part characterized as a process of ethnic mixture, to which those stigmatized by the concept "negro" or "indio" are excluded. If access to new resources for those classed as "negro" and "indio" in modernizing Latin American nations is blocked, then there is no reason for denying that processes of discrimination leading to *de facto* segregation are underway in the wet littoral, and elsewhere.

The processes sketched thus far are familiar as a concomitant of world industrialization. In this hemisphere a *rule of hypodescent* is invoked only in the United States to drive racism to its limits of absurdity, and because of this Latin American concepts of racial mingling are often opposed to the United States hypodescent system. Marvin Harris (1964:56) gives a good definition of this concept:

> "Hypo-descent" means affiliation with the subordinate rather than the superordinate group in order to avoid the ambiguity of intermediate identity . . . children of interracial marriages in the United States are uniformly Negroes . . . That a half-white should be a Negro rather than a white cannot be explained by rational argument. The rule of hypo-descent is . . . an invention which we in the United States have made in order to keep biological facts from intruding into our collective racist fantasies. With it, we have gone so far as to create Alice-in-Wonderland kinds of Negroes about whom people say, "He certainly doesn't look like a Negro."

Because we do not find such a degree of racism in Latin America, many North American and Latin American scholars insist in the face of evidence such as I have just presented, that racism does not "really" exist, and that segregation cannot "really" develop in any but an anglo milieu. Where North Americans usually err in the interpretation of race relations in Latin America is in lumping (as hypodescent racism demands) *all people locally classed as "negro"* with all those people who the North American investigator would class as "Negro," or "black." And where Latin Americans usually err is in giving inordinate weight to the concept of miscegenation as though all "problems" with blackness will disappear as nations become increasingly mixed.

Ambiguity about calculating who is, or who is not, to be classed "negro" in no way negates the fact that a "negro" category exists in Ecuador and in Colombia, as in every other Latin American nation and territory, and that people who share a gene pool of West African characteristics, together with aggregating cultural traits, are the only ones other than "indios" to be routinely excluded when speedup in economic opportunities takes place.

Furthermore, the absence of a hypodescent rule in no way pre-

vents Ecuadorians and Colombians from invoking ancestry of unde-
sirable racial features, if it is convenient to do so. The penetrating,
stigmatizing phrase, *"adonde es tu abuela,"* "where is your grandmother?," is used in the Pacific Lowlands by both blacks and whites
(and mixed) to remind mulattoes and zambos of the blackness in their
mixture. The potential for extending the concept of blackness to include some of the mixed exists. Whether or not it will become more
important as (or *if*) economic development speeds up is probably
dependent on the social demography in the developing zones. If the
mestizo-mulato contrast becomes strategic to national culture bearers,
then I would suggest that the concept "mulato" will fade, as it has in
the United States, and people will be categorized as "mestizo" *or*
"negro." Alternatively those in the "negro" category may be regrouped
as "zambo" or "mulato"—as they frequently are in Ecuador—but
here again what is crucial is whether or not these categories will
continue to contrast with the national "mestizo" ethnic construct.
But regardless of the various permutations and combinations occur-
ring in racial calculations in the wet littoral, and elsewhere, one signal
phenomenon remains. Blackness is the opposite of whiteness, and
national concepts of "mixed" in Colombia and Ecuador stand opposed
to "black" just as white is the opposite of black.

In the position taken here it does not matter that some members
of the black category will rise in status with or without the "lighten-
ing" genes; what matters is that the social category defined by a
national cultural criterion of blackness is cognitively relegated to the
bottom of the economic and social hierarchy. When racial features
are associated with class and cultural features, *and* built into a national cultural category, then the viability of a particular Afro-
Hispanic mode of cultural adaptation is blocked or limited by racist
social constraints. That such a social constraint—whiteness in superior
relationship to blackness—is the very one invoked in the North American industrial-capitalist complex is equally relevant. It is this very
North American complex that is now instrumental in "developing"
nations such as Colombia and Ecuador, and extracting their resources
such as timber and oil.

The processes I have sketched are paralleled by events taking place
elsewhere on the continent of South America—in Guyana (Smith
1962), Colombia (personal observations and field work), Peru (Faron
1970), Bolivia (Léons 1970), Brazil (Azevedo 1966, Fernandes 1969),
and elewhere in the world as well (cf. van den Berghe 1967). I cannot
help but wonder whether countries such as Ecuador and Colombia
are entering a phase of "preadaptation" to contemporary industrial

economy, where segregration along color lines is one relatively convenient, though deplorable, means of sorting aggregates into access
classes. By preadaptation I follow Morton Fried (1967:154):

> I take this to refer in sociocultural evolution to aggregating minor changes
> which themselves exert only small visible effects on the *status quo,* but
> suddenly occupy different functional roles when the society is transformed.

The supra-national frontier cultural ecology of this 450 year old
Afro-Hispanic culture is being transformed into parts of national
societies. As the national societies consolidate their mainstream cultures, then Afro-Hispanic culture becomes one of many "subcultures"
from a national perspective. At this time, in Ecuador, and perhaps
to a lesser degree in Colombia, the development of the national
society seems totally tied to policies of resource extraction of United
States and European based companies. It will not be long before the
natural resource base of northwest Ecuador, and southwest Colombia,
will be inadequate to sustain the balanced adaptation to money and
subsistence economies. When this occurs economic incorporation of
this Afro-Hispanic culture into the bottom stratum of the respective
nations will be complete.

Such incorporation of people now participating in this one Afro-
Hispanic culture will place them in the same structural position as
those classed as "black," "Negro," "colored," "preto," "noire," "nègre,"
etc., in other nations in the Americas. This positioning generates a
corporate sharing of dual macro-identities, best stated as *national
versus black.* This duality can be arranged to simultaneously assert
the supra-national "Black Americas" (Bastide 1967) versus the sub-
unit of their respective "mestizo" nations. Since I do not know where
the current unfolding of Pan-Black awareness across this hemisphere
will lead, I cannot suggest ways by which it may effect peoples of
this particular Afro-Hispanic cultural adaptation.

My purpose in this book has been to document the cultural adaptation of one of many analogous adaptations to a particular type of
supra-national ecological setting. I have considered some of the rich
resources existing in the culture of black frontiersmen in a segment
of the wet Pacific littoral of Colombia and Ecuador. Their cultural
resources are becoming increasingly rich, imbued more and more with
elements which they aggressively choose from many new sources introduced through expanding national infrastructures and through new
modes of world-wide communication. I have also considered the effects
of economic development on the social demography as urbanization
and accompanying forms of western urbanism penetrate the frontier.

Such development is now bringing racist barriers to black participation in a white-dominated political economy.

The *buckra,* or *white problem,* for black people which began with the European-sponsored African slave trade to the New World colonies *is still the crucial one.* As Afro-American peoples converge in their common New World black experiences, then perhaps solutions to this buckra problem will be found, and enacted.

NOTES

1 Part of this section (pp. 177-180) is elaborated and expanded from my earlier work (Whitten 1965:90-92) and is republished here by permission of Stanford University Press.

2 The specific Catholic order referred to is a German one, called in Ecuador *Misión Comboniana Arquidiócesis de Munich,* all of the priests and nuns of which are Italian in Esmeraldas province.

3 Following my earlier analysis (Whitten 1965:170-183) "Conservative," and "Liberal" parties were usually allied through the *Consejo Parroquial* which, ostensibly, should represent only one party. "Socialist," "Independent," and "Communist," parties frequently allied in opposition to the *Consejo.* Harmony between several parties came about, in 1963, when ". . . Liberal and Socialist parties act in concert. This harmony is reached when members of the upper-class initiate action indirectly, through formal organizations, supported by ritual kinship ties with organization members." (Whitten 1965:194) Bringing together of socialist and liberal strands of political ideology involved reinforcement of black *costeño* and *"light costeño"* kinship and affinal ties. Such reinforcement could occur when conservative and liberal alliances formed to resist ever-present opposition. It was also argued that failure of political goal-oriented behavior tended to underscore ethnic, kinship, and class lines. With the power of the military regime co-opting the strength of the Catholic church through economic grants, and with the merger of liberal and conservative parties, no costeño-sponsored goal-oriented behavior seems to have succeeded since 1963. The result seems, indeed, to be an underscoring of ethnic, class, and kinship lines with the possible result of schismatic factionalism and a muddling of political purpose across such lines (cf. Beals and Siegel 1966). By 1970 the national situation had further crystallized as Velasquistas became part of the new military-church one party establishment.

4 The Ecuadorian Banco de Vivienda which is the institution here referred to was originally begun as a U.S.A.I.D. sponsored agency to stimulate the development of rural housing. Such housing really got started under military dictatorship when the *Junta Autónoma del Ferrocarril Quito-San Lorenzo* (agency responsible for the development of the area around the Quito-San Lorenzo railroad, the development of San Lorenzo, the development of the port, and establishment of modern facilities in the northern sector) transferred the land for a new town to the *Misión Comboniana,* and agreed to transport building materials without charge. The mission, together with the *Junta Militar,* provided funds for the *Banco de Vivienda* in San Lorenzo which was administered exclusively through the Catholic church.

GLOSSARY

Abanico. Woven fire fan

Adivinanza. Riddle

Administrador de mina. Administrator, or overseer, of mine during the colonial era.

Aguardiente. Rum

Ahijado, a. Godchild

Alabado. Hymn of praise, wake for deceased adult

Alma. Soul

Almocafre. Adze-like tool used in placer gold mining

Andar. To walk, strut

Angelito. "Little angel;" soul-spirit of deceased child

Aro. Round drying frame for animal skins

Arrullo. Spiritual sung during wakes for deceased children and for the propitiation of saints

Asiento. A contract granting monopolistic rights to provide slaves to the Spanish Indies during the 16th and 17th centuries

Atarraya. Circular casting net

Audiencia. Royal court of colonial era roughly equivalent to the United States circuit court; an administrative instrument of Spanish control

Azotea. Lit., "Verandah;" a raised platform garden in the Pacific Lowlands

Bajonera. Woman who harmonizes with solista in the currulao

203

Barbacoa. Platform for drying fish

Barrio. Named section of a town

Batea. Large oblong or round wooden bowl

Belén. A parade to propitiate and entertain the saints

Blanco. White

Bombero. Man who plays the bombo

Bombo. Large double headed drum

Bordonero. Male musician who plays lower notes on xylophone

Bozal. Slave fresh from Africa

Bruja. Witch, ghoul

Brujo. Sorcerer, diviner

Buckra. White; a West African term widely distributed in New World Afro-American cultures

Burros. Carved posts holding thatch on top of a house

Cachimbo. Clay pipe

Cajita. Coffin for deceased child

Calabazo. Calabash shell, used for carrying water or winnowing rice

Calandra. Trot line

Calor. Heat, anger which endangers others, strong psychobiological drive

Canoa ranchera. Canoe fixed with covered shelter

Cantadora. Female singer

Cantina. A social context usually set in a small drinking room, called kiosko

Capitán de cuadrilla. The slave head of a slave gang in placer mining

Casa. House, household

Casa de la marimba. House in which the currulao is held

Catanga. Shrimp pot

Ceviche. A national Ecuadorian and Colombian dish made of fish or shellfish, limes, hot pepper, tomatoes and onions

Chigualo. Wake for a deceased child

Chinchorro. A drag net

Cholo. Pejorative ethnic designation which links economic and social standing with phenotype or stipulated ancestry. A term of endearment when used reciprocally between social equals

Chontaduro. New World peach palm

Cielo. Sky

Cimarrón. Runaway black slave

Cimarronismo. Guerrilla activity initiated by runaway slaves

Cocina. Kitchen

Comadre. Co-parent in compadrazgo system, female

Comisario nacional de policía. Local representative of Supreme Court of Justice in Ecuador

Compadre. Co-parent in compadrazgo system, male

Compadrazgo. A system of establishing co-parents. Part of the padrinazgo system

Concha. Mussel

Conchera. Woman who gathers mussels

Concuñado, a. Distant in-law

Conocer. To know, to know carnally

Corral. Fish trap with sliding door used on rivers

Costeño. A person from the coast

Criollo. For blacks during slave times referred to a New World born slave

Cuadrilla. Work gang. Slave gang during colonial era

Cuarto. Sleeping room

Cuento. Story, tale

Cununero. Man who plays cununo

Cununo. Cone-shaped drum resembling conga drum

Cuñado, a. Brother-in-law, sister-in-law

Currulao. Marimba dance with xylophone as central instrument

Damajagua. Wood bark from which bark cloth is made

Décima. Poem, stanza of a poem

Diablo. Devil

Esterado. Split bamboo fish screen

Estero. Tidal estuary in the mangrove swamp

Feo. Ugly, in terms of racial features

Finca. Farm

Fogón. Hearth, cooking platform in the cocina

Gloria. Heaven

Glosador. Lead male singer in the currulao

Grito. Stylized falsetto call used in singing and in certain types of greetings

Guarapo. Beer made from sugar cane juice

Guasá. Bamboo tube rattle shaken by women in the currulao

Guerrillero. Guerrilla

Guineo. Banana

Hechicera. Spell, hex

Hembra. Female

Hielo de difunto. Cold radiating from a corpse

Hombre. Man

Indígena. Indian, native of the New World

Indio. Perjorative term for Indian

Infierno. Hell

Jefe. Person particularly responsible to someone of higher standing for the labor or behavior of others

Jefe de la casa. Household head

Jefe de la minga. Central figure in cooperate work group

Jefe Político. Chief executive officer of an Ecuadorian canton

Juyungo. Pejorative term used by Cayapa Indians for black person

Ladino. Hispanicized African, very clever person

Libre. Free; refers to black person in the Colombian Chocó

Loa. A sacred décima sung by a man during an arrullo to a saint

Macho. Male

Madrina. Godmother

Mampora. Banana

Mar. Sea

Marimba. Xylophone, central instrument in the currulao

Marimberos. Those who play the xylophone; all musicians in the currulao

Mazamorra. Tail sluice of placer mine

Mazamorrero. Independent placer miner

Mestizo. Person of stipulated Indian-European descent

Minga. Cooperative labor group

Monte. Forest, jungle, heavy brush

Montubio. Pejorative Ecuadorian ethnic designation which links economic and social standing with imputed regional ethnic culture

Moreno. Polite term for black person

Moro. Moor, unbaptized child

Motorista. Person who operates canoe and motor as a commercial enterprise.

Mujer. Woman, wife

Mulato. Mulatto; person of stipulated African-European descent

Negro. Black

Novenario. Ceremony for the spirit of a deceased adult; second wake

Oidor. Judge in the Audiencia system

Oriente. Amazonian Lowlands of Ecuador and Colombia

Padrinazgo. A system establishing godparents for godchildren. Part of the compadrazgo system

Padrino. Godfather

Palenque. Stronghold of self liberated slaves

Pando. A basket for river fishing

Panela. Brown sugar, sugar loaf

Papachina. An aroid which resembles taro

Payón. Oven

Peso. Colombian currency

Petate. Sleeping mat

Piezas de Indias. A measure of slave labor

Pieza de mina. Slave mine worker

Pieza de roza. Slave field hand

Pildé. Banisteriopsis species, a hallucinogenic vine

Pilón. A deep wooden mortar for pounding rice

Pipa. Green coconut used for drinking water

Primo, a. Cousin; stipulated or fictive relative of unspecified kinship
   relationship

Purgatorio. Purgatory

Quebrada. Bottom area or broken ground away from major river
   which is used for agriculture

Rancho. Temporary dwelling

Rascadera. An aroid resembling taro

Rastrojo. Stubble, planted field

Respondedora. Female singer in the currulao

Rezandera. Prayer singer in the alabado

Roza. Clearing for agriculture

Sala. Main room of a house

Señor. Overseer, overlord, slave master during slavery

Señor de cuadrilla. Slave owner

Serrano. Person from the Sierra

Sierra. Andean highlands

Solista. Lead female singer in currulao

Sucre. Ecuadorian currency

Tagua. Ivory nut

Teniente político. Chief executive officer of an Ecuadorian parish

Tierra. Earth

Tiplero. Male musician who plays higher notes on xylophone

Trapiche. Sugar mill

Trasmayo. Large drag net

Tumba. Ceremony performed to drive lingering ghost-spirit from this world

Tunda. Prominent malign fear creature

Velorio. Lit., "Wake;" saint propitiation in the Pacific Lowlands

Visión. Ghost, apparition, fear creature

Zambo. Person of stipulated African-Indian descent

REFERENCES CITED

ACOSTA-SOLIS, MISAEL
1959   *El Noroccidente Ecuatoriano.* Quito: Junta Autónoma del Ferrocarril Quito-San Lorenzo.

ALLAND, ALEXANDER, JR.
1967   *Evolution and Human Behavior.* Garden City: Natural History Press.
1970   *Adaptation in Cultural Evolution: An Approach to Medical Anthropology.* New York: Columbia University Press.

ALTSCHULER, MILTON
n.d.   *River Indians of Ecuador: A Study of Cayapa Law and Personality.* Manuscript.

AZEVEDO, THALES DE
1966   *Cultura e Situacão Racial no Brasil.* Rio de Janeiro: Editôra Civilizacão Brasileira S.A.

BANTON, MICHAEL
1965 (ed)   *The Relevance of Models for Social Anthropology.* New York: Praeger.
1967   *Race Relations.* New York: Basic Books.

BARRETT, SAMUEL A.
1925   *The Cayapa Indians of Ecuador,* 2 Vols. New York: Heye Foundation.

BARTH, FREDRIK
1956   Ecologic relationships of ethnic groups in Swat, North Pakistan. *American Anthropologist* 58:107-189.
1959   *Political Leadership Among Swat Pathans.* London: Athlone Press.
1966   *Models of Social Organization.* Royal Anthropological Institute Occasional Paper 23. London: Royal Anthropological Institute of Great Britain and Ireland.

211

BASTIDE, ROGER
1967   *Les Amériques Noires: Les Civilisations Africaines dans le Nouveau Monde.* Paris: Payot.

BASTIEN, RÉMY
1959   *Comment,* On the relation between plantation and creole cultures, by Richard N. Adams. In, *Plantation Systems of the New World.* Pan American Union, Social Science Monographs 7:79-81. Washington, D.C.

BATES, MARSTEN
1960   *The Forest and the Sea: a Look at the Economy of Nature and the Ecology of Man.* New York: New American Library (A Mentor Book).

BEALS, ALAN R. AND BERNARD J. SIEGEL
1966   *Divisiveness and Social Conflict: an Anthropological Approach.* Stanford: Stanford University Press.

BENNETT, CHARLES F., JR.
1962   The Bayano Cuna Indians: an ecological study of livelihood and diet. *Annals of the Association of American Geographers* 52:32-50.
1968   *Human Influences on the Zoogeography of Panama.* Ibero-Americana 51. Berkeley and Los Angeles: University of California Press.

BOHANNAN, PAUL AND FRED PLOG (eds)
1967   *Beyond the Frontier: Social Process and Cultural Change.* Garden City: The Natural History Press.

BOISSEVAIN, JEREMY
1968   The place of non-groups in the social sciences. *Man: Journal of the Royal Anthropological Institute of Great Britain and Ireland* 3:542-556.

BRUNER, EDWARD M.
in press   The expression of ethnicity in Indonesia. In, Abner Cohen (ed), *Urban Ethnicity.* London: Tavistock.

CABELLO BALBOA, MIGUEL
1945   (reprinted) Verdadera descripción y relación larga de la provincia y tierra de las Esmeraldas . . . In, Miguel Cabello Balboa: *Obras,* I: 5-55. Quito, Ecuador: Editorial Ecuatoriana.

CARNEIRO, ROBERT L.
1967   On the relationship between size of population and complexity of social organization. *Southwestern Journal of Anthropology* 23:234-243.

CARSON, RACHEL
1955   *The Edge of the Sea*. New York: The New American Library (A Mentor Book).

CASAGRANDE, JOSEPH B., STEPHEN I. THOMPSON, AND PHILIP D. YOUNG
1964   Colonization as a research frontier: the Ecuadorian case. In, Robert Manners (ed), *Process and Pattern in Culture: Essays in Honor of Julian H. Steward*. Chicago: Aldine.

CHAPMAN, CHARLES E.
1918   Palmares: the Negro Numantia. *Journal of Negro History* 3:29-32.

COSTALES SAMANIEGO, ALFREDO
1957   Algunas artefactos prehistóricos de los Esmeraldeños. *Llacta* 2(3). Quito: Instituto Ecuatoriano de Antropología y Geografía.

CURTIN, PHILIP D.
1969   *The Atlantic Slave Trade: A Census*. Madison: University of Wisconsin Press.

DOZER, DONALD M.
1962   *Latin America: An Interpretive History*. New York: McGraw-Hill.

EDER, HERBERT W.
1963   *El Río y El Monte: A Geographical Reconnaissance of the Río Siguirisúa Valley, Chocó District, Colombia*. Report on field work carried out under Office of Naval Research contract, Project 388067, Department of Geography, University of California, Berkeley.

ERASMUS, CHARLES J.
1961   *Man Takes Control*. Minneapolis: University of Minnesota Press.

ESCALANTE, AQUILES
1964   *El Negro en Colombia*. Bogotá: Universidad Nacional de Colombia, Monografías Sociológicas 18.

1971   *La Minería del Hambre: Condoto y La Chocó Pacífico.* Barranquilla: Colón.

ESQUEMELING, JOHN
1967   *The Buccaneers of America.* New York: Dover. (Reprint of 1893 edition).

ESTRADA, EMILIO AND BETTY J. MEGGERS
1961   A complex of traits of probable transpacific origin on the coast of Ecuador. *American Anthropologist* 63:913-939.

ESTUPIÑÁN BASS, NELSON
1966   *El Último Río.* Quito: Casa de la Cultura Ecuatoriana.

FARON, LOUIS C.
1962   Marriage, residence and domestic group among the Panamanian Chocó. *Ethnology* 1:13-37.
1970   Ethnicity and social mobility in Chancay Valley, Peru. In, Walter Goldschmidt and Harry Hoijer (eds), *The Social Anthropology of Latin America,* 224-255. Los Angeles: Latin American Center.

FERNANDES, FLORESTAN
1969   *The Negro in Brazilian Society.* New York: Columbia University Press.

FIRTH, RAYMOND
1951   *Elements of Social Organization.* London: Watts.

FORTES, MEYER
1949   *The Web of Kinship Among the Tallensi.* London: Oxford University Press.
1953   The structure of unilinear descent groups. *American Anthropologist* 55:17-41.
1958   Introduction. In, Jack Goody (ed), *The Developmental Cycle in Domestic Groups.* Cambridge Papers in Social Anthropology, 1. Cambridge: Cambridge University Press.
1969   *Kinship and the Social Order.* Chicago: Aldine.

FOSTER, GEORGE
1960   *Culture and Conquest: America's Spanish Heritage.* Viking Fund Publications in Anthropology 27. New York: Wenner-Gren Foundation for Anthropological Research.

FREILICH, MORRIS (ed)
1970   *Marginal Natives: Anthropologists at Work.* New York: Harper and Row.

FRIED, MORTON
  1967   *The Evolution of Political Society: An Essay in Political An-
         thropology.* New York: Random House.

FRIEDEMANN, NINA S.
  1966-1969   Contextos religiosos en una área negra de Barbacoas
         (Nariño, Colombia). *Revista Colombiana de Folclor* 4(10):63-
         83.

FRIEDEMANN, NINA S., AND JORGE MORALES GÓMEZ
  1966-1969   Estudios de negros en el Litoral Pacífico Colombiano:
         Fase I. *Revista Colombiana de Anthropologia* 14:55-78.

GONZÁLEZ, NANCIE L. SOLIEN
  1969   *Black Carib Household Structure.* Seattle: University of
         Washington Press.

GOODENOUGH, WARD H.
  1970   *Description and Comparison in Cultural Anthropology.* Chi-
         cago: Aldine.

GRINKER, ROY R., SR. (ed)
  1967   *Toward a Unified Theory of Human Behavior.* New York:
         Basic Books.

HARRIS, MARVIN
  1964   *Patterns of Race in the Americas.* New York: Walker.
  1969   *Review of,* Michael Banton, *Race Relations. Current An-
         thropology* 10:103-104.

HELMS, MARY W.
  1969a The purchase society: adaptation to economic frontiers. *An-
         thropological Quarterly* 42:325-342.
  1969b The cultural ecology of a colonial tribe. *Ethnololgy* 7:76-84.
  1971   *Asang: Adaptations to Culture Contact in a Miskito Com-
         munity.* Gainesville: University of Florida Press.

HERRING, HUBERT
  1961   *A History of Latin America.* 2nd Ed. New York: Knopf.

HERSKOVITS, MELVILLE J.
  1945   The processes of cultural change. In, Ralph Linton (ed), *The
         Science of Man in the World Crisis,* 143-170. New York:
         Columbia University Press.

HOFSTADTER, RICHARD AND SEYMOUR MARTIN LIPSET (eds)
  1968   *Turner and the Sociology of the Frontier.* New York: Basic
         Books.

HONIGMANN, JOHN J.
  1959   *The World of Man.* New York: Harper and Row.

HUDSON, RANDALL O.
  1964   The status of the Negro in northern South America, 1820-
         1860. *Journal of Negro History* 49:225-239.

HUDSON, W. H.
  1916   *Green Mansions.* New York: Knopf.

JARAMILLO URIBE, JAIME
  1963   Esclavos y señores en la sociedad Colombiana del siglo
         XVIII. *Anuario Colombiano de Historia y de La Cultura*
         1:3-62.

JEFFREYS, MERVYN D. W.
  1971   Maize and the Mande myth. (With C. A. comment). *Current
         Anthropology* 12:291-320.

KING, JAMES F.
  1939   *Negro Slavery in the Viceroyalty of New Granada.* Ann
         Arbor: University Microfilms. (Ph.D. thesis, University of
         California, Berkeley).
  1945   Negro slavery in New Granada. In, *Greater America: Essays
         in Honor of Herbert Eugene Bolton.* Berkeley: University of
         California Press.

LATHRAP, DONALD W.
  1970   *The Upper Amazon.* New York: Praeger.

LÉONS, MADELINE BARBARA
  1970   Stratification and pluralism in the Bolivian Yungas. In,
         Walter Goldschmidt and Harry Hoijer (eds), *The Social An-
         thropology of Latin America.* Los Angeles: Latin American
         Center.

LÉVI-STRAUSS, CLAUDE
  1953   Social structure. In, Alfred L. Kroeber (ed), *Anthropology
         Today: An Encyclopedic Inventory,* 524-553. Chicago: Uni-
         versity of Chicago Press.
  1967   *Structural Anthropology.* New York: Doubleday.

LINTON, RALPH (ed)
   1945   *The Science of Man in the World Crisis.* New York: Columbia University Press.

LOMAX, ALAN
   1970   The homogeneity of African—Afro-American musical style. In, Norman E. Whitten, Jr. and John F. Szwed (eds), *Afro-American Anthropology: Contemporary Perspectives*, 181-203. New York: The Free Press.

MANNERS, ROBERT (ed)
   1964   *Process and Pattern in Culture: Essays in Honor of Julian H. Steward.* Chicago: Aldine.

MAYER, ADRIAN C.
   1966   The significance of quasi-groups in the study of complex societies. In, Michael Banton (ed), *The Social Anthropology of Complex Societies,* 97-122. New York: Praeger.

MEGGERS, BETTY J.
   1966   *Ecuador.* New York: Praeger.

MEGGERS, BETTY J., CLIFFORD EVANS AND EMILIO ESTRADA
   1965   *Early Formative Period of Coastal Ecuador: The Valdivia and Machalilla Phases.* Smithsonian Contributions to Anthropology 1. Washington: Smithsonian Institution.

MERIZALDE DEL CARMEN, PADRE BERNARDO
   1921   *Estudio de la Costa Colombiana del Pacífico.* Bogotá: Impresos del Estado Mayor General.

MILES, AUDREY
   1968   The minority volunteer. *Peace Corps Volunteer* 6 (11):16-20.

MINTZ, SIDNEY W.
   1970   Foreword. In, Norman E. Whitten, Jr. and John F. Szwed (eds), *Afro-American Anthropology: Contemporary Perspectives,* 1-16. New York: The Free Press.

MITCHELL, J. CLYDE
   1966   Theoretical orientations in African urban studies. In, Michael Banton (ed), *The Social Anthropology of Complex Societies.* ASA Monograph 4. London: Tavistock.
   1969 (ed)   *Social Networks in Urban Situations.* Manchester: Manchester University Press.

MÖRNER, MAGNUS
  1967   *Race Mixture in the History of Latin America.* New York: Little, Brown.

MURPHY, ROBERT C.
  1939a The littoral of Pacific Colombia and Ecuador. *The Geographical Review* 29:1-33.
  1939b Racial Succession in the Colombian Chocó. *The Geographical Review* 29:461-471.

OBERG, KALERVO
  1955   Types of social structure among the lowland tribes of South and Central America. *American Anthropologist* 57:472-487.

ORTIZ, ADALBERTO
  1943   *Juyungo: Historia de un Negro, Una Isla y Otros Negros.* Buenos Aires: Editorial Americalee.

OSBORNE, ANN
  1968   Compadrazgo and patronage: a Colombian case. *Man: Journal of the Royal Anthropological Institute of Great Britain and Ireland* 3:593-608.

PAVY, PAUL DAVID, III
  1967   The provenience of Colombian Negroes. *Journal of Negro History* 47:36-58.
  1968   *The Negro in Western Colombia.* Ann Arbor: University Microfilms (Ph.D. thesis, Tulane University).

PHELAN, JOHN LEDDY
  1967   *The Kingdom of Quito in the Seventeenth Century: Bureaucratic Politics in the Spanish Empire.* Madison: University of Wisconsin Press.

PITT-RIVERS, JULIAN
  1969   Mestizo or Ladino? *Race: A Journal of Race and Group Relations* 10:463-47.

POLANYI, KARL
  1966   *Dahomey and the Slave Trade: An Analysis of an Archaic Economy.* Seattle: University of Washington Press.

PRESCOTT, WILLIAM H.
  1874   *History of the Conquest of Peru.* 2 Vols. Philadelphia: Lippincott.

PRICE, THOMAS J.
1955 *Saints and Spirits: A Study of Differential Acculturation in Colombian Negro Communities.* Ann Arbor: University Microfilms. (Ph.D. thesis, Northwestern University).

RAMOS, ARTHUR
1939 *The Negro in Brazil.* Washington, D.C.: Associated Publishers.

REICHEL-DOLMATOFF, GERARDO
1960 Contribuciones a la etnografía de Los Indios del Chocó. *Revista Colombiana de Antropologia* 11:169-188.
1965 *Colombia.* New York: Praeger.

SACO, JOSÉ ANTONIO
1938 *Historia de la Esclavitud de la Raza Africana en el Nuevo Mundo y en Especial en Los Paises Américo-Hispanos.* Habana: Colección de Libros Cubanos, por Fernando Ortiz: Libreria Cervantes.

SAHLINS, MARSHALL
1964 Culture and environment: the study of cultural ecology. In, Sol Tax (ed), *Horizons of Anthropology,* 132-147. Chicago: Aldine.
1965 On the sociology of primitive exchange. In, Michael Banton (ed), *The Relevance of Models for Social Anthropology.* New York: Praeger.

SAHLINS, MARSHALL, AND ELMAN SERVICE (eds)
1960 *Evolution and Culture.* Ann Arbor: University of Michigan Press.

SERVICE, ELMAN
1962 *Primitive Social Organization.* New York: Random House.

SHARP, WILLIAM F.
1968 El Negro en Colombia: manumisión y posición social. *Razón y Fábula* 8, Julio-Agosto: 91-107.

SMITH, RAYMOND T.
1962 *British Guiana.* London: Oxford University Press.
1963 Culture and social structure in the Caribbean: some recent work on family and kinship studies. *Comparative Studies in Society and History* 6:24-46.

SOUTHALL, AIDAN (ed)
1961 *Social Change in Modern Africa.* London: Oxford University Press.

STEWARD, JULIAN H.
1955 *Theory of Culture Change.* Urbana: University of Illinois Press.
1963 Evolution and process. In, Alfred L. Kroeber (ed), *Anthropology Today: An Encyclopedic Inventory,* 313-326. Chicago: University of Chicago Press.

THOMSEN, MORITZ
1969 *Living Poor: A Peace Corps Chronicle.* Seattle: University of Washington Press.

UHLE, MAX
1927 *Estudios Esmeraldeños.* Anales de la Universidad Central. Quito, Ecuador 39 (262): 219-279.

VALENTINE, CHARLES A.
1968 *Culture and Poverty: Critque and Counter Proposals.* Chicago: University of Chicago Press.

VAN DEN BERGHE, PIERRE L.
1967 *Race and Racism: A Comparative Perspective.* New York: Wiley.

VELÁSQUEZ, M., ROGERIO
1957 La medicina popular en la costa Colombiana del Pacífico *Revista Colombiana de Antropologia* 6:195-258.
1961a Ritos de la muerte en el alto y bajo Chocó. *Revisto Colombiana de Folclor* 2(6):9-76.
1961b Instrumentos musicales del alto y bajo Chocó. *Revista Colombiana de Folclor* 2(6):77-111.
1962 Gentilicios Africanos del occidente de Colombia. *Revista Colombiana de Folclor* 3(7):107-148.

WAGLEY, CHARLES
1959 The concept of social race in the Americas. *Actas del XXXIII Congreso Internacional de Americanistas,* I:403-417. San José, Costa Rica. Reprinted in Dwight Heath and Richard N. Adams (eds), *Contemporary Cultures and Societies of Latin America* (1965:531-545). New York: Random House.

WEST, ROBERT C.
1952 *Colonial Placer Mining in Colombia.* Baton Rouge: Louisiana State University Press.
1957 *The Pacific Lowlands of Colombia: A Negroid Area of the American Tropics.* Baton Rouge: Louisiana State University Press.

WHITTEN, NORMAN E., JR.

1965   *Class, Kinship, and Power in an Ecuadorian Town: The Negroes of San Lorenzo.* Stanford: Stanford University Press.

1968   Personal networks and musical contexts in the Pacific Lowlands of Colombia and Ecuador. *Man: Journal of the Royal Anthropological Institute of Great Britain and Ireland* 3:50-63.

1969   Strategies of adaptive mobility in the Colombian-Ecuadorian littoral. *American Anthropologist* 71:228-242.

1970a   Network analysis and processes of adaptation among Ecuadorian and Nova Scotian Negroes. Chapter 8 In, Morris Freilich (ed), *Marginal Natives: Anthropologists at Work.* New York: Harper and Row.

1970b   Network analysis in Ecuador and Nova Scotia: some critical remarks. *Canadian Review of Sociology and Anthropology* 7:269-280.

WHITTEN, NORMAN E., JR. AND JOHN F. SZWED (eds)

1970   *Afro-American Anthropology: Contemporary Perspectives.* New York: The Free Press.

WHITTEN, NORMAN E., JR. AND DOROTHEA S. WHITTEN

1972   Social strategies and social relationships. In, Bernard J. Siegel (ed), *Annual Review of Anthropology I.* Palo Alto: Annual Reviews Incorporated.

WHITTEN, NORMAN E., JR. AND ALVIN W. WOLFE

1973   Network analysis. In, John J. Honigmann (ed), *Handbook of Social and Cultural Anthropology.* Chicago: Rand McNally.

WOLF, ERIC

1959   Specific aspects of plantation systems in the New World: community subcultures and social class. In, *Plantation Systems of the New World.* Pan American Union, Social Science Monographs 7:136-147. Washington, D.C.

1969   *Peasant Wars in the Twentieth Century.* New York: Harper and Row.

ZELINSKI, WILBUR

1949   The historical geography of the Negro population of Latin America. *Journal of Negro History* 34:153-221.